Accountancy and the Changing Landscape of Integrated Reporting

Ioana Dragu
Babes-Bolyai University, Romania

A volume in the Advances in Finance, Accounting, and Economics (AFAE) Book Series

IGI Global
DISSEMINATOR OF KNOWLEDGE

Published in the United States of America by
IGI Global
Business Science Reference (an imprint of IGI Global)
701 E. Chocolate Avenue
Hershey PA, USA 17033
Tel: 717-533-8845
Fax: 717-533-8661
E-mail: cust@igi-global.com
Web site: http://www.igi-global.com

Library of Congress Cataloging-in-Publication Data

Names: Dragu, Ioana, 1987- author.
Title: Accountancy and the changing landscape of integrated reporting / by Ioana Dragu.
Description: Hershey : Business Science Reference, [2017]
Identifiers: LCCN 2017019848| ISBN 9781522536222 (hardcover) | ISBN 9781522536239 (ebook)
Subjects: LCSH: Financial statements--Romania. | Accounting--Romania. | Ro?sia Montan?a Gold Corporation.
Classification: LCC HF5681.B2 D63 2017 | DDC 657/.309498--dc23 LC record available at https://lccn.loc.gov/2017019848

This book is published in the IGI Global book series Advances in Finance, Accounting, and Economics (AFAE) (ISSN: 2327-5677; eISSN: 2327-5685)

British Cataloguing in Publication Data
A Cataloguing in Publication record for this book is available from the British Library.

Advances in Finance, Accounting, and Economics (AFAE) Book Series

ISSN:2327-5677
EISSN:2327-5685

MISSION

In our changing economic and business environment, it is important to consider the financial changes occurring internationally as well as within individual organizations and business environments. Understanding these changes as well as the factors that influence them is crucial in preparing for our financial future and ensuring economic sustainability and growth.

The **Advances in Finance, Accounting, and Economics (AFAE)** book series aims to publish comprehensive and informative titles in all areas of economics and economic theory, finance, and accounting to assist in advancing the available knowledge and providing for further research development in these dynamic fields.

COVERAGE

- E-Accounting
- Economics of Innovation and Knowledge
- Economic Indices and Quantitative Economic Methods
- Applied economics
- Statistical Analysis
- Accounting Standards
- Behavioral Economics
- Finance
- Evidence-Based Studies
- International Economics

IGI Global is currently accepting manuscripts for publication within this series. To submit a proposal for a volume in this series, please contact our Acquisition Editors at Acquisitions@igi-global.com or visit: http://www.igi-global.com/publish/.

The Advances in Finance, Accounting, and Economics (AFAE) Book Series (ISSN 2327-5677) is published by IGI Global, 701 E. Chocolate Avenue, Hershey, PA 17033-1240, USA, www.igi-global.com. This series is composed of titles available for purchase individually; each title is edited to be contextually exclusive from any other title within the series. For pricing and ordering information please visit http://www.igi-global.com/book-series/advances-finance-accounting-economics/73685. Postmaster: Send all address changes to above address.

Titles in this Series

For a list of additional titles in this series, please visit:
http://www.igi-global.com/book-series/advances-finance-accounting-economics/73685

Alternative Decision-Making Models for Financial Portfolio Management Emerging Research and Oportunities
Narela Spaseski (International University of Sarajevo, Bosnia and Herzegovina)
Business Science Reference • ©2018 • 333pp • H/C (ISBN: 9781522532590) • US $175.00

Ranking Economic Performance and Efficiency in the Global Market Emerging Research ...
Benjamen Franklen Gussen (University of Southern Queensland, Australia & Australian Law and Economics Association, Australia)
Business Science Reference • ©2018 • 306pp • H/C (ISBN: 9781522527565) • US $195.00

Financial Entrepreneurship for Economic Growth in Emerging Nations
Atsede Woldie (University of South Wales, UK) and Brychan Thomas (University of South Wales, UK)
Business Science Reference • ©2018 • 304pp • H/C (ISBN: 9781522527008) • US $225.00

Technological Integration as a Catalyst for Industrial Development and Economic Growth
Bryan Christiansen (PryMarke, LLC, USA) and Ülkü Yüksel (The University of Sydney Business School, Australia)
Business Science Reference • ©2017 • 272pp • H/C (ISBN: 9781522523192) • US $185.00

Handbook of Research on Economic, Financial, and Industrial Impacts on Infrastructure ...
Ramesh Chandra Das (Katwa College, India)
Business Science Reference • ©2017 • 466pp • H/C (ISBN: 9781522523611) • US $230.00

Handbook of Research on Policies and Practices for Sustainable Economic Growth and ...
George M. Korres (University of Aegean, Greece) Elias Kourliouros (University of Aegean, Greece) and Maria P. Michailidis (University of Nicosia, Cyprus)
Business Science Reference • ©2017 • 440pp • H/C (ISBN: 9781522524588) • US $255.00

For an enitre list of titles in this series, please visit:
http://www.igi-global.com/book-series/advances-finance-accounting-economics/73685

IGI Global
DISSEMINATOR OF KNOWLEDGE

701 East Chocolate Avenue, Hershey, PA 17033, USA
Tel: 717-533-8845 x100 • Fax: 717-533-8661
E-Mail: cust@igi-global.com • www.igi-global.com

Table of Contents

Preface

We consider integrated reporting as an essential stage in the evolution of the financial and non- financial reporting environment and this research aims to contribute to IR adoption and implementation. Further on, the integrated reporting approach is meant to change the traditional view on corporate reporting, and in time the business environment will understand better its external and internal benefits in term of cost reduction, reputation, corporate image, stakeholder engagement, etc. (Phillips, Watson, & Willis, 2011). However, before implementing IR, organizations have to understand the true meaning of the integrated reporting concept, the connection between financial and non-financial information, and the origins of this reporting trend, as it represents a continuity of non-financial reporting initiatives, that in the initial stage were seen as separate information channels from the financial data. Still, the integrated report is not just an aggregated report, where non-financial information is simply condensed in the annual report, along with the financial one, but a revolutionary reporting system where information elements are connected and interrelated, as social and environmental impacts affect the financial performance.

This book will be of great interest for academics and practitioners (employees, accountants, auditors, experts, etc.) in the same time, as well as regulators. Thus, it should serve the corporate environment that decided to apply IR reporting techniques, either from voluntary, or mandatory concerns, from employees (CEO, managers, financial analysis, etc.) to the other elements of business (customers, suppliers, providers of financial capital: banks, financial institutions, etc.). The academic environment (universities and their curricula, professors and course materials, students, PhD candidates working on their thesis, researchers etc.), and including those providing training for higher qualifications in the financial and accounting field, and related fields (international organizations), all seek to keep themselves update with the ultimate trends in corporate reporting. Regulators, auditors, accountants, analysis, are all concerned with understanding the best means of evaluating the IR information and the integrated reports.

REFERENCES

Phillips, D., Watson, L., & Willis, M. (2011). Benefits of comprehensive integrated reporting. *Financial Executive*, *27*(2), 26–30.

Chapter 1
The Landscape of Integrated Reporting

ABSTRACT

The aim of the current chapter is to set the main coordinates of the study. We make a broad literature review analysis in order to understand the process of integrating non – financial information in the annual report and the interrelations between sustainability/corporate social responsibility and financial information. The early integrated reporting literature is based on the socio- environmental literature, and explains the nature of disclosure, and integration, as key-elements for an integrated report. Corporations should be aware of what information to disclose in the IR and what integration actually means. In addition, an integrated report is not just a mixture of financial, sustainability, and CSR information. All these elements have to be connected and interrelated based on a business model approach.

OVERVIEW UPON THE NON- FINANCIAL INFORMATION LITERATURE

This section of the book contains an overview on disclosure studies in the field of corporate reporting (Table 1). We use meta-analysis (Chavent *et al.*, 2005) for presenting the process of disclosure. Meta- analysis represents a literature review with the purpose of finding interrelations between studies or even finds common issues with the currently developed research. In our case it is meant to bring new insights on disclosure mechanisms and

DOI: 10.4018/978-1-5225-3622-2.ch001

Table 1. Summary of disclosure studies

Citation	Type of Disclosure	Sample	Variables	Methodology	Results - Variables or Factors That Influence the Level of Disclosure
Singhvi, 1968; Singhvi and Desai, 1971; Buzby, 1975; Stanga, 1976	general disclosure	40 - 155 companies	Size, industry, rate of return, earnings margin, audit firm, type of management, number of stockholders, listing status	disclosure index; univariate/ multivariate regressions	Size, industry, management, number of stockholders, listing status,
Firth, 1979; McNally et al., 1982; Firth, 1984;	voluntary disclosure	52 - 180 companies	size, rate of return, growth, audit firm, industry, listing status; Corporate governance, cultural and firm-specific	disclosure index; univariate	size, listing status, industry
Tai *et al.*, 1990; Wallace and Nasser 1995; Owusu-Ansah, 1998.	mandatory disclosure	28 - 84 companies	Independent non-executive directors, family control, profitability, leverage, size, audit firm, ownership, age, multinational affiliation, profitability, industry, liquidity	disclosure index; OSL	Multinationality, accountant's qualification, size
Cooke, 1989a; Cooke 1992;	voluntary and mandatory disclosure	35 - 138 companies	Listing status, parent company relationship size, number of shareholders, Cultural, legal, Culture, national, financial systems	multivariate/liniar regressions	Common law, culture
Williams, 2001	* voluntary environmental and social disclosure	356 companies	Culture, political and civil system, legal system, level of economic development,	Content analysis (number if sentences); 3 linear regressions	Uncertainty avoidance, masculinity, political and civil systems
Gray *et al.*, 2001	* social and environmental disclosure	100 companies	Profit, turnover, capital employed, industry classification, number of employees	8 measures of disclosure (CSEAR Social and Environmental Disclosure Database; O.L.S regressions	not relevant

Source: Adapted from Chavent et al., 2005.

determinants. Although this is only the first part of a broader research on the topic of integrated reporting, we have to begin by constructing disclosure scales that should measure IR disclosure levels and contribute to finding the determinants of disclosure phenomena (Chavent *et al.*, 2005).

The criteria used for grouping the main research studies in the area of corporate disclosure literature are the *type of disclosure*. For each disclosure group, we identify the sample, variables, methodology, and results. Disclosure studies can be categorized in voluntary disclosure research, mandatory disclosure investigations, voluntary-mandatory debate papers, general disclosure studies, and voluntary environmental and social disclosure, social and environmental disclosure.

Lima and Pereira (2011) investigate the taxonomy of disclosure. The scholars distinguish between association, discretionary, and efficiency types of disclosure. The first one can be successfully used to find correlations or associations within disclosure items and financial ratios/investor behavior/ profit maximization etc. being set as a *causality relationship*. The second type investigates the reasons for different corporate behavior/disclosure strategies/diffusion or adoption of certain reporting practice etc. and is useful for finding the *determinants* of a process/procedure/information disclosure etc. The efficiency based disclosure refers to establishing the set of information that should be disclosed in order for an organization to be efficient and to disclose/present the information in an efficient manner. In our view this relates to determining the most suitable *disclosure framework* according to the corporation needs but in the same time fulfilling stakeholders' expectations. Even though Lima and Pereira (2011) presented the three main types of disclosure in this specific order, we consider that our researcher in integrated reporting should first clarify which is the most relevant information to be included in a disclosure: *efficiency-based disclosure (1)*. The next stage consists of finding the main determinants of the analyzed disclosure - *discretionary-based disclosure (2)* so that we understand which factors can influence the degree of disclosure. Finally, we are also interested in defining the *correlation (3)* between the information disclosure level and the external factors (Figure 1).

An investigation on financial and non-financial information assumes narrative disclosure. Merkl-Davis and Brennan (2011) find sociological explanations for narrative disclosures- *legitimacy, stakeholders, and institutional theories*. Further on, Smith (2004) and Merkl-Davis and Brennan (2011) argue that narrative disclosure is more common for discretionary-based disclosure studies. Beattie *et al.* (2004) consider that an analysis of narratives

Figure 1. Taxonomy of disclosure
Source: Author's design.

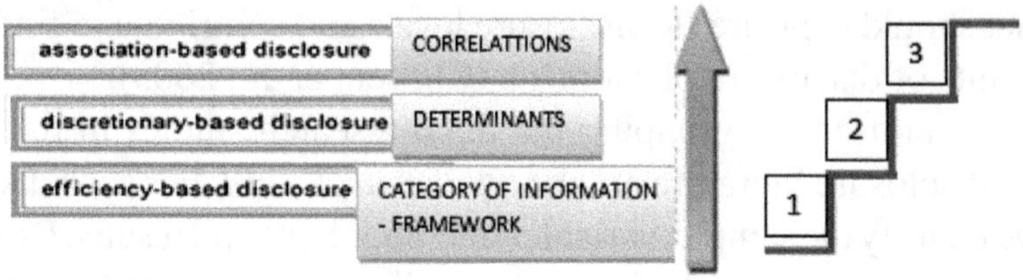

in annual reports should be suitable for investigating disclosure taxonomies for financial and non-financial information. Research on narrative disclosure is conducted by Beattie *et al.*, (2004), Eccles *et al.* (2012), Merkl-Davis and Brennan (2011), De Villiers *et al.* (2011) etc. and involves content analysis, disclosure index determination, key performance indicators computation, and other forms of investigating voluntary narrative information. Campbell and Slack (2006) investigate the relevance of narrative voluntary disclosure from the perspectives of preparers and users of annual reports. Their purpose is to understand if users find the disclosed information useful and if preparers of annual reports understand the needs of users and comply with them in an efficient manner. In other words, narrative disclosure should be consistent with the needs and expectations of stakeholders. In our opinion, the capacity of an organization to incorporate the proper narrative disclosure should be measured based on a *disclosure scale*. Although the disclosure scale represents our original contribution to the current research, we are extracting elements from disclosure literature for defining the referential points of the scale that ensures the relevance of our findings (Figure 2).

Figure 2 presents a model of disclosure scale that fluctuates from minimum requirements- in the form of mandatory disclosure- to medium and maximum disclosure levels – voluntary disclosure items. We consider that the financial information could be classified as a mandatory requirement because it is requested by standards and regulations. Indeed, some countries have specific laws that regulate environmental, social, and governmental information by demanding corporations to disclose a minimum set of ESG-environmental social and governmental information (Ioannou and Serafein, 2011). Therefore, we placed the ESG information at the interplay between mandatory and voluntary disclosure. However, if we refer to an integration of these elements, we can move forward until we reach the top of the scale as the interconnectivity of economic, social, and environmental disclosure

Figure 2. Construction of a disclosure scale for a successful narrative disclosure
Source: Author's design.

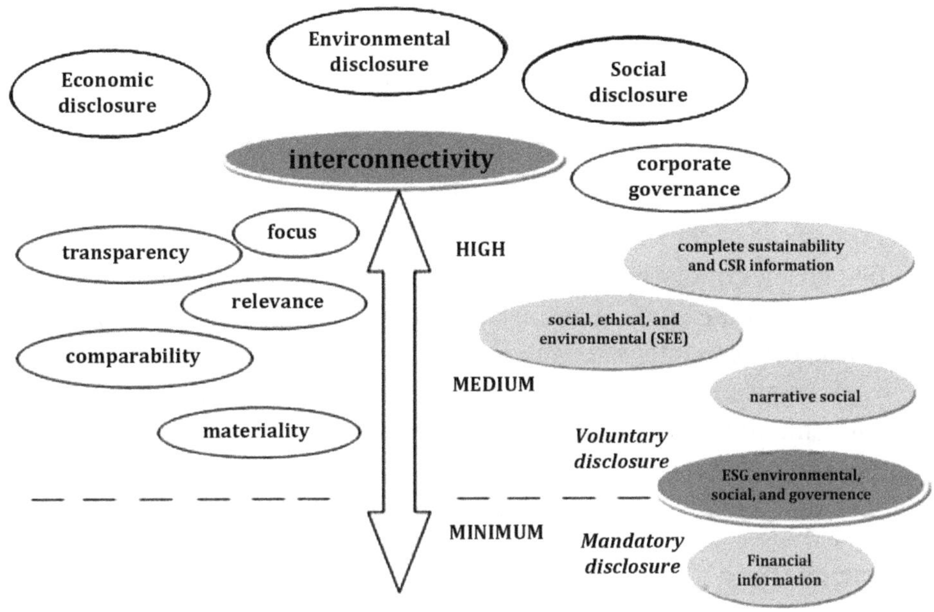

(Watson and Monterio, 2011, Wilkinson *et* al., 2004; Clarkson *et al.*, 2008) ensures while materiality, comparability (Radley, 2012), relevance, and focus are met, the narrative disclosure attains its purpose: *impact* on stakeholders (Cooper and Owen, 2011).

DISCUSSING THE INTERRELATIONSHIP BETWEEN IR AND CORPORATE GOVERNANCE

Ultimately, *impact* on stakeholders is measured through economic, social, environmental, and corporate governance *performance*. Soukopová *et al.* (2011) argue for the importance of proper economic performance integration in an annual report, adding corporate governance performance to a successful narrative disclosure. The narrative social disclosure (Campbell and Slack, 2006) encounters a positive evolution from medium to high disclosure levels, as social, ethical and environmental (SEE) information becomes material and relevant for investors and analysts (Solomon and Solomon, 2006; Campbell and Slack, 2006). Our disclosure scale aims to complete, on a step by step basis, the gaps in disclosure frameworks. Therefore, reporting transparency and focus are meant to improve the disclosure process (Mammat, 2009), while the ESG (economic, social, and governance) performance impact (Mammat, 2009; Watson and Monterio, 2011; Wilkinson *et al.*, 2004) should result in a complete and successful narrative disclosure.

CONCLUSION

The first chapter of our book makes a trespassing through the most relevant disclosure literature studies, and in the end we include a discussion on the connection between integrated reporting and corporate governance. Further on, we acknowledge the relevance of the current study for the corporate environment, informing companies of what an IR really represents and how to apply correctly for an IR.

REFERENCES

Beattie, V., McInnes, W., & Fearnley, S. (2004). A methodology for analysing and evaluating narratives in annual reports: a comprehensive descriptive profile and metrics for disclosure quality attributes. *Accounting Forum, 28*(3), 205-236. doi:10.1016/j.accfor.2004.07.001

Buzby, S. L. (1975). Company size, listed versus unlisted stocks, and the extent of financial disclosure. *Journal of Accounting Research, 13*(1), 16–37. doi:10.2307/2490647

Campbell, D., & Slack, R. (2006). Public visibility as a determinant 18 of the rate of corporate charitable donations. *Business Ethics (Oxford, England), 15*(1), 19–28. doi:10.1111/j.1467-8608.2006.00425.x

Chavent, M., Ding, Y., Fu, L., Stolowy, H., & Wang, H. (2005). *Disclosure and Determinants Studies: An Extension Using the Divisive Clustering Method (DIV).* 10.2139/ssrn.869924

Clarkson, P. M., Li, Y., Richardson, G. D., & Vasvari, F. P. (2008). Revisiting the relation between environmental performance and environmental disclosure: An empirical analysis. *Accounting, Organizations and Society, 33*(3), 303–327. doi:10.1016/j.aos.2007.05.003

Cooke, T. E. (1989a). Disclosure in the corporate annual reports of Swedish companies. *Accounting and Business Review, 19*(74), 113–124. doi:10.1080/00014788.1989.9728841

Cooke, T. E. (1992). The impact of size, stock market listing and industry type on disclosure in the annual reports. *The International Journal of Accounting, 38*(2), 173–194.

Cooper, S., & Owen, D. (2011). Corporate Social Reporting and Stakeholder Accountability: The Missing Link. *Accounting, Organizations and Society, 32*(7-8), 649–667. doi:10.1016/j.aos.2007.02.001

De Villiers, C., & Van Staden, C. J. (2011). Where firms choose to disclose voluntary environmental information. *Journal of Accounting and Public Policy, 30*(6), 504–525. doi:10.1016/j.jaccpubpol.2011.03.005

Eccles, R., Ioannou, I., & Serafeim, G. (2012). *The Impact of a Corporate Culture of Sustainability on Corporate Behaviour and Performance*. Working Paper. Harvard Business School. Available at http://www.hbs.edu/research/pdf/12-035.pdf

Firth, M. (1979, Autumn). The impact of size, stock market listing, and auditors on voluntary disclosure in corporate annual reports. *Accounting and Business Research,* 273-280.

Firth, M. (1984). The extent of voluntary disclosure in corporate annual reports and its association with security risk measures. *Applied Economics, 16*(2), 269–277. doi:10.1080/00036848400000036

Gray, R., Javad, M., Power, D. M., & Sinclair, C. D. (2001). Social and environmental disclosure and corporate characteristics: A research note and extension. *Journal of Business Finance & Accounting, 28*(3-4), 327–356. doi:10.1111/1468-5957.00376

Ioannou, I., & Serafeim, G. (2011). *The Consequences of Mandatory Corporate Sustainability Reporting*. Harvard Business School Research Working Paper No. 11-100.

Lima, E. & Pereira C.A. (2011). Comparative analysis of the index of disclosure and the importance given by stakeholders to information considered relevant for accountability in Philanthropic Institutions of Higher Education of Brazil (PIHEB). *African Journal of Business Management, 5*(34), 13116-13129.

Mammat, J. (2009). *Integrated Sustainability Reporting and Assurance, Conference paper*. CIS Corporate Governance Conference. Retrieved from http://www.ciscorpgov.co.za/present/CIS%20WEBSITE/Mammatt_Integrated%20Sustainability%20Reporting%20and%20Assurance.pdf

McNally, G. M., Eng, L. H., & Hasseldine, C. R. (1982). Corporate financial reporting in New Zealand: An analysis of user preferences, corporate characteristics and disclosure practices for discretionary information. *Accounting and Business Review*, *13*(49), 11–20. doi:10.1080/00014788.1982.9729725

Owusu-Ansah, S. (1998). The impact of corporate attributes on the extent of mandatory disclosure and reportingby listed companies in Zimbabwe. *The International Journal of Accounting*, *33*(5), 605–631. doi:10.1016/S0020-7063(98)90015-2

Phillips, D., Watson, L., & Willis, M. (2011). Benefits of Comprehensive Integrated Reporting. *Financial Executive*, *27*(2), 26–30.

Radley, Y. (2012). *The value of extra- financial disclosure. What investors and analysts said*. Accounting for Sustainability, Global Reporting Initiative. Retrieved from https://www.globalreporting.org/information/news-and-press-center/Pages/Investors-and-analysts-use-extra-financial-information-in-decision-making-suggests-new-research.aspx

Singhvi, S. (1968). Characteristics and implications of inadequate disclosure: A case study of India. *The International Journal of Accounting*, *3*(2), 29–43.

Singhvi, S., & Desai, H. (1971). An empirical analysis of the quality of corporate financial disclosure. *Accounting Review*, *46*(1), 129–138.

Smith, M. (2004). Editorial, Corporate Financial Communication and Voluntary Disclosure. *Accounting Forum*, *28*(3), 201–203. doi:10.1016/j.accfor.2004.08.004

Solomon, J. F., & Solomon, A. (2006). Private Social, Ethical and Environmental Disclosure. *Accounting, Auditing & Accountability Journal*, *19*(4), 564–591. doi:10.1108/09513570610679137

Soukopová, J., Hrebicek, J., Stencl, M., & Trenz, O. (2011). Integration of economic, environmental, social and corporate governance performance and reporting in enterprises. *Acta Universitatis Agriculturae et Silviculturae Mendelianae Brunensis, 59*(7), 157-166.

Stanga, K. G. (1976). Disclosure in published annual reports. *Financial Management*, *5*(Winter), 42–52. doi:10.2307/3665456

Tai, B. Y. K., Au-Yeng, P.-K., Kwok, M. C. M., & Lau, L. W. C. (1990). Non-compliance with disclosure requirements in financial statements: The case of Hong Kong companies. *Journal of International Financial Management and Accounting*, *13*(2), 125–152.

Wallace, R. S. O., & Naser, K. (1995). Firm-specific determinants of comprehensiveness of mandatory disclosure in the corporate annual reports of firms listed on the stock exchange of Hong Kong. *Journal of Accounting and Public Policy*, *14*(4), 311–368. doi:10.1016/0278-4254(95)00042-9

Watson, L.A., & Monterio, B.J. (2011, July). The Next Stage in the Evolution of Business Reporting – The Journey Towards an Interlinked, Integrated Report. *The Chartered Accountants*, 75-78.

Wilkinson, Fergusson, Bowyer, Brown, Ladefoged, Monkhouse, & Zdanowicz. (2004). *Sustainable Development in the European Commission's Integrated Impact Assessment for 2003*. Final Report for the UK Department of the Environment, Food and Rural Affairs (DEFRA). Institute for European Environmental Policy (IEEP).

Williams, M. S. (2001). Is intellectual capital performance and disclosure practices related? *Journal of Intellectual Capital*, *2*(3), 192–203. doi:10.1108/14691930110399932

Chapter 2
Non-Financial Reporting Initiatives

ABSTRACT

This section of our book explains the main non-financial reporting initiatives. From reporting schemes (developed at micro or macro level, or even global reporting guidelines), to specific regulation in France, USA, Denmark, Sweden, South Africa, the first reporting initiatives on non-financial sector were meant to contribute to the development of corporate reporting field, being an initial step in the revolution of IR.

REPORTING SCHEMES AND FIRST REGULATION ATTEMPTS IN THE AREA OF NON-FINANCIAL REPORTING

The most prominent non-financial reporting initiatives were undertaken by worldwide organizations, such as Global Reporting Initiative, AccountAbility, EFRAG- European Financial Reporting Advisory Group, SASB- Sustainability Accounting Standards Board, Climate Disclosure Standards Board, IIRC- International Integrated Reporting Council, FEE- Federation of European Accountants, SA IRC- South African Integrated Reporting Committee, AA 1000, Accounting for Accountability, and other professional organisms.

In 2010 the UN Global Compact Leaders' Summit was discussing the effects of the crises for the global economy, stating the need for a sustainable approach when rebalancing the economy (UN Global Compact-Accenture, 2010).

DOI: 10.4018/978-1-5225-3622-2.ch002

One of the most recent actions of the IIRC involves the introduction of the Corporate Reporting Dialogue (CRD). This represents a tool for comparing the content of participants' frameworks or standards through an IR perspective. CRD participants include IASB, FASB, IPSASB, CDSB, SASB, GRI, and ISO[1].

Eccles *et al.*, (2010a) performed an analysis upon non-financial reporting tendencies within the business world. The scholars mentioned large discrepancies between Europe and other continents, as the European Commission highly promotes non-financial information disclosure. Contrary to European countries, Japan, China and U.S. maintain low disclosure levels of non-financial reporting.

KPMG (2008a) survey analyses trends in corporate reporting including the top 250 companies of the Fortune 500 (G-250), as well as the top 100 companies in 16 countries. It noted that over 80% of the G250 produce sustainability reports. On average, 45% of the top 100 companies in each of the surveyed countries produce sustainability reports - Japan and the United Kingdom are leaders with 93% and 91% respectively. South Africa is some way behind at 45%, but it is one of the leaders in integrating the sustainability report into the annual report.

Later on, in 2010, KPMG raised other issues on integrated reporting, like the importance of communication with stakeholders or integrating the sustainability information into the financial reporting (KPMG, 2010). More recent studies issued by KPMG (2012) present a very suggestive image of the integrated report, being at the interplay of stakeholders', managers', and investors' needs and expectations.

During the last 20 years, corporate non-financial reporting has developed from predominately single-issue reports (mostly focusing on the environment) to multi-issue reports or sustainability reports. The single-issue reports sometimes already covered different topics such as community engagement, ethics, and supply chain management, but only sustainability reports also

Table 1. Use of reporting schemes by G250 and N100

Type of Scheme	G250 (%)	N100 (%)
GRI Guidelines	77	69
Internally-developed company schemes	20	19
National reporting schemes	19	17
Other schemes	13	13

Source: KPMG, 2008a: 71.

reflect the economic and socioeconomic aspects of the reporting company (CRRA, 2010: 5). Currently, this trend of developing multi-issue reporting goes further towards 'integrated reporting', which means sustainability reporting integrated within the financial or annual report. This is one of the major topics in the debate on the future of sustainability reporting.

Initiatives for issuing non-financial reporting regulations were conducted by certain influential countries or organizations, as well as international stock exchanges (ACCA, 2011). South Africa, France, United States, Denmark and Sweden played an active role in implementing requirements for extra financial information as prerequisites for integrated reporting adoption (Table 2).

The Nouvelles Regulations Economiques, issued by France in 2001 established a framework for sustainability disclosure with respect to "corporate governance, social and community impacts, environmental management, and workplace practices" (ACCA, 2011: 12). Eleven years after, France was going to mandate extra financial information and promote an IR approach in reporting (RSE, 2012). In 2002, the US regulates disclosure of corporate governance, code of conduct, and environmental information, through the Sarbanes–Oxley Act. The Danish Financial Statements Act enforced by Denmark in 2001 states the main requirements for sustainability reporting. In Sweden, state-owned companies are requested to disclose on sustainability and assurance for this type of non-financial information according to the Guidelines for external reporting by state-owned companies issued in 2007. South Africa mandated IR in 2010 through the enforcement of the King Code of Governance Principles and the King Report on Governance (ACCA, 2011).

Table 2. Non-financial regulation

Year	Country	Regulation	Impact
2001	France	Nouvelles Regulations Economiques	ESG information
2001	Denmark	Danish Financial Statements Act	environmental and sustainability reporting
2002	US	Sarbanes–Oxley Act	code of conduct; environmental performance.
2007	Sweden	Guidelines for external reporting by state-owned companies	sustainability reporting
2009	South Africa	King Code of Governance Principles and the King Report on Governance (King III)	mandatory IR
2012	France	Grenelle II	extra financial information and IR approach

Source: Author's design.

If previously we presented a set of non-financial initiatives developed at national/country level, from now on we describe the most prominent international organizations and their role in promoting IR (Table 3).

The European Alliance for Corporate Social Responsibility has been set up in year 2006 at the initiatives of the European Commission and European business community, and since then promotes corporate social responsibility and social-environmental integration. Four international stock exchanges (TMX Group, NYSE Euronext, BM & FBOVESPA, Bourse de Luxembourg) demand for reporting on sustainability indices. The Johannesburg Stock Exchange claims that listed companies have to fully report on their non-financial information that becomes mandatory. Similar requirements are issued by Bursa Malaysia that adds corporate social responsibility practice and assurance. Singapore Stock Exchange promotes voluntary disclosure on sustainability items, while Shanghai Stock Exchange engages in mandatory reporting for environmental items when the operations conducted by the companies are affecting the environment (ACCA, 2011).

On September 12, 2011, IIRC issues a Discussion paper *Towards Integrated Reporting – Communicating Value in the 21st Century* through which it creates the foundation of the IIRC framework to serve both producers and users of integrated reports. Next year, they introduced a Prototype Framework, while in April 2013 they release a Consultation Draft and in December 2013

Table 3. International initiatives for promoting non-financial information[2]

Year	Organization/Institution	Initiative	Purpose
2006	European Commission; European business community	European Alliance for Corporate Social Responsibility	corporate social responsibility and social-environmental integration
2009	TMX Group; NYSE Euronext; BM & FBOVESPA; Bourse de Luxembourg	development of sustainability indices; general requirements	useful for investors; voluntary nature
2011	Corporate Sustainability Reporting Coalition	United Nations' member states round tables	framework for integrating sustainability information In the annual report
2013-2012	Johannesburg Stock Exchange; Bursa Malaysia	JSE Listings Requirements; Bursa Malaysia's Listing Requirements	Mandatory disclosure of non-financial information
2011	Singapore Stock Exchange	Guide to Sustainability Reporting for Listed Companies	voluntary sustainability reporting
2012	United Nations (Conference on Sustainable Development (Rio+20))	Sustainable Stock Exchanges (SSE)	global dialogue

Source: Author's design.

they already had the final version for the Framework (www.iirc.com). If the *discussion paper* was the first step in introducing the *content elements* and *principles* of an integrated report, as well as providing definitions for the main terms related to integrated reporting, the *prototype* is a detailed presentation of those elements and principles, or key concepts, while the *consultation draft* was issued with the purpose of gathering important feedback from all the stakeholders in order to obtain a complete and comprehensive version of the framework. In addition, the IIRC has created a database for integrated reports in which they provide examples of reports that follow the content elements and principles of the framework, sustained by Blacksun organization that published case studies on integrated reporting (Steyn, 2015; Kooiker, 2014).

CONCLUSION

The second chapter illustrated the step-by-step introduction of the non-financial reporting initiatives at company level, then national level, and internationally and global stage. At first, these initiatives were defined under the form of guidelines, having a voluntary approach. Then, they emerged into specific mandatory requirements, through national legislator acts: Nouvelles Regulations Economiques (France), Danish Financial Statements Act (Denmark), Sarbanes–Oxley Act (US), Guidelines for external reporting by state-owned companies (Sweden), etc.

REFERENCES

ACCA. (2011). *Adoption of integrated reporting by the ASX 50- A joint report from ACCA and the Net Balance Foundation*. Retrieved from www.accaglobal.com\

CRRA. (2010). *Global Winners and Reporting Trends. Experienced stakeholders judge the world's leading CR reports*. Retrieved from http://www.corporateregister.com/pdf/CRRA10.pdf

Kooiker, K. G. H. (2014). *Towards a new corporate reporting model? Analysing stakeholder opinions concerning the role of business in society and integrated reporting*. Available at http://essay.utwente.nl/65567/

KPMG. (2008). *International Survey of Corporate Responsibility Reporting 2008*. KPMG International.

KPMG. (2010). *Integrated reporting: Closing the loop of strategy*. Retrieved from http://www.kpmg.com/ro/en/issuesandinsights/articlespublications/press-releases/pages/integrated-reporting.aspx

KPMG. (2012). *Integrated Reporting Performance insight through Better Business Reporting*. Retrieved from www.kpmg.com/integratedreporting

RSE. (2012). *The Grenelle II Act in France: a milestone towards integrated reporting*. Institut RSE survey n° 7. Available at https://www.yumpu.com/en/document/view/38199171/the-grenelle-ii-act-in-france-a-milestone-towards-capital-institute

Steyn, M. (2015). Senior executives' perspectives of integrated reporting regulatory regimes as a mechanism for advancing sustainability in South African listed companies. *Southern African Business Review*, *18*(3), 142–174.

UN Global Compact-Accenture. (2010). *CEO Study- A New Era of Sustainability, CEO reflections on progress to date, challenges ahead and the impact of the journey toward a sustainable economy*. Available at http://apo.org.au/research/new-era-sustainability-ceo-reflections-progress-date-challenges-ahead-and-impact-journey

ENDNOTES

1. http://corporatereportingdialogue.com/landscape-map/.
2. Although Johannesburg Stock Exchange, Bursa Malaysia, and Singapore Stock Exchange are all national stock exchanges, we consider them as part of the international non-financial reporting initiatives because they encourage worldwide listed organizations to follow non-financial reporting requirements.

Chapter 3
The Concept of Integrated Reporting

ABSTRACT

Chapter 3 defines the process of integration, and deeply explains the concept of integrated report. We provide a wide range of literature review sources, for the purpose of establishing the characteristics of integrated reporting. Integrated reports cannot be fully understood until we clarify the meaning of the first word: integrated. This section of the book concentrates on defining the term of integration. Kirkpatrick and Lee (1999) links the notion of integration to sustainable development and economic, social, and environmental impacts on the decision-making process. Krajnc and Glavic (2005) mentions that corporations need to integrate the information related to sustainable development so that it becomes useful for decisions.

UNDERSTANDING THE INTEGRATION PROCESS

There have been many approaches to study the *integration* process, from sustainability index combination (Krajnc & Glavic, 2005), to impact assessment integration: economic, social, environmental (Wilkinson *et al.*, 2004), and to corporate social reporting (Frias-Aceituno, 2012). Previous work of Ramjerdi et al. (2008) studied integrated indicators, finding four levels of integration, namely: *very strong, strong, weak, very weak.* Eggenberger and Partidio (2000) distinguish between five forms of integration, namely: substantive, methodological, procedural, institutional, political. Substantive integration is

DOI: 10.4018/978-1-5225-3622-2.ch003

both local and global in the same time, and assumes environmental, social, climate aspects. The methodological integration involves the cumulating of social, economic, and environmental information. Procedural integration represents the implication of stakeholders in the decision making process. The institutional integration involves government, agencies and institutions involvement, while political type of integration relates to the integration of regulations (Eggenberger & Partidio, 2000). All the integration types can be applied in our research, except substantive integration, as this one refers to behavioral aspects more than reporting practices.

From the IIRC perspective, *integration* means the interdependence/ correlation between financial and non-financial information, as it results from the first draft- framework issued in 2013 (Figure 1).

One year later, IIRC had a final framework, that added some general guidance on preparation and presentation of the report, rephrased some IR elements or principles, or changed their order in the framework.

However, the IIRC mentions that the above elements and principles are not mandatory and companies can still apply IR on a correct manner without necessarily including all these items. According to the IIRC vision of the *integration* process, we should consider the various forms of capitals from

Figure 1. IR content elements and principles according to the draft framework of IIRC
Source: Extracted from the IIRC website.

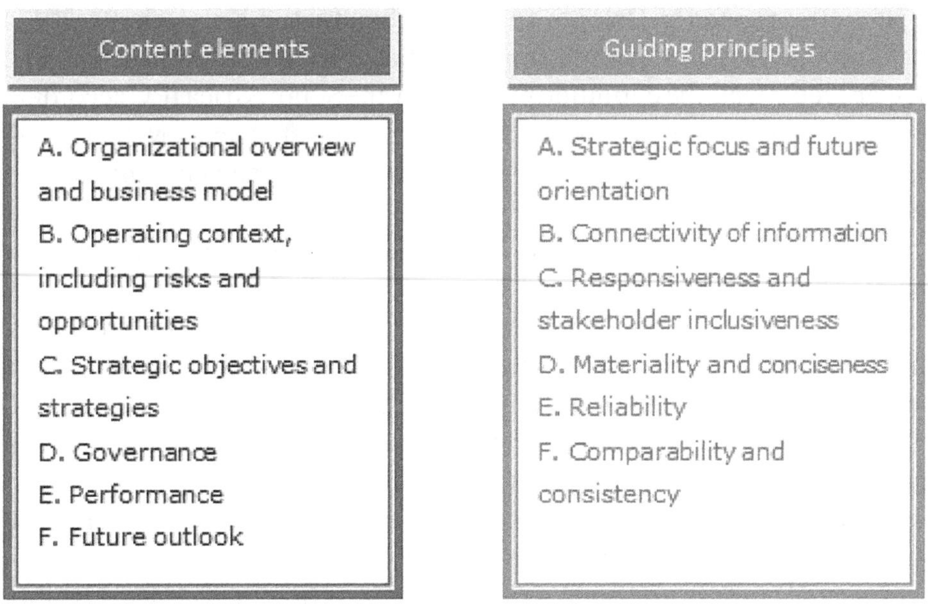

an IR, namely: financial capital, manufactured capital, intellectual capital, social and relationship capital, human capital, and natural capital.

INTEGRATED REPORTING: DEFINITIONS AND CHARACTERISTICS

In order to provide a deep understanding of the concept of integrated reporting (Figure 2) we have gathered various definitions, opinions and facts upon the concept of integrated reporting. Integrated reporting has its roots in the notion of triple bottom line (Elkington, 1998). The concept of integrated reporting is mentioned for the first time by White (2005) who performs an analysis upon various corporations' reports. By 2010, the scholars and academics were becoming more interested in the topic of integrated reporting, enlarging the international literature. Therefore, the notion of integrated reporting has evolved from the triple bottom line (Elkington, 1998), being inoculated by scholars and academics in their studies on corporate reporting (White, 2005, Eccles *et al.,* 2010b; Abeysekera, 2012; Adams *et al.,* 2011; Armbrester *et al.,* 2011; Eccles & Krzus, 2010; Eccles & Krzus, 2011; Hanks & Gardiner, 2012; Krzus, 2011; Roberts, 2011).

Eccles *et al.* (2010b) state that the process of integration involves actually an inclusion of the ESG[1]- environmental, social, and governmental information, into the annual report that contains mainly financial information. A publication issued by Deloitte Touche Toohmatsu Limited (Deloitte, 2011) distinguishes between two meanings attributed to integrate reporting. The first one represents the definition provided by the South Africa IRC according to which the integrated report addresses its stakeholders, by presenting the story of the organization in a proper and clear language that should facilitate the understanding of the users of the reports. The IRC states very clear that the financial, economic, social and environmental value has to be maintained on short, medium and long time periods. In one of their reports, Ernst & Young (2011), mention that the CFO is responsible for presenting the "sustainability story" (p.5) of the corporation. In addition, investors have become more interested in the non-financial aspects, along with the financial ones. Moody's and Standard & Poor are starting to recall for sustainability policies, while ratings and indices on sustainability are being developed for measuring sustainability reporting practices. The second definition (Deloitte, 2011) has been issued by the IIRC and mentions the connection between the strategy, financial performance, governance, and sustainability

Figure 2. The concept of integrated reporting
Source: KPMG, 2012: 17.

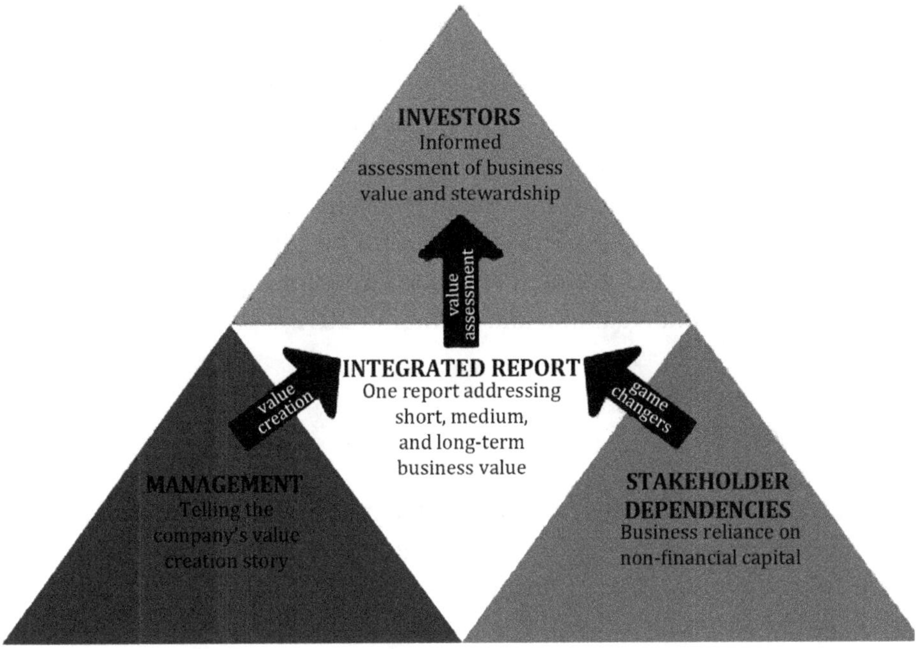

elements- social, environmental, and economic pillars (Robinson and Tinker, 1998; Raar, 2012), as integrated reports contribute to efficient sustainable decisions by providing a holistic view of organizations' performance to the stakeholders[2], especially investors.

Further on, the topic of integrated reports has been highly debated within literature. Nowadays corporations can diffuse and adopt integrated reporting trends, while integrated reporting practices can fill the research gap regarding this new topic and represent a basis for scholars that conduct studies on the matter. Eccles *et al.* (2010b) provide advice on how to approach integrated reporting. The academics explain how companies can develop integrated reports and how to develop attitudes for changing to integrated reporting. Academics and scholars aimed to study the main characteristics of integrated reports. Farrar (2011) establishes eight elements that characterize integrated reporting, namely: integrated thinking, stewardship for manufactured, human, intellectual, natural and social capital, strategic objectives and value creation, long term vision, transparency and trust, flexibility, avoiding complexity and extended reports, and implementing technologies and innovation. A study developed by Rossouw (2011) sets other eight characteristics for integrated reports: disclosure of forward-looking information, assurance on the quality of this type of information, annually disclosure, positive aspects and challenges, holistic and integrated manner of presentation, financial results within a certain context, reporting integration for all performance areas, assurance on material sustainability or non-financial issues. Both Farrar and Rossouw consider the trend of integrated reporting in their research.

Previous studies in the field of corporate disclosure reveal that that mandatory requirements for integrated reporting lead to increase of ESG disclosure (Solomon and Maroun, 2012) and all mandatory non-financial requirements are generate corporate responsible organizations and a sustainable business environment (Ioannou and Serafeim, 2012).

CONCLUSION

The third chapter presented the process of integration and the extended concept of integrated reporting. Starting from *integration* as a process, we define connections of integrated reporting to sustainability, social responsibility, sustainable development, as well as social, economic, environmental, and governmental information.

REFERENCES

Abeysekera, I. (2012). A template for Integrated Reporting. *Journal of Intellectual Capital*, *14*(2).

Aceituno, F., Ariza, R., & Sanchez, G. (2012). Is Integrated Reporting determined by a country's legal system? *Journal of Cleaner Production*, *44*, 44–45.

Armbrester, K., Clay, T., & Roberts, L. (2011, April). Integrated Reporting: an irreversible tipping point. *Accountancy SA*, 28-29.

Biau, C. (2011). The 'Governance Gap', or missing links in transnational chains of accountability for extractive industry investment. *Journal of Sustainable Finance & Investment*, *1*(3-4), 251–260.

Deloitte. (2011. Integrated Reporting: A Better View? In *Global Sustainability and Climate Services*. Author.

Eccles, R., Krzus, M. P., & Tapscott, D. (2010b). *One Report: Integrated Reporting for a Sustainable Strategy* (1st ed.). Wiley Publisher.

Eccles, R. G., & Krzus, M. P. (2010). *One Report: Integrated Reporting for a Sustainable Strategy*. Hoboken, NJ: John Wiley.

Eccles, R.G., & Krzus, M.P. (2011). A Chronology of Integrated Reporting. Harvard Business School Accounting & Management Unit Case No. 411-049. Available at Alerts/PressRelease/Pages/IASB-and-IIRC-sign-MoU.aspx

Eggenberger, M., & Partidrio, M. R. (2000). Development of a framework to assist the integration of environmental, social and economic issues in spatial planning. *Impact Assessment and Project Appraisal, 18*(3), 201–207. doi:10.3152/147154600781767448

Elkington, J. (1998). *Cannibals with Forks: The Triple Bottom Line of 21st Century Business*. New Society Publishers.

Ernst & Young. (2011). *Climate Change and Sustainability. How Sustainability has expanded the CFO's role*. Retrieved from http://www.ey.com/US/en/Services/Specialty-Services/Climate-Change-and-Sustainability-Services/How-sustainability-has-expanded-the-CFOs-role

Farrar, J. (2011). *Integrated Reporting: can it solve the sustainability information gap?* Retrieved from http://www.zdnet.com/blog/sustainability/integrated-reporting-can-it-solve-the-sustainability-information-gap/1635

Frias-Aceituno, Rodriquez-Ariza, & Garcia-Sanchez. (2012). The role of the board in the dissemination of integrated corporate social reporting. *Corporate Social Responsibility and Environmental Management*. Available at http://onlinelibrary.wiley.com/doi/10.1002/csr.1294/pdf

Hanks, J., & Gardiner, L. (2012). *Integrated Reporting: Lessons from the South African Experience*. Retrieved from https://openknowledge.worldbank.org/ handle/10986/11052

Kirkpatrick, C., & Lee, N. (1999). Integrated appraisal and decision-making. *Environmental Impact Assessment Review, 19*(3), 227–232. doi:10.1016/S0195-9255(99)00012-8

Krajnc, D., & Glavic, P. (2005). A model for integrated assesment for sustainable development. *Resources, Conservation and Recycling, 43*(2), 189–208. doi:10.1016/S0921-3449(04)00120-X

Krzus, M. P. (2011). The Case for Integrated Reporting. In Trust Meltdown II: The Financial Industry Needs a Fundamental Restart. Boston: Innovation Publishing.

Raar, J. (2012). *Can early environmental reporting research offer insights into Integrated Reporting guidelines comparability?* Paper in proceedings of the 11th A-CSEAR.

Ramjerdi. (2008). *Developing Composite Indicators for Policy Makings: A Brief Methodological Framework and Considerations.* Institute of Transport Economics Norwegian Centre for Transport.

Roberts, L. (2011, Dec.). Integrated Reporting - the Status Quo. Accountancy SA.

Robinson, J., & Tinker, J. (1998). Reconciling ecological, economic and social imperatives. In J. Schnurr & S. Holtz (Eds.), *The Cornerstone of Development: Integrating Environmental, Social and Economic Policies*. Ottawa, Canada: International Development Research Centre.

Rossouw, R. (2011). *Integrating Sustainability Reporting*. Presentation delivered at the Women in Finance Conference. Retrieved from http://www.slideshare.net/Reana1/integrated-sustainability-reporting

Solomon, J., & Maroun, W. (2012). *Integrated reporting: the influence of King III on social, ethical and environmental reporting*. London: The Association of Chartered Certified Accountants. Available at http://www.accaglobal.com/content/dam/acca/global/PDF-technical/integrated-reporting/tech-tp-iirsa.pdf

White, A. L. (2005). *Fade, Integrate or Transform? The Future of CSR*. Business for Social Responsibility. Retrieved from www.bsr.org

ENDNOTES

1 The ESG concept has the same meaning as sustainability and CSR under the responsible corporate leadership patronage (Smith, 2011), being even qualified as a component of CSR (Biau, 2011).

2 The reference to *stakeholders* makes clear link to CSR, so we deduce that IR does not mean only the connection between financial performance and sustainability elements, but also CSR elements (Roberts, 1992; McGuire et al., 1998).

Chapter 4
Theories on Integrated Reporting

ABSTRACT

This chapter seeks to explain the main theories used for studying integrated reporting. Scholars and academics conducted research on non-financial information (investigating environmental/social/governance reports), and even on integrated reports (still few studies in this field) involving a set of theories: institutional and neo-institutional theory, legitimacy theory, positive accounting theory, agency theory, accounting constellation theory, etc.

EXPLAINING THE MAIN THEORIES RELATED TO INTEGRATED REPORTING

Jackson and Apostolakou (2010), Matten and Moon (2008), Granovetter (2000), Granovetter (1985), and Ball *et al.,* (2010) use *institutional theory* or *neo-institutional theory* in their research to prove that institutions of economic, cultural, educational, financial, and political nature maintain a significant influence upon worldwide organizations. Jensen and Berg (2011) conduct an empirical research upon 309 corporations selected from various sources, namely GRI reports list, GRI dataset with best traditional sustainability reports, CRRA Reporting Award 2010, Eccles & *et al.* (2010b). Results show that integrated reporting is highly correlated with the stage of economic development, national corporate responsibility, countries' values system, trade unions, private expenditure of tertiary education, ownership

DOI: 10.4018/978-1-5225-3622-2.ch004

dispersion. The authors failed to prove the influence of the political factor, underlining the inconsistency of data regarding the years for which information has been collected, given the fact that the analysis does not consider the presumption of major changes in the political system. Finally, we consider that the institutional theory can be successfully introduced in a research paper aiming to find the determinants of integrated reporting. The relevance of this paper for our research resides in the fact that Aceituno *et al.* (2012) use the coercive and normative approaches of the IT isomorphism (from the three dimensions of coercive, mimetic, and normative). We apply the segment of mimetic isomorphism of IT in our own research. The mimetic isomorphism refers to engagement in reporting practices because other companies did this before and are considered as models. Coercive isomorphism means to act in a certain manner as a result of rules expressed by external forces (Othman *et al.,* 2011). Normative isomorphism assumes doing what is considered to be right from a professional point of view, e.g. countries based on a civil law policy are more stakeholder oriented than those that practice common law and focus on shareholders mostly (Aceituno *et al.*, 2012).

We can add the legitimacy theory on the IR theories' list, especially from the perspective of stakeholders' legitimacy (Bebbington *et al.,* 2014; De Villiers *et al.,* 2006). Carnegie and Napier (2010) explain the relevance of the legitimacy theory in connection to stakeholders' needs and expectations, as not only investors are affected by the activity of the organization, because the main client of the company is the "society as a whole" (Carnegie & Napier, 2010: 20; Barone *et al.,* 2013; De Villiers *et al.,* 2006).

The diffusion and adoption theory for organizational practices (Jensen & Berg, 2012; Dillard *et al.,* 2004) originated from the institutional theory, as the latter states the influence of certain factors in the practices adopted by corporations (Jackson & Apostolakou, 2010; Matten & Moon, 2008).

Further on, integrated reporting emerged from the need to reduce information asymmetry (Jensen & Berg, 2012). Jensen and Meckling (1976) provide a concrete definition of this term correlated with the *agency theory*[1], as the unification of agent and principals' interests, by cost monitorization and residual diminishment. The principle of cost monitorization stated in the theory is applied when implementing IR, from efficient resource allocation, to long- term value creation through the contribution of financial capital (and other forms of capital) and the forward- looking perspective. Regarding the reasons management has to add monitoring costs in case of integrated reports, the agency theory cannot bring any argument, as these respective costs are neither the result of regulatory pressure nor the specific requirements of principals (or shareholders). Therefore, as Gray *et al.* (1995) argues, the agency theory cannot have the same impact on voluntary disclosures as in mandatory ones.

Integrated reporting can also be connected with the *positive accounting theory*, as it allows corporations the possibility of making choices on the policies for cost reduction (Wulf *et al.,* 2014, De Jong *et. al*, 2006). The limitation of this theory when applied to IR comes from the fact that it does not provide any evidence on the IR impact for cost reduction/ cost controlling[2].

Finally, although all these corporate reporting theories enlightened us on why organizations implement IR (stakeholders' pressure or fulfilling stakeholders' needs, cost reduction and controlling, efficient resource allocation, eliminate information asymmetry), they do not show the concrete benefits for the users of IR. In other words, do not focus on users, but on report preparers (and eventually the legislative actions to promote IR development). Therefore, we are going to present two theories that consider the whole actors involved in the IR process: *accounting constellation* and *positive accounting theory.*

From the perspective of the integrated reporting evolution and the value creation principle of IR, we have an additional theory of *accounting constellation*. International literature describes this theory as the connection between institutions, norms, processes, and practice (Burchell *et al.*, 1985; Hopwood *et al.*, 1994). When applied to IR, the constellation theory outlines the promoters of integrated reporting: GRI, A4S, OECD, IASB-IFRS, ACCA, ICAEW, FRC- UK Financial Reporting Council, CIMA- Chartered Institute of Management Accountants, FEE, IFAC, AICPA- American Institute of Certified Public Accountants, SASB, AA1000, SA8000, European Union and its new directive proposals[3], big 4 audit companies (PwC, KPMG, Erns&Young, Deloitte).

Disclosure literature presents a series of theoretical frameworks that are fundamental for studies on corporate reporting behavior (Matten and Moon, 2008; Jensen and Berg, 2012). Matten and Moon (2008) constructed a national

Figure 1. Theoretical framework
Source: Author's design.

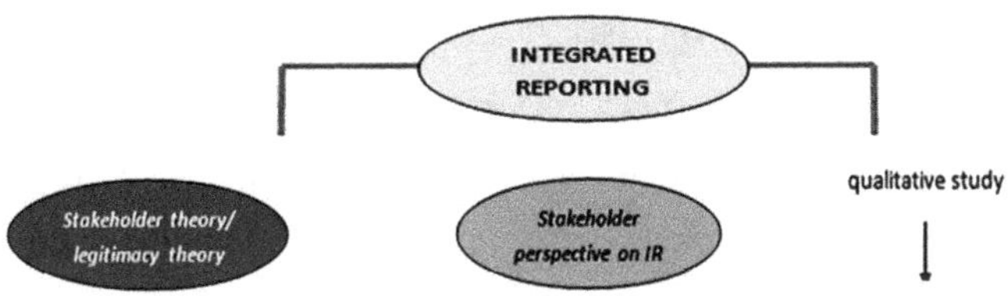

institutional framework analyzing the corporate reports from the corporate social responsibility pressure perspective in an institutional context. Based on previous conceptual frameworks from literature (Jensen and Berg, 2012), we develop our own research framework:

As the framework suggests, we have one type of research: qualitative. The qualitative research assumes the implication of stakeholder and legitimacy theories within the research upon integrated reporting. The literature review explains the economic, social, and environmental dimensions of an integrated report, showing how IR can be assessed from different stakeholders' perspectives. Furthermore, the case study on a Romanian company represents the practical approach, explaining the impact of an oil and gas corporation upon all the implicated parts, from a social, environmental, and economic perspective.

CONCLUSION

Chapter 4 presents the main theories used in correlation with corporate reporting research. Two of the mentioned theories represents the basis for our own research, and finally had a major role in defining the research framework. Thus, we fundament our study on both stakeholder and legitimacy theory, with the aim of demonstrating different stakeholders' perspectives on IR.

REFERENCES

Ball, A., & Craig, R. (2010). Using neo-institutionalism to advance social and environmental accounting. *Critical Perspectives on Accounting*, *21*(4), 283–293. doi:10.1016/j.cpa.2009.11.006

Barone, E., Ranamagar, N., & Solomon, J. (2013). A Habermasian model of stakeholder (non)engagement and corporate (ir)responsibility reporting. *Accounting Forum*. doi:10.1016/j.accfor.2012.12.001

Bebbington, J., Unerman, J., & O'Dwyer, B. (Eds.). (2014). *Sustainability accounting and accountability*. Routledge.

Burchell, S., Clubb, C., & Hopwood, A. G. (1985). Accounting in its social context: Towards a history of value added in the United Kingdom. *Accounting, Organizations and Society*, *10*(4), 381–413. doi:10.1016/0361-3682(85)90002-9

Carnegie, G. D., & Napier, C. J. (2010). Traditional accountants and business professionals: Portraying the accounting profession after Enron. *Accounting, Organizations and Society*, *35*(3), 360–376. doi:10.1016/j.aos.2009.09.002

DeJong, A., Rosellón, M., & Verwijmeren, P. (2006). The economic consequences of IFRS: The impact of IAS 32 on preference shares in the Netherlands. *Accounting in Europe*, *3*(1), 169–185. doi:10.1080/09638180600920350

De Villiers, C. J., & Van Staden, C. J. (2006). Can less environmental disclosure have a legitimating effect? Evidence from Africa. *Accounting, Organizations and Society*, *31*(8), 763–781. doi:10.1016/j.aos.2006.03.001

Dillard, J. F., Rigsby, J. T., & Goodman, C. (2004). The making and remaking of organization context. *Accounting, Auditing & Accountability Journal*, *17*(4), 506–542. doi:10.1108/09513570410554542

Donaldson, T., & Preston, E. L. (1995). The Stakeholder Theory of the Corporation: Concepts, Evidence, and Implications. *Academy of Management Review*, *20*(1), 65–91.

Eccles, R., Cheng, B., & Saltzman, D. (2010a). *The Landscape of Integrated Reporting Reflections and Next Steps*. Harvard Business School, The President and Fellows of Harvard College. http://people.hbs.edu/rec%20D%20-%20cles/2011SU_Features_EcclesSaltzman.pdf

Granovetter, M. (1985). Economic action and social structure: The problem of embeddedness. *American Journal of Sociology*, *91*(3), 481–510. doi:10.1086/228311

Granovetter, M. (2000). A theoretical agenda for economic sociology. *Center for Culture, Organizations and Politics*. Available at https://escholarship.org/uc/item/4mk4g08q

Gray, R., Kouhy, R., & Lavers, S. (1995). Corporate social and environmental reporting: A review of the literature and a longitudinal study of UK disclosure. *Accounting, Auditing & Accountability Journal*, *8*(2), 47–77. doi:10.1108/09513579510146996

Hopwood, A. G., Burchell, S., & Clubb, C. (1994). Value-added accounting and national economic policy. In *Accounting as Social and Institutional Practice*. Cambridge Studies in Management. Retrieved from http://www.capitalinstitute.org/sites/capitalinstitute.org/files/docs/Institut%20RSE%20The%20grenelle%20II%20Act%20in%20France%20June%202012.pdf

Jackson, G., & Apostolakou, A. (2010). Corporate social responsibility in Western Europe: An institutional mirror or substitute? *Journal of Business Ethics*, *94*(3), 371–394. doi:10.1007/s10551-009-0269-8

Jensen, C. J., & Berg, N. (2012). Determinants of Traditional Sustainability Reporting Versus Integrated Reporting. An Institutionalist Approach. *Business Strategy and the Environment*, *21*(5), 299–316. doi:10.1002/bse.740

Jensen, M. C., & Meckling, W. H. (1976). Theory of the Firm: Managerial behavior, agency costs and ownership structure. *Journal of Financial Economics*, *3*(4), 305–360. doi:10.1016/0304-405X(76)90026-X

Matten, D., & Moon, J. (2008). Implicit and explicit CSR: A conceptual framework for a comparative understanding of corporate social responsibility. *Academy of Management Review*, *33*(2), 404–424. doi:10.5465/AMR.2008.31193458

Othman, S., Darus, F., & Arshad, R. (2011). The influence of coercive isomorphism on corporate social responsibility reporting and reputation. *Social Responsibility Journal*, *7*(1), 119–135. doi:10.1108/17471111111114585

Wulf, I., Niemöller, J., & Rentzsch, N. (2014). Development toward integrated reporting, and its impact on corporate governance: A two-dimensional approach to accounting with reference to the German two-tier system. *Journal of Management Control*, *25*(2), 135–164. doi:10.1007/s00187-014-0200-z

ENDNOTES

1 In management literature (Donaldson and Preston, 1995), the *agency theory* represents the relationship between shareholders, or *principals*, and the management of the organization, as *agent*.

2 This limitation is more prominent in case of mandatory IR (South Africa - King III Corporate Governance Code) or tentative to become mandatory IR (UK - Companies Act 2006) because *regulatory costs* are compulsory. However, even for specific regulation in the field of IR, the norms might leave space for the company to choose which elements to present in the report, so the theory can be applied without any issue.

3 In 2014 the European Parliament issued a Directive on disclosure of non-financial and diversity information by large companies and groups.

Chapter 5
Accountancy and International Perspectives on Integrated Reporting

ABSTRACT

The aim of the IIRC is to break down all the country and industry barriers through adoption and implementation of integrated reporting; ultimately obtaining a common set of standards that would define IR as the "corporate reporting norm" (IIRC, 2013, p. 1). FEE highlights that regulators should have a crucial role in the evolution of IR, as well as the global standard setters.[1]

INTEGRATED REPORTING AT AN INTERNATIONAL LEVEL

In Australia, integrated reporting is still applied on a voluntary basis, though this state has been a promoter of IR from the beginning. A report issued by G100 in 2014 stated that „Australia should not prematurely adopt/mandate integrated reporting. The Framework can be used to inform voluntary reporting initiatives" (G100, 2014)[2].

Since 2009, South Africa has a leading role in regulating the area of IR, through King Code of Governance Principles and the King Report on Governance (King III). It represents the first country that included IR on the list of Johannesburg Stock Exchange (JSE) requirements.[3] Denmark tried to follow the initiative of South Africa through their *Danish Act* but failed as its requirements stand for disclosing non-financial information in a manner that

DOI: 10.4018/978-1-5225-3622-2.ch005

lacks integration (Eccles *et al.*, 2012). In 2008, China introduced the mandatory non-financial reporting for those companies listed at Shenzhen Stock Exchange (SZSE). One year earlier there has been a similar approach in Malaysia where the Prime Minister decided that listed firms should report on CSR information (Saleh *et al.*, 2010). However, UK was one step before, issuing the Companies Act in 2006 (Reisberg, 2009). According to Ioannou and Serafein (2014), other countries had some initiatives for regulating non-financial reporting, by introducing the social reports (Netherlands[4] and France), or the environmental report (Germany, Austria, Switzerland). France had a spectacular evolution in this sense, from the Nouvelles Regulations Economiques issued in 2001 on ESG- environmental, social, and governance- information to Grenelle II (2012) focused on extra financial information and following an IR approach. Sweden issued in 2007 several guidelines for sustainability reporting, and the US became known in the field of environmental performance reporting through the Sarbanes–Oxley Act (2002). Other similar approaches towards IR were raised by Brazil and their national IR network (one of the first regional networks) and Singapore, where the SAC (Singapore Accountancy Commission) was initiating the research in the field of integrated reporting focusing on value creation (IIRC, 2014).

Starting with 2012, we witness several international coordinated actions for regulating IR. The first Memorandum of Understanding (MOU) was signed by IIRC with IFAC in 2012, the same year when the IIRC was launching the Pillot Programme 2012 Yearbook, and an emerging database of integrated reports, while registering feedback from the Investor Network (IIRC, 2014). Two years later, on 4th of February 2014, the IFRS was signing a Memorandum of Understanding with the IIRC, having the main purpose of promoting reporting harmonization, as well as developing common frameworks, guidelines, and standards (IFRS, June 2011; IFRS, 2013).

There is an international debate on integrated reporting, whether it should be voluntary or mandatory. The promoters of voluntary reporting consider that IR should not be standardized (Sull, 2005). Sull (2005) argues that less flexibility and higher constraints coming with enforceable norms will not lead to corporation's success. Figure no. 25 presents the shift from strategies, values, resources, relationships, and frames, to blinders, routines, dogmas, millstones, shackles. Too much framing can make the managers blind in front of new opportunities or other possible innovative solutions. Concentrating 100% on processes will lead to an inefficient routine, while hardening the resources for building competitive advantage can drive millstones, or diminish the value of resources. Then, if managers consolidate relationships with key-customers, the company may become too addicted to depending on important clients (so in case they lose them, the organization will suffer high losses). Finally, too much focus on core values can, in time, decrease the interest of customers in a company, as values can become dogmas, and this is not advisable in a world that is continuously changing. The dynamic of voluntary application of reporting framework will replace the inertia of mandatory actions.

A study conducted by ACCA and Longitude Research (ACCA, 2014) shows that organizations are reluctant to adopting IR, although investors call for a transparent integrated reporting of the financial results and of the decisions being made. The majority of the respondents in the ACCA survey claim the need for IR that would convey a better image for the company itself. Therefore, financial data is no longer enough for the investor that nowadays becomes *socially responsible* (Radley, 2012). However, corporations still continue to publish separate sustainability/ social/ environmental reports, that are meant to serve investors and other stakeholders' needs, and are not open to issue integrated reports. The explanation could be that even if the business environment is in favour of the idea of an integrated reporting system, they take into account the risks of changing third reporting vision, the new techniques/ technology, and costs that an IR approach might bring, including the involvement of external experts, not to mention the complexity

Figure 1. The need for norms and standardization
Source: Sull, 2005: 3.

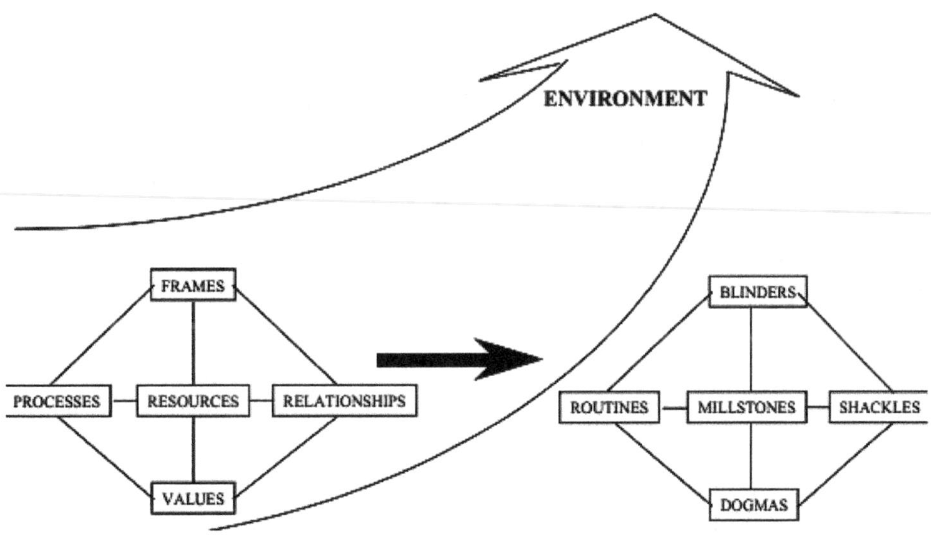

of providing assurance for such a report. Finally, the ACCA survey reveals that most of the interviewed organizations intend to consider IR for the near future period, with the main purpose of serving investor's needs of finding non-financial information in the same place with the financial one, in a single, unified, report. The investor perspective is also underlined by the 2014 IIRC Yearbook (IIRC, 2014), where companies from the financial sector (Mainfirst Bank, Eumedion, Primavenue) provides insights on how the investor assimilates the information from integrated reports, and the importance of IR for enhancing long-term investments.

The big4 audit company, PwC, argues that integrated reporting can improve the analysis for investment decisions (PwC, 2014). Investment analysts state that reporting quality influences a company's financing cost, or the corporation ability to attract funds and investments. PwC explains the results of their study applied at international level and conducted on 85 professional investment analysts. Thereof, it seems that most of the respondents consider that *concise and clear information* leads to better investment decisions. In addition, any relevant annual report should present the company business model, and mention the whole cycle of generating liquidities- from a value creation perspective-, as well as strategy for the present and for the future. Further on, the investor analysts will need to know the cases of lack in effectiveness, and how these can be reduced. Also, corporations should include in the reports the connection between reporting elements such as risks, opportunities, KPIs, strategies, etc. At the end, PwC underlines that presenting the non-financial information (on social, environmental, governance, environmental, human nature) in an association with the financial data, explaining strategies, opportunities, and risks, represents a strong point in front of investors.

Serafein and Ecless (2010), discuss the implications of issuing a set of integrated reporting regulations. The scholars take into account the perspective of European Commission on non-financial information disclosure elements. According to Serafeim and Ecless (2010), the main issues on European Commission agenda should be the integration of non-financial information with the financial data in the annual report and the determination of what characterizes those companies publishing this information in their reports. All these could be considered in a future global reporting standard on IR.

Scholars and academics (Ruth, 1989; Carnegie and Napier, 2010; Matis *et al.,* 2012) define accounting profession as the legitimate knowledge, expertise, and professionalism of accountants. Regarding the terminology, international literature mentions the usage of "accounting profession" versus "accountancy profession" (Carnegie and Napier, 2010). Both represent the same concept, so any of the two can subsidize the other, the only difference being that in UK "accountancy" is more frequently used than "accounting", while in US people prefer the term "accounting" instead of "accountancy".

The notion of professional accountant is strongly linked to accounting profession (Carnegie and Napier, 2010), cumulating a series of characteristics: independence, trust, expertise, education, professional knowledge, ethics etc. Professional accountants have to continuously update their knowledge and skills and adapt to the continuous evolution of the accounting and reporting environment (new standards, changes in accounting norms, additional legal requirements).

Unlike financial reporting, where accountants have high expertise, sustainability reporting requires innovation and communication with experts in specific issues related to sustainability – that may involve experienced personnel, scientists, engineers, etc. The main role of accounting specialists will be to connect the non-financial indicators to future financial outcomes, ultimately having a direct impact on decision-making processes. Such examples include carbon footprint measurements, sustainability indexes, life cycle analysis, environmental profit and loss accounts for covering GHG emissions, air and water pollution, etc (Clarkson *et al.,* 2008). This idea is strengthened by the academic Robert Eccless in an interview for ACCA's Accounting Futures Journal, where he states that accountants are main actors in the evolution of integrated reporting, as of their skills and expertise in financial measurements and reporting mechanisms, but still need to assimilate new measures for non-financial information, and contact other people with experience and capabilities in this area (ACCA, 2011). From an entrepreneur perspective, Paul Druckman argues that there will be a definite shift in the role accountancy profession, from 100% financial reporting orientation, to a new integrated reporting approach. The practitioner further explains that nowadays the accountant is by nature interested in data and information as a whole, not only numbers – as considered in the past as a general stereotype. Thereof, the accountancy profession has the capabilities and the proper judgment to be able to improve the content of integrated reports, of course asking for additional resources - human or technical – for better assessment of non-financial information when the case (ACCA, 2011).

DeCoster and Rhode (1971), Bedeian *et al.* (1986) and Granleese and Barrett (1990) argue that accountancy profession should aim to change the traditional perspective of the accountant as an 'impersonal', individualistic, figures-oriented, limited person who understands only his sector of activity. However, the other extreme of having a perfect image of the accounting profession causes a higher danger of ending in international scandals such as Enron case of fraud (Carnegie and Napier, 2010). These tough lessons generated a need of change in the accountancy profession, with direct effects on the competition between accounting and audit firms (Squires *et al.*, 2003). In addition, the 'professional status' ...'remains accounting's biggest challenge' (Carnegie and Napier, 2010: 18), as it should be attained through consistent efforts (Chandler and Edward, 1994).

Further on, the professional accountant and the accountancy profession itself could not function properly without the professional accounting body. The professional accounting body represents an association of the accounting profession that ensures the fulfillment of certain requirements, also providing a license for practice, like the one of *chartered accountant*. In addition, its members have to follow a code of conduct, to apply the policies of the association, and comply with requirements issued by the professional accounting body with respect to obtaining certificates or qualifications in the field (Arnold, 2005).

Finally, the highest authority in accounting norms and compliance belongs to the accounting standard setting- body. This can be defined as "a body issuing standards applicable to all companies and recognized in law to an informal grouping for the discussion of issues related to accounting rules" (FEE, 2008: 4).

Further on, one has to distinguish between *accounting standard- setting body* and *professional accounting bodies*. The accounting standard- setting body represents the accountancy profession's global representative body and the main authority in accounting standards, norms, international regulation; the professional accounting body is setting its own standards, codes of conduct, policies, requirements, that have to be fulfilled by all members and affiliates (at international or national level). In addition, the accounting standard-setting body issues accounting standards, and the professional accounting body translates these standards into conduct, policies, requirements, while monitoring their implementation in corporate reporting practice. We add that for some countries the *professional accounting body* and the *accounting standard setter body* are the same entity, while in others we can make a distinction between the two. In Romania, for example, the standard setter in the accounting area is the Finance Ministry, and the professional accounting bodies are CECCAR- The Body of Expert and Licensed Accountants of Romania and CAFR- The Chamber of Financial Auditors of Romania.

On an international scale, the most representative standard setters are IASB- International Accounting Standards Board, IFRS- International

Financial Reporting Standards, Foundation, respectively IFAC- International Federation of Accountants. IASB has the main objective of establishing a single set of high-quality global accounting standards. Along IASB priorities agenda, we mention the implementation of an accounting platform and preparation of a suitable framework for the convergence of national and international accounting standards. At European level, IFRS adoption is closely supervised by ARC- Accounting Regulatory Committee and EFRAG- European Financial Reporting Advisory Group. IFAC serves the interest of 2.5 million accountants, contributing to the evolution of the international accounting standards and accountancy profession. On 7th March 2003, IFAC was issuing a memorandum for FASB- Financial Accounting Standards Board from United States, and IASB- International Accounting Standards Board from United Kingdom, having the purpose of finding the convergence between the North- American accounting norms and the International Accounting Standards. This agreement is also know known as the convergence project of US GAAP (American accounting norms) and IFRS (international accounting norms). IFAC had a major role in developing accounting norms that are specific for the audit/ ethic code/ public sector/ education areas. IPSASB- International Public Sector Accounting Standards Board, was set up at the initiative of IFAC. The international standards issued by IPSASB, known as IPSAS (International Public Sector Accounting Standards), provide guidance and support for the public sector for promoting a transparent and high-quality reporting system. IFAC has a total of 143 member bodies, 22 associates, and 4 affiliations worldwide.

If we take a closer look to the IIRC composition, we realize that for sure integrated reporting is strongly connected to the accountancy profession. Paul Druckman, the CEO of the IIRC, is an important member of ICAEW- Institute of Chartered Accountants in England and Wales and FRC- UK Financial Reporting Council. He initiated a series of actions for promoting integrated reporting, from worldwide events such as workshops and conferences, to technology improvements in reporting, or other IIRC programmes that highlight the IR costs and benefits, or advice on IR implementation. Secondly, we have Mervyn E. King, Chairman of the IIRC, who is also Chair of the King Committee on Corporate Governance and Supreme Court judge in South Africa. His main achievements in IR area were the development of integrated thinking trend, as well as the legislative initiatives in South Africa.

We can add important names of people from the IIRC council, also members of accountancy profession organizations worldwide (Hans Hoogervorst - Chairman of *IASB*; Ian Ball - Principal Advisor at *IFAC* and

Chairman of Chartered Institute of Public Finance and Accountancy- *CIPFA* International; Pater Baker- President of the World Business Council for Sustainable Development –*WBCSD;* Alex Malley – CEO for *CPA* Australia; Barry Melancon *AICPA*- American Institute of Certified Public Accountants President and CEO; Charles Tilley- Chief Executive, *CIMA*- Chartered Institute of Management Accountants; Terence Nombembe- *SAICA* CEO; Helen Brand- Chief Executive, *ACCA*; Robert Eccles- Chairman of *SASB*; Dennis Nally- Chairman of *PwC*.; Steve Almond- Global Chairman, *Deloitte* Touche Tohmatsu; Martin Van Roeker- CEO at *BDO*; Richard Cjambers- President and CEO of *The Institute of Internal Auditors*; Larry Bradley- *KPMG* Global Head of Audit, and many others). Hans Hoogervorst was in charge of signing the memorandum between FASB-IASB and IIRC in 2013, from the IASB side, while Paul Druckman signed as an IIRC authority. Through the MOU[5], the accounting organizations agreed on working together to achieve common targets in the corporate reporting field. During the 20+Rio Conference from 2012, Peter Baker strengthened the idea that IR is needed in a corporate environment that is continually changing, as companies have to adapt their businesses for driving performance. The same approach was sustained by Alex Malley, who claimed that IR represents the future of corporate reporting and underlined its relevance for performance measurement. Barry Melancon, from AICPA, considered IR as being an opportunity for investors that can make decisions based on the complete package of information that goes beyond financial data. Charles Tilley is another supporter of IR who considers that this can increase the reports' credibility in front of the investors (especially shareholders). Terence Nombembe supports the idea that IR originated from South Africa and Mervyn King's legislator initiatives that mandates integrated reporting. Helen Brand from ACCA organized round tables on integrated reporting, in the same time encouraging worldwide organizations to adopt and implement IR. Robert Eccles, as from the academic sphere, had consistent contribution in the development of IR, through all his papers on IR adoption and implementation (Eccles *et al.,* 2010b; Eccles *et al.,* 2012). Steve Almond from Deloitte sustains that IR is strongly connected to the value creation process and the organizations' resources used to create value though its capitals. In addition, Deloitte UK issued a guide for corporation leaders on how IR can be applied. Besides value creation, audit companies underline the relevance of reporting future performance, as Larry Bradley from KPMG sustains. Therefore, all these people, members of IIRC and relevant names from accountancy profession, maintain a high impact on the development of IR.

The Global Body for Professional Accountants, **ACCA,** has strong connections with the IIRC- from sharing the same headquarter, to the ACCA's recent initiative (starting with 2014) of including integrated reporting guidelines in its courses and curricula (Table 1). However, the ACAA had a major role in the evolution of IR by introducing – even since 2007 - topics in their examinations that became later the *IIRC content elements.*

Clare Minchington, ACCA executive director, resumes very clear the ACCA direction in what concerns integrated reporting, focusing on the 6 capitals, communication, long-term vision, and finally the impact through decisions that are being made:

We recognized the importance of building trust, of looking at wider capitals (not just financial), communicating with authenticity and ensuring that organizations have a long-term vision which they use to explain their decision making and strategy externally.

Ultimately, the head of ACCA seems to be optimistic from the point of view of IR evolvement in time, as this reporting scheme should find support on both practical and regulatory axes- as companies will be open to experiencing IR while professional accounting bodies should provide further guidance and encourage its development.[6] ACCA also organized a series of discussions and roundtables on the subject of integrated reporting, and was even included in the pilot programme, by applying the IR on its own reports.

As for the future, ACCA indents to increase the IR information requested in their courses, with the purpose of supporting integrated reporting adoption and implementation, and even seeks to create new materials in their exam curricula to express IR outcomes. The initiative of ACCA is followed by

Table 1. ACCA curricula on IR

IIRC Content Elements	Professional Papers
Organisational overview	P1, P3
Governance	P1, P4
Opportunities and risks	P1, P3, P4, P7
Strategy and resource allocation	P3, P4, P5
Business model	P3, P5
Performance	P2, P5, P7
Future outlook	P3

Source: Author's design.

other professional accounting bodies, such as CIMA - Chartered Institute of Management Accountants, that also included IR materials in their courses. CIMA- Chartered Institute of Management Accountants consider that integrated reporting is relevant for both private and public sector, underlining the importance of value creation. The main connection between CIMA and IR is represented by Charles Tilley, Chief Executive in CIMA and member of the IIRC Council, being involved in the technical part of integrated reporting evolution, who had a huge contribution in developing the first version of the IR framework. Finally, CIMA supports the IR initiative because of the mutual benefits of increased accountability, the holistic view of reporting more than financial information, and building sustainable value.[7]

We have analyzed particularly the private sector because this is the subject of our book. However, if most of accounting professional bodies focused on private sector organizations, CIPFA- Chartered Institute of Public Finance and Accountancy joined efforts with the IIRC to initiate the Public Sector Pioneer Network in order to promote integrating reporting adoption in the public sector. [8]

IFAC - International Federation of Accountants has issued a publication on how can professional accountants influence integrated reporting adoption and implementation. The report demonstrates that the integration of governance, strategy, resource allocation, value creation, and accountability represents the key to business performance. The study conducted by IFAC involved interviewing several professional accountants on the above mentioned aspects regarding corporate reporting. We provide some extractions from their report regarding the professional accountant perspective on integrated reporting:

Participating in creating an integrated annual report (versus a traditional annual report) has taught me that it is necessary to understand what is really important to our stakeholders. This has ultimately changed my view on what information should be used to inform strategy and planning, and what we should report on as an organization—to really explain our results in terms of both financial as well as non-financial performance. Pure financial results do not tell the whole story. Some organizations might not be as financially profitable as other organizations in the short term, but the story behind that could be that they are operating more responsibly, and in a way that meets the needs of their key stakeholders, which could lead to greater success in the long term."; "Our understanding of our non-financial performance and impact, and its relationship to our financial performance, is only going to develop further. There is a necessity for the accounting profession to have a broader education so they can understand non-financial issues and integrate them with financial aspects. In this way, accountants will be able to play a key role in influencing underlying reporting structures, processes, and systems to support organizations to prepare for truly integrated thinking and reporting (IFAC, 2012: 38).

One of the main actions made by IFAC to prove total support for integrated reporting was to request G20 countries an active participation in the IR framework development (IIRC, 2010). We should also mention IPSASB – International Public Sector Accounting Standards Board that in July 2013 and March 2015 issued three *Recommended Practice Guidelines (RPG)*: RPG 1, RPG 2, and RPG 3 which are all related to non-financial information/ or information that is additional to the financial statements. RPG 1 concerns the *Long-Term Sustainability of an Entity's Finance.* This requires public entities to report on financial statements and long-term fiscal sustainability information, projects implementation period, sources of significant revenue, outflows of capital, changes in projections between reporting dates, time horizon used for the projections, changes in the indicators used to report long-term fiscal sustainability information, legislation and regulation, policy, demographic and economic assumptions (IPSASB, 2013). RPG 2 regards *Financial Statement Discussion and Analysis* and provides advice on how to discuss and analyze financial statements, by obtaining a better understanding of cash flows, financial position and performance. RPG 3 on *Reporting Service Performance Information* refers to guidelines of good practice when reporting information on service performance.

AICPA- American Institute of Certified Public Accountants states that the accounting profession has an impact on sustainability activities. They highlight the fact that the accountant has the expertise and experience to connect sustainability to financial performance. AICPA welcomes the release of IR framework as integrated reports should serve investors in decision-making meeting the real challenges of adapting the traditional assurance to new reporting trends[9] processes and create value in time.[10] During the conference launched by AICPA together with PwC in 2014, the perspective of assurance for integrated reporting was presented, sub submitting the real challenges of adapting the traditional assurance to new reporting trends.[11]

The comments provided by FEE (FEE, 2008) underline the main differences between a traditional financial report and an integrated report. FEE consider that nowadays we witness a trespassing from the presentation of information in isolation, to an integration (or integrated information) approach. Then, if in the past we had only the financial capital, now we add five more capitals on the list (manufactured, human, intellectual, natural, social). From the perspective of medium and long-term vision, reporting has met an evolution from a past and financial oriented information to future orientation, connected and strategic information. Ultimately, if in the past reporting was too rigid because of compliance matters; nowadays it becomes more flexible, as companies can adapt their reporting style. The only issue remains assurance on IR, which should provide more credibility for these reports. In addition, on October 16, 2014, FEE was organizing a *Roundtable on Integrated Reporting Assurance*.

ICAEW- The Institute of Chartered Accountants in England and Wales, is one of the promoters of integrated reporting cause. On 28th October 2014, the accounting profession body was organizing a *Convention on Corporate Governance and Sustainability* that had a special session on *integrated reporting*. Few days earlier the same month, in the ICAEW Chartered Accountants' Hall took place the UK roundtable on Assurance over Integrated Reporting. Robin Fifth, ICAEW CFO, mentions the main challenges of integrated reporting implementation, in terms of reporting on the 6 capitals, KPIs, and communicating the information in a transparent and concise manner. The main connection between ICAEW and IIRC is the current CEO *Paul Druckman*. Paul Druckman is also CFO for FRC- UK Financial Reporting Council. ICAEW anticipated the value creation debate of IR (ICAEW, 2010), while the real implementation of disclosure on *long-term value creation* started in fact with the IIRC initiative (IIRC, 2013).

According to IFAC, PAIB - Professional Accountants in Business, and CPA Australia, integrated reporting will generate improvements in governance (IFAC, 2012). These institutions/ accounting professional bodies have organized a forum for discussing ESG- economic, social, and environmental factors, as well as financial and non-financial information integration. This forum was followed by a meeting in Melbourne Australia, at which the IIRC had representatives also. The purpose of the meeting was to develop the idea that IR can contribute to better governance practices, while defining special measurements for assessing social, economic, and environmental performance.

Regarding the assurance of integrated reports, IFAC supports the idea of introducing standards for IR assurance, and passes this responsibility to the IAASB (International Auditing and Assurance Standards Board)[12].

Finally, we provide a chronological synthesis on the concrete actions initiated by the accountancy profession in the area of integrated reporting:

All the actions from the accounting profession environment mentioned above underline its importance for the development of integrated reporting.

Figure 2. Accountancy profession and IR
Source: Author's design.

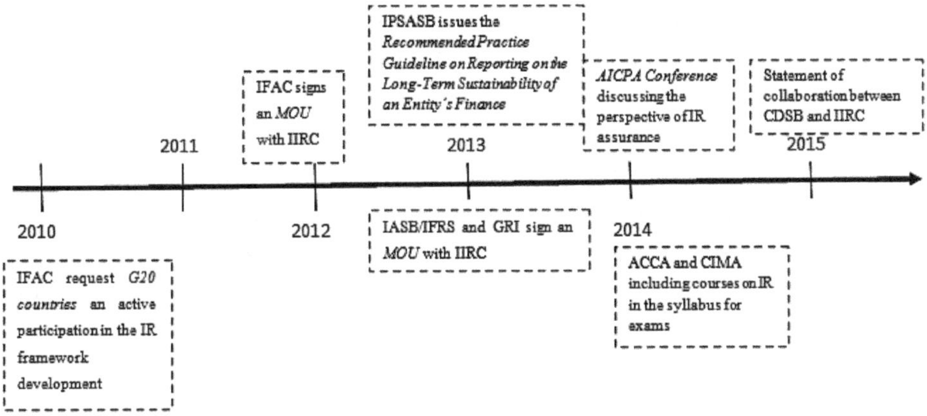

Figure 3. Distribution of IR discussion paper respondents per category
Source: IIRC, 2012: 12.

By Stakeholder Group:

36	Reporters
31	Accounting bodies
25	Professional services (other than accounting)
25	Coalitions/Professional groups
22	NGOs/NFPs
19	Investors/Investor groups
12	Academics
11	Government agencies
10	Standard setters
10	Individuals
9	Professional services – Accounting
2	Intergovernmental agencies
2	Stock exchanges

By Country:[7]

45	UK
26	USA
16	Australia
15	Germany
12	Global
11	Italy
10	each of: South Africa and Spain
7	Canada
6	each of: Brazil, China (including HK), and India
5	each of: France and The Netherlands
4	each of: Sweden and Switzerland
3	each of: Malaysia, New Zealand, and Russia
2	each of: Belgium, Denmark, Japan, and Singapore
1	each of: Austria, Finland, Granada, Israel, Korea, Mexico, Norway, Sri Lanka, and Tanzania

7 The significant number of UK respondents reflects the fact that the global project originated in the UK and, accordingly, the awareness of it was perhaps greater in 2011 for UK organizations.

Still, some academics (Adams and Larrinaga González, 2007; Adams and Whelan, 2009; Adams, 2015) are reluctant to admit that accountancy profession has a leading role in the evolution of IR, while diminishing the contribution of other international organizations with an interest in IR.

The emerging initiative of integrated reporting, launched by the IIRC through a Discussion Paper (DP) in 2011, encountered many echoes from stakeholder groups and countries that provided feedback responses to the DP and thus contributed to the initial development stage of IR (Figure 3). This strengthens the argument expressed previously that IR is the result of various organizations' implication, not only from accounting sphere, and becomes international, with strategies of future implementation and adoption at national level.

CONCLUSION

This chapter outlined the most relevant stages in the evolution of integrated reporting at an international level. We showed that accounting profession (IFAC, IASB/IFRS, IPSASB, ACCA, CIMA, GRI etc.) has had a great impact in the development of IR.

REFERENCES

ACCA. (2014). *Accountants for business- Understanding investors: the changing corporate perspective*. Available at http://www.accaglobal.com/content/dam/acca/global/PDF-technical/financial-reporting/pol-afb-ui04.pdf

Adams, C., & Larrinaga González, C. (2007). Engaging with organisations in pursuit of improved sustainability accountability and performance. *Accounting, Auditing & Accountability Journal*, *20*(3), 333–355. doi:10.1108/09513570710748535

Adams, C. A. (2015). The International Integrated Reporting Council: A call to action. *Critical Perspectives on Accounting*, *27*, 23–28. doi:10.1016/j.cpa.2014.07.001

Adams, C. A., & Whelan, G. (2009). Conceptualising future change in corporate sustainability reporting. *Accounting, Auditing & Accountability Journal*, *22*(1), 118–143. doi:10.1108/09513570910923033

Arnold, P. J. (2005). Disciplining domestic regulation: The World Trade Organization and the market for professional services. *Accounting, Organizations and Society*, *30*(4), 299–330. doi:10.1016/j.aos.2004.04.001

Bedeian, A. G., Mossholder, K. W., Touliatos, J., & Barkman, A. J. (1986). The accountants stereotype: An update for vocational counsellors. *The Career Development Quarterly*, *35*(2), 113–122. doi:10.1002/j.2161-0045.1986.tb00771.x

Chandler, R., & Edwards, J. R. (1994). *Recurring issues in auditing. Professional debate 1875-1900*. New York: Garland.

DeCoster, D. T., & Rhode, J. G. (1971). The accountant's stereotype: Real or imagined, deserved or unwarranted. *Accounting Review*, *46*, 651–664.

Fédération des Experts Comptables Européens. (2008). *Accounting Standards Setting in Europe*. Available at http://www.iasplus.com/en/binary/resource/feestudy.pdf

Granleese, J., & Barrett, T. F. (1990). The social and personality characteristics of the Irish Chartered Accountant. *Personality and Individual Differences*, *11*(9), 957–964. doi:10.1016/0191-8869(90)90278-Y

ICAEW (Institute of Chartered Accountants in England and Wales). (2010). *New Reporting Models for Business: Information for Better Markets Initiative*. London: ICAEW.

IFAC. (2012). *Integrating Governance for Sustainable Success*. Available at http://www.cpaireland.ie/docs/default-source/media-and-publications/other-publications/integrating-governance-for-sustainable-success.pdf?sfvrsn=2

IFRS. (2013). *IASB and IIRC formalise cooperation on work to develop integrated corporate reporting framework*. Retrieved from http://www.ifrs.org/

IFRS Advisory Council. (2011). *Integrated Reporting*. Retrieved from http://www.ifrs.org/The-organisation/Advisory-bodies/IFRS-Advisory-Council/meetings/2011-Advisory-Council-meetings/Documents/AC061110.pdf

IIRC. (2012). *Summary of Responses to the September 2011 Discussion Paper and Next Steps*. Available at http://integratedreporting.org/wp-content/uploads/2012/06/Discussion-Paper-Summary1.pdf

IIRC. (2013). *The International IR Framework*. Available at http://integratedreporting.org/wp-content/uploads/2015/03/13-12-08-THE-INTERNATIONAL-IR-FRAMEWORK-2-1.pdf

IIRC. (2014). *Yearbook 2014*. Available at http://integratedreporting.org/yearbook2014/timeline-assets/timeline

IIRC, International Integrated Reporting Committee. (2010). *Committee Members*. Retrieved from http://www.integratedreporting.org/node/6

Ioannou, I., & Serafein, G. (2014). *The Consequences of Mandatory Corporate Sustainability Reporting: Evidence from Four Countries*. Harvard Business School. Available at http://www.hbs.edu/faculty/Publication%20Files/11-100_7f383b79-8dad-462d-90df-324e298acb49.pdf

IPSASB. (2013). *Recommended Practice Guideline- Reporting on the Long-Term Sustainability of an Entity's Finances*. Final Pronouncement.

Matis, D., James, K., Mustata, R. V., & Bonaci, C. G. (2012). Romanian accounting profession: Erudition and perspectives. *International Journal of Critical Accounting*, *4*(2), 120–144. doi:10.1504/IJCA.2012.046378

PwC. (2014). *Corporate performance: What do investors want to know? Powerful stories through integrated reporting*. Available at http://www.pwc.com/en_GX/gx/audit-services/corporate-reporting/publications/investor-view/assets/pwc-investors-survey-powerful-stories-through-integrated-reporting.pdf

Reisberg, A. (2009). Shadows of the Past and Back to the Future: Part 11 of the UK Companies Act 2006 (in) action. *European Company and Financial Law Review*, *6*(2-3), 219–243. doi:10.1515/ECFR.2009.219

Ruth, D. H. (1989). Financial Accounting Knowledge, Conceptual Framework Projects and the Social Construction of the Accounting Profession. *Accounting, Auditing & Accountability Journal*, *2*(2).

Saleh, M., Zulkifli, N., & Muhamad, R. (2010). Corporate social responsibility disclosure and its relation on institutional ownership: Evidence from public listed companies in Malaysia. *Managerial Auditing Journal*, *25*(6), 591–613. doi:10.1108/02686901011054881

Serafein & Eccles. (2010). Mandatory Environmental, Social, and Governance Disclosure in the European Union. *Harvard Business Review*.

Squires, S. E., Smith, C. J., McDougal, L., & Yeack, W. R. (2003). *Inside Arthur Andersen: Shifting values, unexpected consequences*. Upper Saddle River, NJ: FT Prentice-Hall.

Sull, D. (2005). *Why Good Companies Go Bad and How Great Managers Remake Them.* Harvard Business School Press. Available at http://donsull.com/wp-content/uploads/2013/07/ft_why_good_go_bad.pdf

ENDNOTES

1 http://www.fee.be/news/default.asp?library_ref=2&category_ref=214&content_ref=1504

2 http://www.group100.com.au/policies/g100-views-integrated-reporting-july-2014.pdf

3 www.saica.co.za

4 On March 2013, the Netherlands Institute of Chartered Accountants (NBA) participated, along with IFAC, CIMA, PwC, ACCA, NBA, WICI, AICPA, Ernst & Young in the publication of a series of background papers on IR: *Business model, Capitals, Connectivity, Materiality, Value creation.* These had the purpose of setting the right coordinates in the corporate environment for a better understanding and implementation of an IR framework in the UK (where the papers were published); http://integratedreporting.org/yearbook2014/timeline-assets/timeline.

5 http://www.ifrs.org/Use-around-the-world/Documents/MoU-IIRC-and-IFRS-Foundation-February-2013.pdf

6 http://www.accaglobal.com/za/en/student/acca-qual-student-journey/sa/features/acca-embeds-integrated-reporting.html

7 http://www.cimaglobal.com/

8 http://www.icaew.com/en/events/2014/october/m141028-debate-on-integrated-reporting-an-emerging-global-trend http://www.accountingforsustainability.org/principles/icaew-hosted-uk-roundtable-on-assurance-over-integrated-reporting http://economia.icaew.com/business/integrated-reporting-in-action

9 http://www.pwc.com/en_US/us/cfodirect/assets/pdf/in-depth/us2014-09-aicpa-conference.pdf

10 http://www.aicpa.org/press/pressreleases/2013/pages/aicpa-commends-iirc-for-release-of-international-integrated-reporting-framework.aspx

11 http://www.pwc.com/en_US/us/cfodirect/assets/pdf/in-depth/us2014-09-aicpa-conference.pdf

12 http://integratedreporting.org/wp-content/uploads/2014/12/29-IFAC.pdf

Chapter 6
IR in Romania:
A National Perspective - Case Study on a Romanian Company

ABSTRACT

This chapter investigates the topic of integrated reporting at national level. We demonstrate that a Romanian company, Rosia Montana Gold Corporation, issued in 2010 an Annual Report that can be considered a real prototype of an integrated report. Derived from the need to fulfill the gaps in corporate reporting (lack of non-financial information in the annual reports, organizations' failure in explaining social/environmental/other impacts, aggregation of CSR/environmental/social reports in the annual reports – without any connectivity to the financial performance, etc.), the new IR trend should be shaped by international accounting organizations and accountancy profession. This is one of the few studies that aimed to develop a conceptual model for the integrated report that can be applied by companies intending to implement this reporting practice. The originality of our book results from the various perspectives contained in our model: from the IIRC content elements and principles, to IASB/IFRS implications for integrated reporting. Finally, we strongly believe that the evolution of integrated reporting will end with a common standard issued by IASB/IFRS in cooperation with IIRC, and even European legislation/ or going further-national requirements. Therefore, research on a complex framework for integrated reporting (that has to address both financial and non- financial focus) and provide extended guidelines for an integrated report, should be useful for standard setters – for regulatory purposes, and companies- for a successful implementation of this reporting scheme.

DOI: 10.4018/978-1-5225-3622-2.ch006

OBJECTIVE OF THE STUDY

This current sub-chapter presents the topic of integrated reporting from a conceptual perspective. We have developed a model for the integrated report that can be applied by companies intending to implement this reporting practice. The proposed IR model is based on the IIRC content elements and principles; disclosure requested in IFRS-IASB accounting standards that is correlated with IR; non-financial information included in the European Commission initiatives; disclosure items from SA8000 and AA1000 social audit standards.

The model has been tested on a Romanian organization- Rosia Montana Gold Corporation. We have chosen Rosia Montana Gold Corporation for our case study because this is one of the few companies in Romania that issues integrated reports. In Romania, integrated reporting is still in its infancy, taking into account that not too many companies have adopted this reporting line (e.g. Petrom or Rosia Montana Gold Corporation). However, it seems that there is an increasing trend for integrated reporting in our country, as since 2006 the corporations that implement an IR system is 7% higher (Daniela Nemoianu, Partner, Head of Advisory la KPMG Romania). In addition, Bucharest Stock Exchange has recently organized an event in conjunction with ACCA for obtaining a better understanding of the IR principles[1].

We analyzed their 2010 Annual Report and searched for the disclosure items contained in our model. Through a case study approach, we discussed the relevance of each category of information or disclosure element and identified the source in the annual report that explains the respective item. The case study method is very much used with the objective of demonstrating good practice or is suitable for areas where we have a lack of empirical or theoretical research (Dumitru et al., 2013). Scholars and academics advocated the case study method for investigating CSR corporate behaviors (Wiig and Kolstad, 2010; Chaudhri and Wang, 2007), sustainability reporting (Dowda et al., 2005; Bell and Morse, 2004), and integrated reports (Dumitru et al., 2013).

The aim of the study was to prove that the 2010 Annual Report issued by Rosia Montana represents a prototype of an integrated report. This case study seeks to contribute to the international corporate reporting literature and corporate practice, by providing new insights of IR good practice and encourage other companies to adopt and implement IR.

RESEARCH METHODOLOGY

In developing the conceptual model of integrated reporting (Figure 1), we started from the IIRC Content Elements and Principles listed in the Final Framework published by the Council on December 2013 (IIRC, 2013). Additional to the previous Consultation Drafts of the IIRC regarding the framework, we have a last content element: basis of preparation and presentation. In our view, not only the content elements and guiding principles are essential for a report to switch from traditional form to an integrated one, but the integrated thinking as key element of integration. According to Busco *et al.* (2013), the concept of integrated thinking assumes the correlation between three basic elements: capital, value creation, and accountability (Archel *et al.,* 2011). Therefore, the integrated report should present all the three dimensions to demonstrate integrated thinking.

However, the IIRC focuses more on the non- financial sphere, and little attention is given to the financial (and accounting) side. We consider that accountancy profession has a major role in the evolution of integrated reporting by providing guidance for the application of integrated reporting, and even working together with the IIRC to issue standards/ regulation for this field (the best proof is the Memorandum signed by IASB/IFRS and IIRC in February 2013). Thus, our model aims to show the impact of IFRS/IASB international accounting standards on integrated reporting by finding common elements between standards' requirements regarding the information disclosed in annual reports and the social and environmental performance outlined by the IIRC (Table 1). The paper by Barbu *et al.* (2012) discusses dimensions of environmental information required by different IFRS/IASB standards. Further on, corporate social responsibility information can also be linked to IFRS/IASB accounting standards requirements (EC, 2007; CPA, 2013).

CONCLUSION

This study represents a consistent contribution for the emerging IR literature. The originality resides from being one of the first attempts to develop a conceptual model/ framework on integrated reporting. In addition, the main challenge in setting this framework was to provide relevant accounting referential/ reporting guidelines, as there is no standard for IR, and the framework developed by IIRC was not anchored into the accounting sphere,

Table 1. IFRS/IASB impact on integrated reporting

Environmental Information					
Intangible assets exploration of mineral resources	IFRS 6	IAS 36			
Emission rights assets	IAS 38	IAS 36	IFRIC 3		
Concessions, licenses, trademarks, and similar items	IAS 38	IAS 36			
Other intangible assets	IAS 38	IAS 36			
Tangible assets	IAS 16	IAS 36			
Tangible assets with exploration of minerals resources	IFRIC 6	IAS 36			
Inventories (waste)	IAS 2				
Environmental provisions (provision for dismantling, removal of assets and the site restoration, Provision for CO2 emissions, Provision for insurance, environmental litigates etc.)	IAS 37	IFRIC 5	IFRIC 6	IFRIC 1	IFRIC 3
Emission rights governmental grant	IAS 20	IFRIC 3			
Fines and taxes for environmental purposes	IAS 37				
Other environmental expenses	IAS 8	IAS 38	IFRS 6		
Contingent liabilities and assets	IAS 37				
CSR Information					
Recognition of provision	IAS 37				
present obligation					
outflow of resources					
reasonable estimate					
Disclosure on CSR information	IFRS 8				
commitment to transparency					
acceptance on obligation to societies in which they work					
avoid reputation risk					
commitment to investors					
CSR information included in financial statements					
CSR information subject to statutory audit					

Source: adapted after Barbu et al., 2012; EC, 2007; CPA, 2013.

Figure 1. The conceptual model for IR
Source: Author's design.

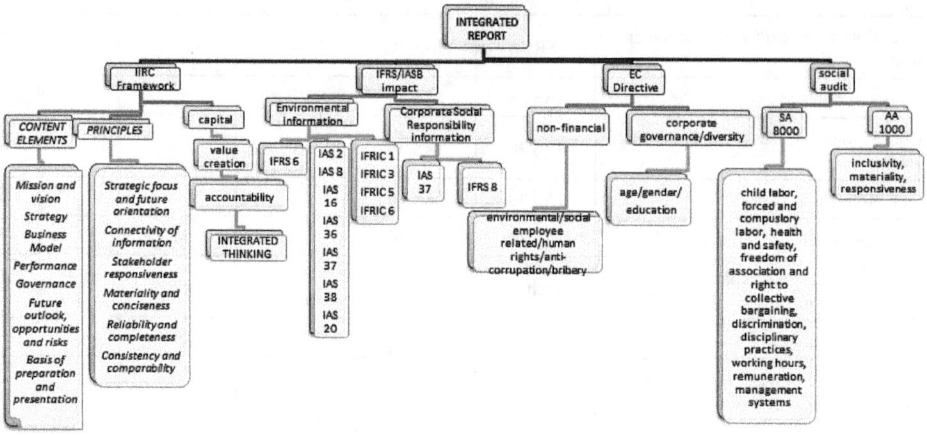

although accountancy profession had a major role in its development. Therefore, we started by defining the impact that IFRS/IASB standards has on the IR field, and identified specific disclosure elements for our model. Then, we started looking at other non-financial regulation attempts, such as the EU Proposal for a Directive on non-financial information, or social audit standards (and the information assessed in a social audit).

REFERENCES

Archel, P., Husillos, J., & Spence, C. (2011). The institutionalisation of unaccountability: Loading the dice of corporate social responsibility discourse. *Accounting, Organizations and Society*, *36*(6), 327–343. doi:10.1016/j.aos.2011.06.003

ENDNOTE

1 www.bvb.ro/InvestorRelations/Overview

Chapter 7
Rosia Montana Gold Corporation Ltd:
Company Background

ABSTRACT

This chapter contains historical data regarding the set-up and evolution/ expansion of the Romanian Company Rosia Montana Gold Corporation. We also mention their reporting practices, as well as main achievements from economic, social, and environmental perspectives.

BRIEF PRESENTATION OF THE COMPANY

Rosia Montana Gold Corporation Ltd. was set up in 1997 in Alba county, Romania. Its equity structure is divided between two main shareholders: Minvest Rosia Montana S.A. (19.31%) and Gabriel Resources (80.69%). With more than 150 employees, Rosia Montana Gold Corporation Ltd. operates in the mining industry, gold and silver exploration area. In Romania, most of the mines have been closed because the state found difficult to adapt to European Union environmental standards. On international scale, the main competitors are from Sweden (Boliden- Dragon Mining), Finlanda (Lappland Goldminers), Spain (Rio Narcea -Kinbauri Gold Corporation), Italy (Sargold), Bulgaria (Dundee Precious Metals Inc.), Turkey (Koza Group – Ovacik), Hungay (Carpathian Gold), Slovakia (Tournigan Gold Corporation), Romania

DOI: 10.4018/978-1-5225-3622-2.ch007

(European Goldfields), and Russia (Highland Gold, Polymetal, Peter Hambro Mining, Trans-Siberian Gold, Polyus, Kamgold).

The company issues annual reports and non- financial reports. For the purpose of the current analysis, we are going to use the *Annual Report and Accounts 2010*, being the most recent report made available by the company. We perform an evaluation on this report in order to check if complies with our model of an *integrated report*. According to the *Annual Report and Accounts 2010,* the company is fully committed to building a sustainable mine at Rosia Montana. The company understands that true sustainability means less corporate contributions, and more to community support. The assessment of the Technical Review Committee regarding the environmental impact performed in late 2010 allowed the company to demonstrate that the Romanian state plans to adopt the most modern mining technics being accountable to the environment, complying with both the law and national and European regulations and best practice. In 2010 they had many initiatives for community health and welfare through educational programs and cultural programmes related to community traditions and cultural heritage.

The direct benefits for the Romanian state result from paid dividends, salary taxes, royalties and other obligations of total, $ 1.8 billion. The remaining $ 2.4 billion will be spent on human resources, electricity, transport, construction, spare parts and other expenses. Creating jobs at local and county level will be a significant benefit brought by the project, specifically: over 3,000 direct and indirect jobs available during the construction phase of the project. After authorization, the Company is prepared to invest about $ 1 million per day during the two and half years of construction.

The company is committed to building a special operation that will bring positive outcomes for the local economy; restore and preserve cultural heritage and at the same time establish world class standards for environmental and social responsibility issues. Therefore, the company continues to demonstrate commitment to the environment through projects of reforestation and cleaning campaigns; energy consumption reduction by reorganizing office space to better meet current and settled rules of "green office" which highlighted recycling and responsible use of paper in the offices of the company. Long-term sustainability of the project depends on relationship with stakeholders (especially employees and community). "By building a best practice modern mine and implementing the highest environmental standards, the Project creates an opportunity to remediate past damage, leaving the region's rivers and soil cleaner than before. The Project will be the first permitted under the EU's stringent environmental laws, creating a model mining project not only

Table 1. Achievements on environmental target in 2010

	Objective	Targets
Forestry and landscaping	Planting of 1,000 hectares of forestry to replace 255 hectares to be deforested	All 1,000 hectares to be planted before the first tree for the Project will be cut
		Entire 300 hectares for TMF to be re-vegetated
		Cetate pit to be filled with water after rehabilitation
		Carnic, Jig and Orlea pits to be rehabilitated and re-vegetated
Tailings Dam Safety	Designed to hold the rainfall from two back to back 1 in 10,000 year extreme flood events within 24 hours	Design capacity – 250 million tonnes
		Required capacity – 215 million tonnes
		Dams designed by MWH, based in the US, one of the world's leading companies in this field
		Norwegian Geotechnical Institute reviewed the design to be one of the safest in the world, able to withstand extreme earthquakes in a low risk seismic region
Water	Rational use of water – aim of recirculation of 85% of industrial water required in the process	Collect and clean historical pollution from the site
		Ensure water life regeneration over 40km of river waters
		Best technologies will eliminate the source of acid rock drainage and enable management of surface run-offs

Source: Extracted from Annual Report 2010: page 13.

for Romania and the EU but for future mining projects worldwide" (extracted from Annual Report 2010: page 12).

Rosia Montana Gold Corporation has reached many of the proposed environmental targets involving international groups and local communities:

The company has funded an independent team of specialists in archaeology using methods and cutting-edge research techniques. All archaeological efforts are conducted in compliance with UNESCO and EU guidelines archaeology. Cultural Heritage Plan includes a protected area comprising the historic village structures and future museum, which will enable pupils, students and experts to study the region's cultural heritage. Over 35 million dollars have been set aside for the investment in cultural heritage. Rosia Montana Gold Corporation "is fully committed to restoring, preserving and honoring Rosia Montana's unique cultural heritage. Over the past five years, more than US$10m has been invested in exploration and recovery of Rosia Montana's cultural heritage, one of the largest privately funded programmes in Europe" (extracted from Annual Report 2010: page 14).

The general objective of the company is to maintain close relationships with the community, involving it in the decision- making process. The community relations department of the company has a detailed database of the population

Table 2. Restoring and preserving cultural heritage

Restoration Works	In March 2010, the Company completed the first building restoration project with the rehabilitation of Building No. 325 using traditional methods and materials, following a two and a half year period of restoration activity. The property is currently being used as a Heritage Information Centre and houses a collection and exhibition of mining, historical and archaeological artifacts.
Building Repairs	The emergency building repairs on the buildings in the protected area are aimed at evaluating primarily the condition of the houses and prioritizing them according to their conservation status and needs. The list of the emergency repairs in the historical center of Rosia Montana exceeds 135 houses and annexes. In 2010 emergency repairs and protection or conservation works were carried out on around 80 houses.
Mining Galleries	In parallel with these initiatives, maintenance and servicing works were carried out on a number of access galleries to underground mining operations on the areas of Catalina Monulesti, Paru Carpeni and Carnic. Over 140 km of galleries have been researched, out of which 7 km (in discontinuous fragments) are from the Roman period.
Outlook	Looking forwards the Company's cultural heritage efforts will continue to focus on maintenance, conservation and restoration of the historic centre as well as the provision of scientific and public research for the cultural heritage programme for Rosia Montana based on two major components: Archaeology (surface and underground) and Architecture.

Source: Extracted from Annual Report 2010: page 15.

affected by the project, including relocated and displaced families, vulnerable people (especially people with property), isolated families. So far 794 homes have been purchased. During the process of relocation, resettlement assistance is provided to all households. The company has supported the affected community throughout the process of relocation, offering legal assistance, relocation assistance and resettlement program of lifestyle (grants for training and education). Rosia Montana Gold Corporation "is committed to fostering the sustainable development of the Rosia Montana community. This includes a comprehensive set of programmes designed to improve living standards, addressing education, skills training, assistance for the elderly, health issues, job and business creation, and respect for the area's archaeological heritage" (extracted from Annual Report, 2010, p. 16).

REFERENCES

A Project for Romania Annual Report and Accounts 2010. (2011, July). Retrieved from https://www.unglobalcompact.org/system/attachments/11239/original/COP_2011_FINAL_GABRIEL_RESOURCES.pdf?1310627394

Chapter 8
Case Study on Rosia Montana:
An Example of an Integrated Report

ABSTRACT

This chapter represents the case study on Rosia Montana Gold Corporation. We assumed from the beginning of our research that the 2010 Annual Report issued by Rosia Montana Gold Corporation has the prototype of an integrated report. As we can deduct from the research methodology section, a report becomes an integrated report if it complies with the conceptual model based on the IIRC content elements and principles, capital, value creation, and accountability, environmental and CSR information extracted from IFRS/IASB requirements.

INTRODUCTION

Figure 1 presents the business model developed by Rosia Montana Gold Corporation that underpins the concept of *integrated thinking*. The *capital* is divided between sustaining capital and closing capital. All the six forms of capital (financial, relational, human, social, manufactured, and natural) are used in producing value and this value is finally reflected in the benefits for the community/society, the environment, and economy at national level demonstrating in the same time a high degree of *accountability*: "From previous mining the site has 100 hectares affected by 18 waste stockpiles and two pits with 140 km of underground galleries generating acid water. Via the Project 500 hectares will be redesigned and the existing contamination and

DOI: 10.4018/978-1-5225-3622-2.ch008

main pollution source will be eliminated. After mining, three pits will be backfilled and vegetated and a lake of 70 hectares will be created in one of the old pits". Besides environmental projects, the company involved in social projects, such as "resettlement site built for local families" that were affected by their activities, often correlated with another benefit for the community- job creation- for example more than 1.000 people were involved in the construction of new houses for local people, contributing to the development of the new Recea district (Annual Report 2010: page 12).

The Report follows closely the IIRC Framework, stating from the beginning the mission and vision of the organization: "Our *mission* is to create value for all of our stakeholders from responsible mining…Our *vision* is to build the Rosia Montana project and to be a catalyst for sustainable economic, environmental, cultural and community development". The two statements also confirm the compliance with the IIRC Principles of *stakeholder responsiveness* and *future outlook*. Further on, the Annual Report presents the company *performance* at all levels: economic, social, and environmental. The economic performance is generated by the financial results (although in 2010 they registered a loss of USD 22,667). The social and environmental performance is demonstrated through the commitment to the community and the environment offering "substantial returns for all stakeholders" (Annual Report 2010: page 4). Although the report mentions a strategic planning process adopted by the board, we do not consider that the company *strategy* or *strategic focus* are explicitly presented and outlined.

On the other hand, a full page of the Annual Report is dedicated to *governance* topic (or corporate governance), where the readers can find information on the board role and responsibilities, strategic planning process and risk management, corporate social responsibility, ethics and integrity, succession planning, etc. The company's *opportunities* are described via environmental impacts (positive ones), while *risk* identification and *risk* management is presented only from financial perspective (credit risk, liquidity risk etc.). Finally, the report does not provide details on *basis of preparation and presentation.* Regarding, IIRC principles, we argue that the information presented in the report is interrelated, and the *connectivity* principle fulfilled. This is supported by the *business model* and *integrated thinking.* In addition, we consider that the information presented in the report is *material, concise, consistent* and *reliable* (as it includes an audit report). Regarding *comparability*, the company did not include non- financial indicators in the report, so that only financial data can be compared with similar companies from the same industry.

Table 1. Disclosure items from IIRC Framework applied for 2010 AR of Rosia Montana

Item From the IR Conceptual Model	Disclosure in the Annual Report 2010
Integrated thinking	business model (Fig. 27)
Capital	financial, relational, human, social, manufactured, and natural
Accountability	environmental projects, social projects (page 12)
IR Content Elements	
Mission and vision	"Our mission is to create value for all of our stakeholders ...Our vision is to .. be a catalyst for sustainable economic, environmental, cultural and community development" (page 4)
Governance	board role and responsibilities, strategic planning process and risk management, corporate social responsibility, ethics and integrity, etc (page 17)
Opportunities	environmental impacts (pages 1-3)
Risk	financial perspective: credit risk, liquidity risk (pages 17-24)
IR Principles	
Stakeholder responsiveness	statements on mission and vision (page 12)
Future outlook	statements on mission and vision (page 12)
Performance	economic, social, and environmental performance (page 4)
Connectivity	business model and integrated thinking (page 11)
Material	Yes
Concise	Yes
consistent	Yes
Reliable	audit report

Source: Author's design.

The 2010 Annual Report includes social and environmental related information (regarding the projects developed at community and environment protection level), and employee related information: "Under the Collective Bargaining Agreement between RMGC and its employees, under certain conditions, employees of RMGC are entitled to a bonus equal to one month of average gross salary when celebrating 3, 5, 10, 15, 20, and 25 years of uninterrupted service."(page 30). The previous citation from the report quotes another element from the framework: *collective bargaining* from the social audit section of our model. Further on, the report presents a part of the SA 8000 requirements, such as information on *health* and *safety* or freedom of association. However, none of the three principles of AA 1000 standards are mentioned in the 2010 Annual Report.

Regarding the disclosure requested in IFRS-IASB accounting standards that is correlated with IR, the table below shows the items contained in the

Figure 1. Rosia Montana Gold Corporation: business model of integrated thinking; capital, value added, accountability
Source: Extracted from the Annual Report 2010: page 11.

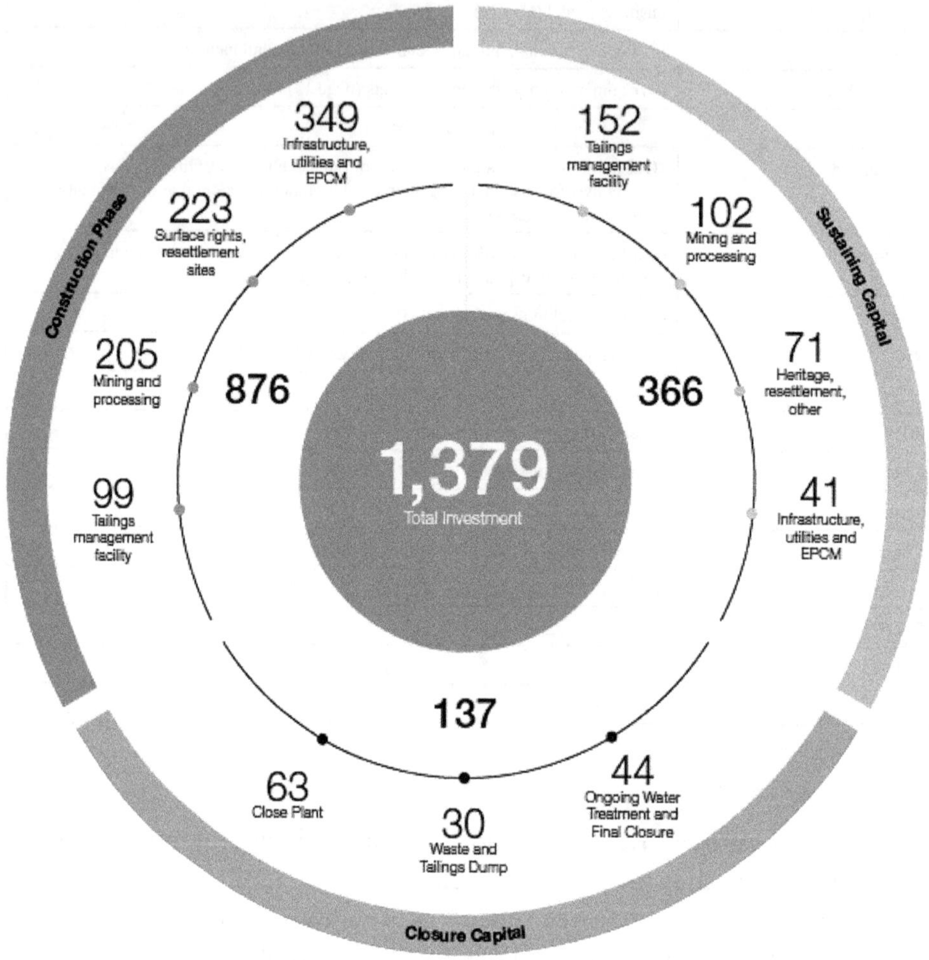

Table 2. Information on social audit disclosed in the 2010 AR of Rosia Montana

Social Audit	Explanation and Source in the Annual Report
Collective bargaining	"Under the Collective Bargaining Agreement between RMGC and its employees...(page 30)
Health and safety	pages 3; 5; 10; 11; 14
Freedom of association	page 16

Source: Author's design.

Table 3. Discussing the common elements between IASB/IFRS and integrated reporting: their application within the 2010 Annual Report of Rosia Montana - Gold Corporation

Standards	Environmental/CSR Information	Explanation and Source in the Annual Report
IAS 36; IAS 38	Concessions, licenses, trademarks, and similar items	exploitation licence; surface concession rights (page 36)
IAS 36; IFRIC 6	Tangible assets with exploration of minerals resources	Estimated future cash flows are calculated using estimated future prices, mineral resources and… *(impairment of long-lived assets section-* page 27)
IAS 2	Inventories (waste)	tailings system managing processed waste rock (page 11)
IAS 37	Recognition of provision	"provision of scientific and public research for the cultural heritage programme for Rosia Montana based on two major components: Archaeology (surface and underground) and Architecture" (page 15)
IFRS 8	Disclosure on CSR information	
	acceptance on obligation to societies in which they work	accountability towards society (community) and environment

Source: Author's design.

2010 Annual Report of Rosia Montana. The report presents the following environmental and CSR related information: concessions, licenses, trademarks, and similar items; tangible assets with exploration of minerals resources; inventories; recognition of provision; acceptance on obligation to societies.

We consider that the 2010 Annual Report of Rosia Montana Gold Corporation is a prototype of an integrated report, containing the majority of the elements from our model. This conceptual model on integrated reporting can provide guidance for the preparers of integrated reports and foster the adoption of integrated reporting.

We add that the development of the IR conceptual model is based on more theories previously discussed in the current book, namely: the constellation theory (as we consider the impact of accountancy profession on the information to be presented in an annual report through the introduction of accounting standards in the model) and the stakeholder theory (because the annual report issued by Rosia Montana has a stakeholder orientation, underlining the community involvement and the fact that companies' operations take into account all the possible environmental effects, making efforts to diminish it).

Figure 2. Applying our conceptual model of Integrated Reporting on the 2010 Annual Report of Rosia Montana - Gold Corporation
Source: Author's design.

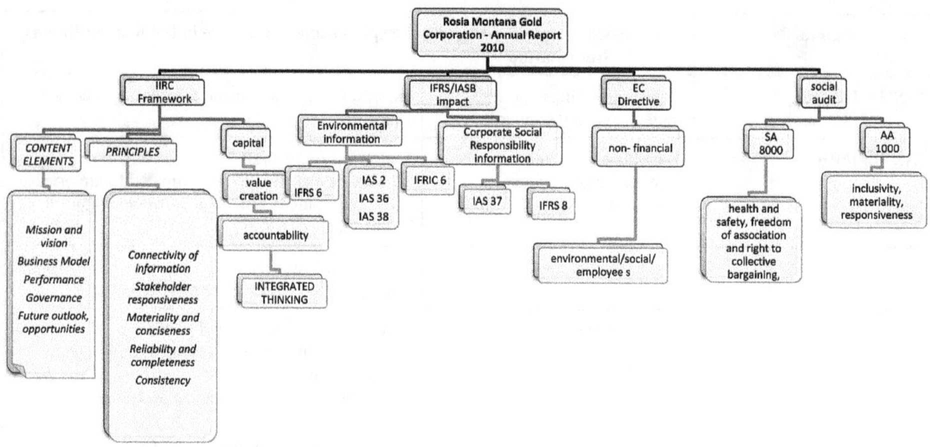

However, one can argue that just presenting the elements from the IR conceptual model in the annual report would not be enough for a report to be called *integrated.* The information has to be connected, for example by presenting a certain financial indicator in correlation with its social/ environmental impacts, or having a unique indicator for expressing more dimension, such as an environmental indicators that cumulates more environmental effects. Still, the concepts of integrated thinking and business model (the core of IR) are present in the Annual 2010 Report of Rosia Montana, and some of the elements from our model detailed very well, demonstrating the company's ability to develop future integrated reports.

We argue that the model can be further developed into a conceptual framework that goes beyond the IIRC principles and content elements, towards a set of requirements included by standard setters in specific regulation. Currently, IASB/ IFRS is joining efforts with IIRC in defining a new standard for the area of integrated reporting, as they state in the signed Memorandum. Furthermore, we believe that research on integrated reporting practice that develop new frameworks/models/prototypes of integrated reporting schemes and test their implementation on companies, can become a catalyst for the evolution of integrated reporting, bringing substantial contribution for this topic.

CONCLUSION

Through the case study approach (and applying in the content analysis technique), we investigated the 2010 Annual Report published by Rosia Montana Gold Corporation to find if this report discloses the information from the conceptual IR model stated above. The results of the analysis show that the report presents almost all the type of information from the conceptual model. In addition, we also noticed that this information is very well structured and contains complete details.

REFERENCES

A Project for Romania Annual Report and Accounts 2010. (2011, July). Retrieved from https://www.unglobalcompact.org/system/attachments/11239/original/COP_2011_FINAL_GABRIEL_RESOURCES.pdf?1310627394

Conclusion

The aim of the current book has been to demonstrate that the accountancy profession maintains a strong influence upon the development of integrated reporting. In the first chapter, we presented the evolution of a literature review in the field of corporate reporting, from non-financial information disclosure mechanisms, to emergent integrated reports, trying to understand how early IR adopters perceived integrated reporting. We continued by analyzing the meaning of the word 'integration' itself, in order to set the main definitions and characteristics of IR. At the end of the chapter we managed to identify the theorization area for integrated reporting, as well as relevant methods and techniques that can be included in a research methodology on IR. During the first chapter we managed to show the importance of IR for the development of corporate reporting, as an essential stage in the evolution of the financial and non- financial reporting environment.

The first chapters represent the center of our research, analyzing the impact of accountancy profession for the IR evolution from a theoretical approach. After setting the main coordinates of accountancy profession, we investigate its influence on integrated reporting, from the IIRC formation and consolidation, to several *Memorandum of Understanding (MOU)* signed between this organization and accounting professional bodies/organizations/standard setters. We acknowledge the challenges for accountants and members of professional accounting bodies in assessing the additional knowledge, skills, and techniques, for working with integrated report.

The last chapters introduce the national perspective on integrated reporting. Therefore, we investigate the stage of IR in Romania and the research has two dimensions. At first, we developed a questionnaire on the integrated reporting, its content, usefulness, costs, benefits, etc. We addressed the questionnaire to Romanian members of accounting professional bodies. The second part of the research involves a case study on a Romanian corporation that started to publish integrated reports. In this case we apply the prototype framework from chapter five to a single report in order to check the conformity. Finally, we would like to underline the contribution of the current book to corporate reporting, in general, but also to IT management literature, as integrated reports assume new techniques, methods, processes, that incorporate technical revolution and of course, follow up IT developments.

Appendix

COMMENT LETTERS

June 17, 2013
To: International Integrated Reporting Council (IIRC)
Lincoln's Inn Fields
London WC2A 3EE
Re: IMA Response to the IIRC Framework Consultation Draft

Dear Sirs and Madams,

As one of the leading and largest global professional bodies focused on advancing the profession of management accounting, IMA® (Institute of Management Accountants) is pleased to offer its comments on the Integrated Reporting Framework Consultation Draft (CD) dated April 16, 2013. IMA, with members in over 120 countries, represents management accountants around the world who help protect investor interests and drive business performance in the areas of financial planning and analysis, business/corporate reporting and analysis, risk management and internal controls, strategic costing, M&A and much more. Management accountants are not "just technical accountants" – they are broad-based business thinkers who serve as trusted advisors inside organizations and are "at the table" on all issues involving strategy and sustainable value creation.

IMA conducted global surveys, both formal and informal, to capture what we expected to be diverse input on the subjects of disclosures and integrated reporting. Internal and external groups that we solicited input from include members of our technical committees, which include preparers and, representatives from rating agencies, auditors, consultants, technologists, investors, academicians and others. Additionally, we reviewed polling question responses from the IMA-sponsored webinar conducted by IIRC staff on May 2, 2013 that drew about 1,000 attendees from around the world.

The Executive Summary that follows is supplemented by official responses to the twenty-four CD questions, submitted as requested via the web-based template and also attached.

Executive Summary

1. IMA concurs that substantial improvement is possible and needed in the area of disclosures to better inform investors and other stakeholders as to the sustainable value creation capacity and capability of the enterprise. In this regard, we appreciate the work of the IIRC in attempting to transform business enterprise reporting and to develop guidance that can be consistently applied, in addition to cultural shifts in the area of integrated thinking.
2. IMA also believes that there are several potential fatal flaws in the CD, outlined here but developed in greater detail below and in the CD question set:
   a. The compelling market need for a single integrated report (i.e., integrated reporting), from investors and other market stakeholders, is not described or articulated. b. The cost/benefit of integrated reporting is also not described or articulated, either in this document or in companion documents. Further, it is possible that interlinked financial and non-financial reports (e.g., statutory financials, MD&A, GRI, OECD, etc.) could produce higher ROI than a single, integrated report.
      c. There is no consideration of existing legal disclosure requirements in various jurisdictions, or other unique environmental conditions specific to a jurisdiction.
      d. In an increasingly complex and competitive global marketplace, we question whether investors and other market stakeholders would want management teams to disclose (potentially) competitively sensitive information about how they achieved profitable growth in a differentiated manner.
      e. It is unclear how independent assurance providers can obtain evidence about the future, which is the stated orientation of the CD.

Additional Points for Consideration

1. We believe by taking a market-driven approach there is a great opportunity to improve the disclosures process, including simplification and better connecting disclosures to the overarching "strategy story" of the organization.
2. There generally is a call to action globally with respect to reforming the external disclosures process which includes simplifying disclosures. For example, according to an Ernst and Young study, in the US over the past two decades the average number of pages in annual reports devoted to footnotes and MD&A has quadrupled. If that rate continues for the next two decades, companies would devote more than 500 pages to notes and MD&A! The FASB Disclosures Framework project focused on financial footnotes is in the evaluative stage, with the Invitation to Comment issued on July 12, 2012. The IASB recently initiated a similar project.
3. IMA endorses the following components of a more effective and efficient external disclosures process, with disclosures that are *material*; *relevant* (to decision-makers - investors, rating agencies, regulators, data aggregators, etc.); *actionable*; *accurate* (recognizing that disclosures beyond audited financials may not have the same level of assurance but can still be connected to the strategy story); *succinct* and *logical; balanced* (leading and lagging indicators; financial, customer, employee and societal measures); *reasonably connected* (to the overarching "strategy story" and goals for the organization, and, to each other, e.g., financial with non-financial measures); and, *cost effective to produce*. In a competitive market, shareholders and other market constituents clearly want the value of the disclosures to exceed the cost to produce and obtain assurance thereon, and do not wish to see a regulatory "social tax" imposed on organizations striving for growth.
4. We question, however, the market drivers, need and value articulated by investors (and other market constituents) for a single, fully integrated report as well as lack of alternatives presented (e.g., interconnected reports), as noted earlier.
5. CFOs and other strategic leaders in the organization (e.g., corporate governance groups, Investor Relations) have demonstrated that they

understand the need for more balanced, leading indicator type of data to drive decisions supporting the strategy with internal application of balanced scorecards, enterprise performance dashboards, and strategy maps, to name a few. Taking this balanced data and using a variant for external disclosures is a function of value to the "target" (market constituents including investors, etc.), cost/benefit and externalities such as the legal, regulatory and competitive environments all of which the IIRC needs to assess.

6. Integrated reporting does not singularly drive integrated thinking as is asserted in companion documents. Well run organizations have long understood that integrated thinking makes for better business and better outcomes and is also a starting point for cross-functional value generation, "un-silo'ing" the organization, etc. What also leads to well run businesses and positive outcomes for business and society are smart business practices, courageous leaders, business processes and cross-functional behavior on behalf of stakeholders.
7. Especially in the early stages of IR development, the focus should be on learning and growth and NOT reating involuntary regulatory-type standards (potentially creating a social tax) before a tangible value and the benefit to investors are more clearly understood.
    a. IMA is not in favor of creating mandatory reporting standards in the learning and growth phase of IR (which could be several years).
    b. IMA is also "not excited" about mandatory "report or explain" approaches. On April 16, 2013 the EU adopted a proposal requiring large companies to disclose ESG information as part of their annual reporting requirement, in effect, report the data or explain why it could or should not be provided. With the rapid rise in voluntary reporting (e.g., GRI), is the IR approach really adding economic value or insight to investors? Are regulators really in the best position to determine the metrics most important to sustainable value creation in highly competitive, global markets?
    c. The SASB (Sustainability Accounting Standards Board) is a San Francisco-based not for profit incorporated in 2011 and charged with developing industry-specific standards for use by companies to report on material ESG issues in standard filings. We encourage SASB, per its charter, to reach out to a broad range of constituents in terms of the cost/benefit of ESG KPIs and the strength of the relationship between these KPIs and the financial/strategy story. On June 12, 2013 SASB issued its Conceptual Framework for a

45-day comment period. We assume the IIRC will stay abreast of developments.

8. Specifically, in the US, for IR to gain traction we believe the focus should be first on addressing disclosure overload including simplified disclosures, and then later better connecting ESG metrics with financial and strategic measures if the cost/benefit analysis makes sense. In the US and other jurisdictions, there also needs to be more focus on intangible assets/IP and associated KPIs as a start (as well as industry vertical KPIs more important to investors in some cases than ESG categories).
9. According to the April 29, 2013 study by the IRRC (Investor Responsibility Research Center) Institute, and the Sustainable Investments Institute, *Integrated Financial and Sustainability Reporting in the US*, all but one company in the S&P 500 issued at least one sustainability related disclosure but only seven companies "integrate" financial and sustainability reporting.

Additionally, according to GRI there has been a triple digit percentage increase in sustainability reports issued by S companies over the past year. A key question is whether the degree of integration is correlated with better returns for shareholders and other market constituents.

As a related question, what level of integration do investors and other market constituents need to make their assessments as to sustainable value generation capacity and capability?

For example, the nine reporting areas in the IRRC report are already discussed in company-level sustainability reports and to some extent in US 10-K filings (environmental management, employment, climate change, hazardous waste, product formulations, waste management, water use, ethics and human rights).

10. Further, regarding the IRRC US study which closely comports with IIRC framework thinking, IMA took an informal sampling of a few of the MNCs implied to be "compliant" with integrated reporting and compared those with 10-Ks, sustainability and/or CSR reports of other registrants. We found little substantive differences on key risk factor disclosures, and, in connecting financial, customer, employee and societal measures to the overarching strategy story.
11. In the US and perhaps in other regulatory regimes, full integration of customer, employee and societal measures with the standard financial external disclosures (process) may not be feasible in terms of timing (e.g.,

financial statements issued to coincide with issuance of the integrated report, GRI, CSR or other), cost effectiveness, assurance level and legal liability. Without a much clearer "investor value proposition", it may not even make good business sense.

12. The notion of linking financial and non-financial measures to the strategy is perhaps a nice end state to envision, but trying to develop precisely quantified and causal linkages across all performance indicators will always be a challenge and the "standard" for non-financial measures may always be directional and "roughly right". On the preparer side, there needs to be a level of professional judgment in reporting and linking non-financial measures to financials and the overall "strategy story". On the user side, there needs to be a level of trust, and, professional skepticism to ask the right questions that management needs to answer in a cohesive manner (to boards, audit committees, investors and other constituents). Overall, effective stakeholder engagement is necessary to build transparency and trust.
13. SMEs (small and medium sized entities) need to be included in the external disclosures discussion. SMEs including private companies have the need to compete for capital, be transparent, demonstrate solid internal controls and link balanced measures to strategy. They tend to be disproportionately impacted by onerous reporting requirements yet account for a majority of jobs growth.

The Path Forward

1. IMA respectfully believes that the end in mind needs to be redefined to better serve organizations and society. It should NOT be to produce a single, integrated report. The end in mind should be to motivate disclosures that better inform investors as to the sustainable value creation capability and capacity of the organization. A good first step would be to clarify and simplify existing disclosures. It may turn out that interlinked or interconnected reports will produce a higher ROI for investors.
2. The ROI and "proof of concept" assessment of integrated reporting should shift more to actual value delivery *participants* (e.g., business owners, business managers, CFOs, preparers, investors, analysts, etc.) relative to value chain *observers* and *monitors* (e.g., academics, consultants and regulators). This will help to develop the required market evidence.

3. A "learning and growth" approach should be taken to IR with tangible step changes such as improving MD&A disclosures, motivating more concise and informative financial reports including reporting on intangibles, creating better connections to the overarching "strategy story", and, supporting new sustainability/ESG frameworks such as GRI (GRI issued the next generation, "G4", of its guidelines on May 22, 2013 in Amsterdam). Mandatory reporting is not recommended and history has often shown that it results in a social tax.
4. Technology enablement including XBRL/structured data standards could play a role to potentially improve the cost/benefit of IR. A new report from the Boston College Center for Corporate Citizenship and E&Y concluded that while two-thirds of companies reporting on sustainability use the GRI framework, the same number says difficulties with data collection are among their largest reporting challenges. In IMA's May 2, 2013 webinar with nearly 1,000 global participants, the responses to the question "which is the most significant barrier to IR in your organization" were: 13% weak external drivers, 21% lack of appetite from the top, 20% strong organizational silos, 32% patchwork of IT programs/legacy systems, and, 14% other.

Closing Remarks

IMA again commends the IIRC for its efforts. We all share the same goal – creating stronger organizations, and, fulfilling our missions to serve the profession and society.

Jeffrey C. Thomson, CMA
President and CEO

Consultation Questions

The IIRC welcomes comments on all aspects of the Draft International <IR> Framework (Draft Framework) from all stakeholders, whether to express agreement or to recommend changes.

The following questions are focused on areas where there has been significant discussion during the development process. Comments on any other aspect of the Draft Framework are also encouraged through the questions.

Please provide all comments in English.

All comments received will be considered a matter of public record and will be posted on the IIRC's website (www.theiirc.org).

Comments should be submitted by Monday 15th, July 2013.

Name: Jeffrey C. Thomson
Email: jthomson@imanet.org
Stakeholder group: Professional bodies – Accounting
If replying on behalf of an Organization please complete the following:
Organization name: Institute of Management Accountants (IMA)
Industry sector: Financials
Geographical region: Global

Key Points

If you wish to briefly express any key points, or to emphasize particular aspects of your submission, or add comments in the nature of a cover letter, then the following space can be used for this purpose. Please do not repeat large amounts of material appearing elsewhere in your comments.

Executive Summary

1. IMA concurs that substantial improvement is possible and needed in the area of external disclosures, to better inform investors and other stakeholders as to the sustainable value creation capacity and capability of the enterprise. In this regard, we appreciate the work of the IIRC in attempting to transform business enterprise reporting and to develop guidance that can be consistently applied, in addition to cultural shifts in the area of integrated thinking.
2. IMA also believes that there are several potential fatal flaws in the CD, outlined here but developed in greater detail below and in the CD question set:
    a. The compelling market need for a single integrated report (i.e., integrated reporting), from investors and other market stakeholders, is not described or articulated.
    b. The cost/benefit of integrated reporting is also not described or articulated, either in this document or in companion documents. Further, it is possible that interlinked financial and non-financial

reports (e.g., financial, MD&A, GRI, OECD, etc.) produce higher ROI than a single, integrated report.

c. There is no consideration of existing legal disclosure requirements in various jurisdictions, or other unique environmental conditions specific to a jurisdiction.

d. In an increasingly complex and competitive global marketplace, we question whether investors and other market stakeholders would want management teams to disclose (potentially) competitively sensitive information about how they achieved profitable growth in a differentiated manner. e. It is unclear how independent assurance providers can obtain evidence about the future, which is the stated orientation of the CD.

The Path Forward

1. IMA respectfully believes that the end in mind needs to be redefined to better serve organizations and society. It should NOT be to produce a single, integrated report. The end in mind should be to motivate disclosures that better inform investors as to the sustainable value creation capability and capacity of the organization. A good first step would be to clarify and simplify existing disclosures. It may turn out that interlinked or interconnected reports will produce a higher ROI for investors.
2. The ROI and "proof of concept" assessment of integrated reporting should shift more to actual value delivery participants (e.g., business owners, business managers, CFOs, preparers, investors, analysts, etc.) relative to value chain observers and monitors (e.g., academics, consultants and regulators). This will help to develop the required market evidence.
3. A "learning and growth" approach should be taken to IR with tangible step changes such as improving MD&A disclosures, motivating more concise and informative financial reports including reporting on intangibles, creating better connections to the overarching "strategy story", and, supporting new sustainability/ESG frameworks such as GRI (GRI issued the next generation, "G4", of its guidelines on May 22, 2013 in Amsterdam). Mandatory reporting is not recommended and history has often shown that it results in a social tax.
4. Technology enablement including XBRL/structured data standards could play a role to potentially improve the cost/benefit of IR. A new report from the Boston College Center for Corporate Citizenship and E&Y

concluded that while two-thirds of companies reporting on sustainability use the GRI framework, the same number says difficulties with data collection are among their largest reporting challenges. In IMA's 5/2/13 webinar with nearly 1,000 global participants, the responses to the question "which is the most significant barrier to IR in your organization" were: 13% weak external drivers, 21% lack of appetite from the top, 20% strong organizational silos, 32% patchwork of IT programs/legacy systems, and, 14% other.

CHAPTER 1: OVERVIEW

Principles-Based Requirements

To be in accordance with the Framework, an integrated report should comply with the principles-based requirements identified throughout the Framework in bold italic type (paragraphs 1.11-1.12).

1. *Should any additional principles-based requirements be added or should any be eliminated or changed? If so, please explain why.*

Possibly add principles that broadly provide information as to how an organization applies quality management techniques in achieving goals, serving customers, internal process efficiencies, etc.

Many of the principles dealing with strategic focus and future orientation are already captured in the MD&A or should be in a directional sense. Describing connectivity as referenced in 3B should be directional and judgment based, not precise, quantitative and prescriptive as these paragraphs sound.

Paragraph 3.16 implies that an integrated report with more metrics is what builds trust.

What builds trust are smart, honest organizations delivering on their goals to serve customers and society.

Paragraph 3.30 says an integrated report should include all material matters in a balanced way and without material error. This is too broad and does not reflect environmental factors such as competitive environment, litigation and reputation risk nor the fact that materiality and assurance are defined differently for financial vs. nonfinancial metrics. We don't understand how this and other principles get applied in the real world of business.

Principle 4.4 states that an integrated report should stand alone. Where is the evidence that this is what market constituents want? Where is the evidence that this adds value to shareholders and society? An integrated report could easily duplicate, thereby adding non-value added cost, key performance metrics contained in financial reports, MD&A, GRI, responsibility reports, etc. The end in mind is not an integrated report - the end in mind are better disclosures that inform market stakeholders as to the sustainable value creation capacity and capability of the organization.

Principles in section 4 - Too much information, not all needed by investors, some subject to reputation and litigation risk depending on jurisdiction. For example, broad understanding of how the organization manages its people capital is important (including succession planning at the top) but 4B is too much detail to produce with minimal value, in addition, it flexes and changes over time.

Principle 4C opportunities and risks are captured in MD&A and/or COSO, ISO, etc. internal controls and risk management frameworks.

Frequency of reporting in principle 5, preparation of the integrated report in conjunction with the annual statutory financial reporting cycle is not realistic in the US and likely other jurisdictions.

Interaction With Other Reports and Communications

The <IR> process is intended to be applied continuously to all relevant reports and communications, in addition to the preparation of an integrated report. The integrated report may include links to other reports and communications, e.g., financial statements and sustainability reports. The IIRC aims to complement material developed by established reporting standard setters and others, and does not intend to develop duplicate content (paragraphs 1.18-1.20).

2. *Do you agree with how paragraphs 1.18-1.20 characterize the interaction with other reports and communications?*

IMA is not convinced that a single, integrated report is necessary to produce disclosures that are more actionable, relevant and concise in describing the sustainable value creation capacity and capability of an organization to investors and other market participants. Please refer to our Executive Summary. Enhanced MD&A, greater adoption of voluntary GRI/G4 standards, and doing a better job of connecting activities to the overarching strategy story in a directional sense could be helpful to investors. Smart investors do not want companies to be spending time and cost duplicating information found in other reports, revealing competitive information, etc. They want smart, well managed companies who deliver what they promised.

IMA also believes that interlinked/interconnected reporting should be assessed by investors as a more effective and efficient alternative to a single, integrated report.

3. *If the IIRC were to create an online database of authoritative sources of indicators or measurement methods developed by established reporting standard setters and others, which references should be included?*
   a. COSO Internal Controls and Risk Management frameworks.
   b. ISO 9001, ISO 14001.
   c. GRI including G4 just released.
   d. XBRL.
   e. SASB.
   f. ESG.

In the spirit of avoiding regulatory mandates, sources from guidance setters vs. standard setters should be strongly considered such as COSO and its refreshed internal controls framework issued May 14, 2013.

Other

4. *Please provide any other comments you have about Chapter 1.*

Paragraph 1.12 should be modified to allow management to explain its determination that some content elements are being omitted because they might result in competitive harm.

Although paragraph 1.6 states emphatically that the audience for an integrated report should primarily be providers of financial capital, this primacy is not reflected in Figure 3 where society seems to be the recipient of the information. Shareholders should be prominently displayed in Figure 3.

CHAPTER 2: FUNDAMENTAL CONCEPTS

The Capitals (Section 2B)

The Framework describes six categories of capital (paragraph 2.17). An organization is to use these categories as a benchmark when preparing an integrated report (paragraphs 2.19-2.21), and should disclose the reason if it considers any of the capitals as not material (paragraph 4.5).

5. *Do you agree with this approach to the capitals? Why/why not?*

Generally we agree with the six capitals approach so long as there is flexibility in defining materiality and level of expected assurance. Broadly understanding an organization's approach to the capitals, including dependencies, resource allocation and optimization, may be helpful to investors and other market stakeholders. It is not clear that an integrated report with all of the principles achieved is the means to this end.

6. *Please provide any other comments you have about Section 2B?*

Paragraph 2.16 should be clarified to state what is meant by the "overall stock of capitals". Is reporting suggested for the net result of value changes in all capitals? The language appears to state that each capital experiences value creation or diminution over time and thus each requires periodic reporting. If correct, this level of reporting could diminish shareholder value and is simply not necessary, practical or valued by investors. Also not practical is paragraph 2.25, requiring that "an organization's net impact on the global stock of capitals could be tallied".

Business Model (Section 2C)

A business model is defined as an organization's chosen system of inputs, business activities, outputs and outcomes that aims to create value over the short, medium and long term (paragraph 2.26).

7. *Do you agree with this definition? Why/why not?*

Generally agree, as this adequately captures the supply and value chains of the organization. See previous comments on Figure 3.

Outcomes are defined as the internal and external consequences (positive and negative) for the capitals as a result of an organization's business activities and outputs (paragraphs 2.35-2.36).

8. *Do you agree with this definition? Why/why not?*

Yes.

9. *Please provide any other comments you have about Section 2C or the disclosure requirements and related guidance regarding business models contained in the Content Elements Chapter of the Framework (see Section 4E)?*

US companies and companies in other jurisdictions are currently challenged with an overload of disclosure requirements for mandatory quarterly and year-end financial reports, which is being addressed by the FASB for US companies (initially focused on notes to the financial statements). Other national disclosures-related improvement projects should be considered by the IIRC in describing the journey to its desired end state.

Other

10. *Please provide any other comments you have about Chapter 2 that are not already addressed by your responses above.*

None.

CHAPTER 3: GUIDING PRINCIPLES

Materiality and Conciseness (Section 3D)

Materiality is determined by reference to assessments made by the primary intended report users (paragraphs 3.23-3.24). The primary intended report users are providers of financial capital (paragraphs 1.6-1.8).

11. *Do you agree with this approach to materiality? If not, how would you change it?*

Materiality and assurance depend on the type of metric being reported. More precise and quantitative for financial KPIs; less so for non-financial KPIs.

Materiality should generally be defined by senior management and the board, but external input from investors may also be helpful from an independence perspective.

12. *Please provide any other comments you have about Section 3D or the Materiality determination process (Section 5B).*

The disclosure described in 5B is too much and does not add net value to the investor. Material matters and level of assurance for KPIs should be disclosed; "describing the process used to identify relevant matters and to narrow them down to material matters, ..., identifying the key personnel involved in the identification and prioritization of material matters, and, identifying the role of those charged with governance in the process" is unnecessary detail for investors and other market stakeholders.

We are unclear how all of the process-related and other disclosures purported to be necessary in a single integrated report avoid exacerbating disclosure overload while achieving the goals of conciseness and relevance.

Additionally, although the CD questions note that the primary intended report users are providers of financial capital, this concept is not contained in Chapter 3. In fact, the inclusion of broader social interests as report users could confuse the preparer's approach to materiality, as the relevant matters to be considered (see 3.25) will naturally depend on which capital is being reported on. The primacy of providers of financial capital should be re-emphasized in chapter 3.

Reliability and Completeness (Section 3E)

Reliability is enhanced by mechanisms such as robust internal reporting systems, appropriate stakeholder engagement, and independent, external assurance (paragraph 3.31).

13. *How should the reliability of an integrated report be demonstrated?*

While desirable in theory, independent assurance from a provider adds to the cost of the integrated report, especially if most of the substantive information is already captured and (somewhat) connected in financial reports, GRI and CSR/responsibility reports, etc.

At the end of the day, the market itself serves as the barometer as to how management is performing and the same would be true for data captured in an integrated report. A level of trust and a healthy dose of professional skepticism on the part of investors and analysts, combined with a general sense as to how an organization applies its professional judgment (especially true for non-financial KPIs/capitals), creates the appropriate "tension" in the value chain and incites the right questions in delivering sustainable value.

We are unclear what is meant in 3.31 by "The reliability of information is affected by its balance and freedom from material error".

14. *Please provide any other comments you have about Section 3E.*

Since the primary orientation of an integrated report is future prospects and providing this information to the public is subject to various laws and regulations (US and presumably other national jurisdictions), an overall qualifier "to the extent permitted by law" would be helpful in several paragraphs in this chapter (especially those dealing with disclosures).

Additionally, given the judgment-based and future orientation of the integrated report, it would seem that independent external assurance providers would have great difficulty in providing such assurance, as suggested in 3.31.

Other

15. *Please provide any other comments you have about Chapter 3 that are not already addressed by your responses above.*

An IMA webinar hosted by the IIRC (over 900 participants) in early May revealed the following, when participants were asked "what is the most challenging principle to implement from the integrated framework"? -

- Strategy focus and future orientation 34%
- Connectivity of information 18%
- Stakeholder responsiveness 13%
- Materiality and conciseness 7%

- Reliability and completeness 12%
- Consistency and compatibility 16%

CHAPTER 4: CONTENT ELEMENTS

16. *Please provide any comments you have about Chapter 4 that are not already addressed by your responses above (please include comments on the Content Element Business Model [Section 4E] in your answer to questions 7-9 above rather than here).*

4.1 Many if not all of the Content Elements are captured in current/enhanced financial disclosures, MD&A and voluntary GRI type sustainability reports.

4.2 As noted, the compelling market-driven case for a single integrated report which we believe duplicates other information has not been made. We understand the connectivity issue, and believe that investors would be more than satisfied with enhanced MD&A and other ideas we have suggested.

4.10 Governance - we believe some level of insight on "people and process capacity" is helpful but not to this degree. The value of the information is far less than the cost to produce, and would exacerbate the disclosures overload situation in some national jurisdictions including the US.

4.33 Future outlook - business issues could include litigation, reputation and competitive risk(s).

CHAPTER 5: PREPARATION AND PRESENTATION

Involvement of Those Charged With Governance (Section 5D)

Section 5D discusses the involvement of those charged with governance, and paragraph 4.5 requires organizations to disclose the governance body with oversight responsibility for <IR>.

17. *Should there be a requirement for those charged with governance to include a statement acknowledging their responsibility for the integrated report? Why/why not?*

Management and their boards have a responsibility to state in broad terms the assurance level of any KPIs (lagging indicators) and KRIs (Key Risk Indicators, leading indicators) that they provide externally on a voluntary or involuntary basis. Since the responsibilities of a body charged with governance are set forth with great specificity in many national jurisdictions including the US, with no current guidance as to what integrated reporting if any the body should take, these responsibilities should be deleted or minimally qualified by the phrase "to the extent permitted by law". It appears that requiring boards of directors to perform management functions like reporting of performance and future prospects could be in violation of current practice and laws.

18. *Please provide any other comments you have about Involvement of those charged with governance (Section 5D).*

None.

Credibility (Section 5E)

The Framework provides reporting criteria against which organizations and assurance providers assess a report's adherence (paragraph 5.21).

19. *If assurance is to be obtained, should it cover the integrated report as a whole, or specific aspects of the report? Why?*

Some level of assurance, more so for financial and qualitative KPIs vs. non-financial qualitative KPIs, should be expected by investors. The cost of assurance, internal (e.g., internal audit) or external (independent experts) should be considered in the overall ROI/cost vs. benefit of integrated reporting.

The definition of "reasonable" assurance will vary between financial and non-financial capitals. Also, at the end of the day, investors/shareholders either trust the organizations they invest in or they do not based on performance, societal status, reputation, etc. A healthy dose of professional skepticism on the preparer side with a professional judgment process on the user side helps to mitigate high assurance costs. More metrics conceptually linked in a "golden thread" to strategy and mission is not necessarily the path to better disclosures. Greater stakeholder engagement also builds transparency and trust.

20. *Please provide any other comments you have about Credibility (Section 5E). Assurance providers are particularly asked to comment on whether they consider the Framework provides suitable criteria for an assurance engagement.*

None.

Other

21. *Please provide any other comments you have about Chapter 5 that are not already addressed by your responses above (please include comments on the materiality determination process [Section 5B] in your answer to question 11 above rather than here).*

None.

OVERALL VIEW

22. *Recognizing that <IR> will evolve over time, please explain the extent to which you believe the content of the Framework overall is appropriate for use by organizations in preparing an integrated report and for providing report users with information about an organization's ability to create value in the short, medium and long term?*

We actually believe that the Framework is well described IF there is market evidence that a single integrated report leads to better external disclosures with a positive ROI/cost vs. benefit. However, at this point in time the market evidence is not there or has not yet been well articulated. As we noted earlier in "The Path Forward" section up front, "The ROI assessment of integrated reporting should shift more to actual value delivery participants (e.g., business owners, business managers, CFOs, preparers, investors, analysts, etc.) relative to value chain observers and monitors (e.g., academics, consultants and regulators). The latter play a valuable role in future, transformational thinking, but "proof of concept" requires a far greater role by value delivery participants as defined".

Development of <IR>

23. *If the IIRC were to develop explanatory material on <IR> in addition to the Framework, which three topics would you recommend be given priority? Why?*
    a. The journey or roadmap toward better external disclosures which hits most of the criteria on which we all agree. As noted earlier, we do not agree that a single integrated report is the end in mind for market participants.
    b. The level of connectivity to the strategy story that balances market need with organizational risks such as litigation, reputation and competition.
    c. How the balanced scorecard, used typically for internal management applications, may apply to IR with "filters" that reflect externalities such as national mandates, litigation issues, competition and more.

Other

24. *Please provide any other comments not already addressed by your responses to Questions 1-23.*

We wanted to emphasize the role of technology enablement including XBRL and other web-based structured data standards to improve the cost/benefit of disclosures reporting, improving comparability and connectivity, etc. Two data points are provided -

- A new report from the Boston College Center for Corporate Citizenship and Ernst and Young concluded that while 2/3 of companies reporting on sustainability use the GRI framework, the same number says difficulties with data collection are among their largest reporting challenges. These results would be even more pronounced for integrated reporting which is broader than ESG/sustainability reporting.
- In IMA's 5/2/13 webinar with nearly 1,000 global participants, the responses to the question "which is the most significant barrier to IR in your organization" were
    - 13% weak external drivers
    - 21% lack of appetite from the top
    - 20% strong organizational silos

- 32% patchwork of IT programs/legacy systems
- 14% other

CIMA WISHES TO THANK THE IIRC FOR THE OPPORTUNITY TO COMMENT, AND AGAIN, WE APPLAUD YOUR EFFORTS TO TRANSFORM DISCLOSURES REPORTING AND MOTIVATE INTEGRATED THINKING.

Jean Rogers, PhD PE
Executive Director
75 Broadway Suite 202
San Francisco, CA 94111
510-816-4175 Cell
jean.rogers@sasb.org
www.sasb.org
July 8, 2013

Dear Members of the International Integrated Reporting Committee,

I write on behalf of the Sustainability Accounting Standards Board (SASB), a 501c3 organization that provides sustainability accounting standards for the disclosure of material sustainability issues by publicly-listed corporations in the U.S, for the benefit of investors and the public. SASB receives strategic guidance from a Board of 13 members and an Advisory Council of 130 members. SASB's standards development work is overseen by a Standards Council of 15 experts in accounting, law and sustainability and vetted by Industry Working Groups with more than 650 experts participating in three sectors to date. These working group members represent $8.8T assets under management and $3.2T market capital.

SASB is invested in the work of the International Integrated Reporting Committee (IIRC) and is honored to provide official comments on the Consultation Draft Integrated Reporting Framework (Draft IRF).

SASB's development of industry-specific disclosure and accounting standards on material sustainability issues complements with the work of the IIRC. Many of the elements of the Draft IRF fully align with elements of SASB's Conceptual Framework, including our respective approaches to materiality, boundary and accounting for capitals.

Specifically, the principles-based approach in the Draft IRF complements SASB's approach, which prescribes sustainability topics that are material at the industry-level, for consideration of inclusion on annual regulatory filing by individual companies based on specific operating context. For topics that companies deem material in their specific operating context, SASB provides comparable metrics to account for company performance. This approach is also consistent with rules of public disclosure in U.S. capital markets, whereby materiality determination is ultimately the responsibility of companies, with ultimate liability of senior management.

Sarbanes-Oxley Act of 2002

Strategically, we view SASB's work of promoting disclosure of material sustainability issues in annual and other SEC filings of publicly listed companies in the U.S. as a practical implementation of the concept of integrated reporting in the context of U.S. capital markets. SASB standards provide specific disclosure and accounting metrics to put the concept of integrated reporting into practice.

However, we believe one element of the Draft IRF—integration with other reports and communications– is not fully compatible with U.S. Federal disclosure regulations and disclosure requirements for publicly-listed companies in the U.S., and therefore could represent a hindrance for a successful implementation of integrated reporting in the U.S.

U.S. Federal law already requires publicly listed companies to disclose material information, defined as "presenting a substantial likelihood that the disclosure of the omitted fact would have been viewed by the reasonable investor as having significantly altered the "total mix" of information made available."2

TSC Indus. v. Northway, Inc., 426 U.S. 438 (1976) and Basic v. Levinson, 485 U.S. 224 (1988)

Specific disclosure requirements are established by federal regulation (Regulation S-K) and require publicly listed companies to disclose material information at the time of initial public offering (Form S-1) and thereafter on an annual and quarterly basis (Form 10-K and 10-Q) and on an on-going basis upon material corporate events (Form 8-K). Similar disclosure requirements are imposed on foreign corporation that issue share to the public in the U.S. (Mainly Form 20-F).

Therefore, Form 10-K and other mandatory SEC filings for publicly listed companies (SEC Filings) are the logical platform for Integrated Reporting by publicly listed in the U.S., for the following reasons:

- SEC Filings are the official conduit of material information between companies and investors and one of the main source of information for capital markets, on which investor base their follow-up information request and valuation models.
- SEC Filings are mandatory for corporations (both U.S. and Foreign) that issue securities to the public in the U.S. Inclusion or omission of information is the ultimate responsibility of senior management, subject to liability of company executives for non-disclosure of material items.
- SEC Filings are a high-level, strategic account of company performance that are intended for the benefit of investors and providers of financial capital (the primary audience of the Draft IRF.
- SEC Filings are meant to present a fair and comprehensive account of companies' performance and ability to create value in the short-, medium- and long-term, including not only operational and financial results but also the management of financial, manufactured and intellectual capitals, governance information and non-financial information that is required to give context to financial results.
- To the extent that the management of natural, human and social capitals is material, as determined by SASB in an industry-specific context, disclosure of company performance in these area is legally required. In addition forward looking information can be included to address key Content Elements of the Draft IRF, such as Opportunities and Risks and Strategy and Resource Allocation. Lastly, the Business Description Section of Form 10-K can be used to address other Content Elements of the Draft IRF including Organizational Overview and Business Model.

If an integrated report is created on top of, or in addition to the Form 10-K and other SEC filings, as prescribed by the Draft IRF in Section 1.18, all information that is material (as understood in the context of the U.S. capital markets) will be redundant with information in SEC Filings. Therefore, to the extent that IR focuses on significant and material value creation from the perspective of investors, implementation of these principles in a cost-effective manner is best done through the mandatory filings in the U.S.

Thank you for the opportunity to provide feedback on the Draft IRF. We encourage the IIRC to have flexibility in implementing its principles on a country by country basis, and to recognize/augment existing reporting systems which are in place. We appreciate your consideration of the point of view outlined in this letter.

Kind regards,
Jean Rogers PhD PE
Executive Director
Sustainability Accounting Standards Board

Philip D. Tarling, CIA, CRMA, CMIIA
Global Chairman of the Board
The Institute of Internal Auditors
247 Maitland Avenue
Altamonte Springs, FL 32701
July 12, 2013
Professor Mervyn King
Chairman, International Integrated Reporting Council
Mr. Paul Druckman
Chief Executive Officer, International Integrated Reporting Council
Response e-mailed to dpresponses@theiirc.org
RE: IIRC's Consultation Draft of the International <IR> Framework

Dear Professor King and Mr. Druckman:

On behalf of the over 180,000 members of The Institute of Internal Auditors (IIA), attached are our comments on the International Integrated Reporting Council's (IIRC) Consultation Draft of the International Integrated Reporting <IR> Framework. As the global standards setting body for the professional practice of internal auditing, we appreciate the opportunity to provide comments on this very important initiative that will impact the internal auditing profession.

Recently, The IIA's President and Chief Executive Officer was appointed to serve on the IIRC. Therefore, as Chairman of the Board, I am pleased to provide The IIA's comments on the Consultation Draft.

Our comments are based on discussions conducted by a core team of internal audit professionals who serve on The IIA's Professional Issues Committee consisting of Certified Public Accountants, Chartered Accountants and Certified Internal Auditors who have worked in the public and private sectors, internal and external auditing, and small, medium, and large domestic and multinational companies. As well, we collaborated with a number of global internal audit thought leaders as we developed our observations and comments.

Our principal comments related to the Consultation Draft are below. Detailed responses to the specifically asked Consultation Questions are provided in Attachment A.

It is evident that the <IR> Framework has been well thought out and conceptualized. As well, it communicates its important messages to reporting organizations in a balanced manner. We recognize and appreciate that The IIA's December 2011 exposure draft feedback was considered, and welcome this opportunity to provide additional observations. Principally,

1. A distinct advantage of <IR> is that it takes a broad view of contributions of the various capitals by going beyond the traditional focus on reporting of historical financial performance. To best elevate the stature of non-financial capitals, we recommend that the IIRC develop the <IR> Framework with users of each type of capital in mind and expand the users to include potential providers and stakeholders of all six types of capitals, while recognizing that the ultimate user remains the financial capital markets.
2. Those charged with governance (TCWG) should look at capitals collectively when identifying an organization's risks that are materially significant. Materiality should be assessed from the perspectives of key stakeholders and owners of all types of applicable capitals since these are the primary report users in addition to the providers of financial capitals.
3. Technology touches all aspects of a business and serves various critical capacities throughout the entire value-creation chain. As a result, effective implementation of state-of-the-art technology provides a definitive competitive advantage toward sustainability. Therefore, we suggest the IIRC consider providing more clarification to users of the framework to better explain how technology relates to the framework's principles and content elements. For example, it would benefit users of the framework to understand how section 3B - Connectivity of Information interrelates with section 5I - Use of Technology.
4. We recommend that the IIRC create a specific link between <IR> and an organizations' Enterprise Risk Management (ERM) capabilities and, where appropriate, the Three Lines of Defense model, as well as providing examples of how they work together to strengthen governance.

The IIA would welcome the opportunity to assist with this, based on its extensive work and experience across these areas.

There is an important advisory role for internal auditors in supporting the implementation of <IR> in organizations around the world. Furthermore, there are important assurance roles that internal auditors can and should play post-implementation.

Certified Internal Auditors (CIAs), as well as, individuals who possess a Certification in Risk Management Assurance (CRMA) are very capable of providing assurance over the integrity of data and adequacy of governance, risk management and controls related to both financial and non-financial capitals. In addition, the internal audit profession can provide assistance by leveraging its "seat at the table" to help influence the global adoption of <IR>.

The IIA welcomes the opportunity to discuss any and all of these observations with you. Please forward all inquires to Glenn Darinzo, IIA Director of Standards and Guidance at Glenn.Darinzo@theiia.org. We look forward to our continued work with the IIRC and supporting efforts to further the value of <IR> within the global internal auditing profession.

Best regards,
Philip D. Tarling, CIA, CRMA, CMIIA
Global Chairman of the Board

IIRC CONSULTATION QUESTIONS ATTACHMENT A

1. Should any additional principles-based requirements be added or should any be eliminated or changed? If so, please explain why.

We are recommending the following underlined clarifications to the Guiding Principles:

Principle 3.2: (Strategic focus and future orientation) - An integrated report should provide insight into the organization's strategy and how that relates to its ability to create or maintain existing value, as well as the associated risks, in the short, medium and long term and to its use of and effects on the capitals.

Principle 3.7: (Connectivity of information) - An integrated report should show, as a comprehensive value creation story, the inter-relatedness and dependencies between the components that are material to the organization's ability to create or maintain existing value, as well as the associated risks, over time.

Principle 3.22: (Materiality and conciseness) - An integrated report should provide concise information that is materially significant to assessing the organization's ability to create or maintain existing value, as well as the associated risks, in the short, medium and long term.

Guiding Principles 3.2, 3.7 and 3.22 assume that the organization creates value. Section 1.2 in the Overview states that "<IR> is a process that results in communication by an organization, most visibly a periodic integrated report, about value creation over time."

While overall value creation is an organization's objective, there will be times when value for one or more capitals is diminished, intentionally or otherwise. We suggest the principles focus on creation of value and fluctuations of value over time, and the risks attendant to the pursuit of value creation. The framework should not assume that value is always created.

For example, natural capital is depleted by many companies in order to achieve their financial and organizational objectives, such as with fisheries and construction companies building dams.

Therefore, we recommend recognizing incidents of value creation, as well as the risks of value depletion. This view is consistent with the concept that "risk" is any deviation from the expected. Risk is not always negative; it can be positive by presenting opportunities. This change would also be consistent with 2.13 "The capitals are stores of value that, in one form or another, become inputs to the organization's business model. They are increased, decreased or transformed through the activities and outputs of the organization…"

2. Do you agree with how paragraphs 1.18-1.20 characterize the interaction with other reports and communications?

We are recommending the following underlined clarifications to paragraphs 1.18 and 1.20:

1.18 - The <IR> process is intended to be applied continuously to all relevant reports and communications, including analyst calls and the investor relations section of an organization's website. An integrated report should have a designated owner, responsible for establishing sound processes and methodologies to compile and review the report, ensuring adequacy of risk management and controls over preparation of the report, and attesting to the accuracy, completeness and fair presentation of the report.

In addition, it is anticipated that a stand-alone integrated report will be prepared annually in line with the statutory financial reporting cycle. Organizations may provide additional reports and communications (e.g., financial statements and sustainability reports) for compliance purposes or to satisfy the particular information needs of a range of stakeholders. The integrated report may include links to these other reports and communications.

1.20 - Although <IR> builds on developments in financial and other reporting, an integrated report differs from other reports and communications in a number of ways. In particular, it has a combined emphasis on: conciseness, strategic focus and future orientation, the connectivity of information, the capitals, the business model, the ability to create value in the short, medium and long term, and providers of financial capital as the primary audience.

3. If the IIRC were to create an online database of authoritative sources of indicators or measurement methods developed by established reporting standard setters and others, which references should be included? If the IIRC were to create an online database of authoritative sources of indicators or measurement methods, we recommend aligning the sources with the sources of capitals and their key stakeholders. For example:
    a. Accounting standard setters such as: IFRS and US GAAP;
    b. Ratings Agencies such as: Standard & Poors, Moody's Investor Service, and Fitch Ratings;
    c. Key Stock Exchanges, such as: The New York Stock Exchange, London Stock Exchange, Frankfurt Stock Exchange, Hong Kong Stock Exchange, Shanghai Stock Exchange;
    d. Regulators that are general or industry-specific, such as U.S. Securities and Exchange Commission (SEC), Financial Industry Regulatory Authority (FINRA), the Federal Reserve System ("Fed"), Financial Conduct Authority (FCA) in the UK, Federal Financial Supervisory Authority (BaFin) in Germany, Securities and Exchange Commission (*Comissão de Valores Mobiliários*, CVM) in Brazil, and Office of the Superintendent of Financial Institutions (OSFI);
    e. Global Reporting Initiative for non-financial;
    f. World Resources Institute for ecosystems services;
    g. Frameworks such as Basel's Frameworks on operational risk, credit risks, governance, effective supervision; CoCo on Internal Control published by The Canadian Institute of Chartered Accountants, Turnbull on corporate governance, COSO ERM Framework, COSO Internal Control - Integrated Framework, ISO 31000 Risk Management. We recommend that the IIRC use the online database of authoritative sources to identify opportunities for improvement

and provide guidance to drive these improvements. The IIRC could also encourage the formation of user groups to share lessons learned and implementation experience. Organizations participating in the <IR> pilot program would be ideal champions for formation of such user groups to encourage early adoption of <IR> and continuous improvement along maturity model lines.

4. Please provide any other comments you have about Chapter 1.

1.2/1.3 - We also recommend that the definition of "Integrated Reporting" include the concept of "integrated thinking" which is defined in the glossary as "The active consideration by an organization of the relationship between its various operating and functional units and the capitals that the organization uses and affects. Integrated thinking leads to integrated decision-making and actions that consider the creation of value over the short, medium and long term." This is the key differentiator and benefit of issuing an integrated report.

1.3 - The context should also consider an organization's internal environment. The organization executes its strategies, plans, governance, oversight, etc., through its people, systems, and processes within its internal environment.

1.5 - Bullet #2 states: "Inform the allocation of financial capital…"

1.6 states: "An integrated report should be prepared primarily for providers of financial capital…" Reports on performance relative to financial capital are readily available but this is not so for other types of capitals. One of the strengths of <IR> is taking a broad view of capitals and going beyond the traditional focus on financial capital. The value of <IR> may not be optimized by focusing predominantly on providers of financial capital. If the IIRC wants to elevate the stature of non-financial capitals, it would make sense to acknowledge the users of reporting across all six capitals. The IIRC should recognize that other decision-makers may be equally interested in integrated reporting (see examples in Table 1). We recommend that the IIRC develop the <IR> Framework with a balanced focus on users of each type of capital expanding the users to include potential providers and stakeholders of the six types of capital. Stakeholders considering investment of this type of capital will use <IR> content to make this type of decision (as examples)

KPMG IFRG Limited Tel +44 (0)20 7694 8871 8 Salisbury Square Fax +44 (0)20 7694 8429 London EC4Y 8BB mark.vaessen@kpmg.co.uk United Kingdom

Appendix

Table 1.

Financial	Do I invest my money?
Manufactured	Do I choose to be in this organization's supply chain? Do I want this organization to be in MY supply chain? Would purchasing/ using this organization's product/ services present reputational risk for my organization? (conflict minerals, clothing from factories in Bangladesh)
Intellectual	Do I engage in R&D with this organization?
Human	Do I go to work for this company?
Social/ Relationship	Does affiliation with this organization enhance or diminish my organization's brand?
Natural	Is use of natural capital efficient and in the public interest? Are their developments contributing to society? As a regulator, do I allow this organization to use ecosystem services (e.g., use water, pollute the air) to do business in my jurisdiction? Should a government entity grant a permit to a company that has consistently under-performed in the natural capital category?

KPMG IFRG Limited, a UK company limited by guarantee, is a member of KPMG International Cooperative, a Swiss entity. Registered in England No 5253019 Registered office: 8 Salisbury Square, London, EC4Y 8BB

Professor Mervyn King
The International Integrated Reporting Council
Submitted via www.theiirc.org/consultationdraft2013
12 July 2013

GLOBAL COMPACT LEAD SUBMISSION: COMMENTS TO THE IIRC'S CONSULTATION DRAFT OF THE INTERNATIONAL INTEGRATED REPORTING <IR> FRAMEWORK - *12 JULY 2013*

Consultation Background

Twenty Global Compact LEAD companies are participating in the "Shaping the Future of Reporting" project, which aims to harness their collective voice and promote better alignment of corporate reporting standards, frameworks and regulations. The group's first objective of 2013 is providing collective feedback to the IIRC on the Consultation Draft of the International Integrated Reporting "<IR>" Framework. As a Global Compact initiative, LEAD's feedback is primarily focused on ensuring that material sustainability issues are adequately addressed1.

1. The Global Compact defines corporate sustainability as *the delivery of long-term value in financial, social, environmental, and ethical terms.*
2. We acknowledge that neither the terms ESG or sustainability appear in the Draft Framework; however the meaning of the terms are widely understood and share the same intent as consideration of the six capitals (e.g., natural capital, social and relationship, human, etc.).

From April to June, Global Compact staff conducted interviews with LEAD project members on the Draft Framework. The interviews were built around three key topics: 1) overall utility of the Framework, 2) alignment with other reporting standards; and 3) materiality.

Nine companies, of diverse geographies and sectors, participated in the interview process. They included companies from Japan, South Africa, Brazil, China, Italy, Denmark, and the United States, and such industries as technology, oil and gas, pharmaceuticals, mining and metals and financial services.

This is the first draft of the submission, summarizing key points that emerged from the consultation. It is important to note that this submission is not meant to replace individual company feedback to the IIRC.

General Comments

Respondents welcome the International <IR> Framework as a principles-based approach to corporate reporting. The companies interviewed affirmed that they are striving to more deeply integrate financial and sustainability issues in corporate disclosures, and the IIRC offers a principles-based framework in response to this trend.

The <IR> Framework is well positioned to address two key priorities for LEAD companies: 1) making the connection between financial and environmental, social and governance (ESG) information and 2) communicating ESG value to mainstream investors.2 The business case for sustainability can often be difficult to measure and share. Respondents affirm that integrated reporting has the potential to connect financial disclosures with sustainability in a way that makes them more relevant for a broader audience than would separate financial or sustainability reports, and that this greater level of integration of reporting practices encourages and supports the integration of sustainability in strategic planning, decision-making and operations.

However two concerns that emerged from the LEAD consultations around the draft <IR> Framework are: 1) the risk that companies may overlook material sustainability issues when applying the current materiality determination process in the Draft and 2) that <IR> will result in creating an additional report instead of enhancing an existing financial report. These comments will be expanded upon in the "Affirmation" and "Feedback" sections of the document.

Affirmation of Key Elements

1. The Framework offers an important step away from "tick-box" reporting practices. Respondents are pleased that the <IR> Framework does not mandate reporting against a laundry list of metrics and instead offers companies guidance on identifying those issues they deem material. Reporting fatigue was widely reported by respondents, stemming from the sense that they feel obligated (or required) to track and communicate indicators that are not material to their operations or are not of interest to their stakeholders. The <IR> Framework has the potential to alleviate this reporting burden, especially in the long-run.
2. Respondents appreciate the management-driven materiality determination and integrated thinking at all levels of a company's operations. A deep understanding of the importance of ESG issues by senior management, and CEOs in particular, was often cited as a key reason why LEAD companies are advanced in their integration of sustainability into business practice. One welcome result from this element of the Draft will be strengthened relations between departments that were previously isolated from each other. This is a key factor that may help propel sustainability into the mainstream for both companies and their providers of financial capital.
3. The principles-based approach to the Framework is well received as an "umbrella" under which existing reporting practices can be implemented (Sec. 1.13). Respondents appreciate that the Framework and its principles dos not contradict those of existing sustainability standards. The Framework's Content Elements are organized to mirror the contents of a traditional financial disclosure (e.g., strategy, performance and future outlook), which facilitates understanding of the link between integrated reporting and financial reporting. These characteristics support uptake

of the Framework by a wide range of companies. Additional guidance should be made available (outside the scope of the Framework) on how to incorporate existing standards for sustainability reporting into an integrated report.

4. The flexibility and individualized nature of the Framework should be balanced with the need for comparability. Respondents raised questions about how comparable integrated reports would be in practice, but supported the emphasis placed on comparability of integrated reports described in Section 3.51-.52. The individual need of each company to "express its own value story" should be balanced with the need to retain comparability with other companies. To support comparability, an appendix with the tools referenced in Section 3.52, such as benchmark data, ratios and quantitative indicators, would be helpful.

Constructive Feedback

1. **Broader Definition of "Providers of Financial Capital":** One concern regarding providers of financial capital as the primary intended user is that it is too narrowly defined to be used by all types of business structures (Section 1.6). To encourage uptake of the Framework among companies ranging from SMEs to publicly listed multinationals to state-owned corporations, it is important that the language surrounding "providers of financial capital" be flexible to meet their diverse needs.
2. **Inclusion of Stakeholder Engagement in Materiality Determination:** While respondents appreciate that 'those charged with governance' must ultimately decide whether a matter is material, respondents agreed that there needs to be explicit reference to stakeholder engagement in this materiality determination process. Respondents affirmed that 'providers of financial capital' as primary intended users focuses the design of an integrated report. However, engagement with stakeholders may allow companies to identify material issues that otherwise would be overlooked.
3. Integrated reporting should improve efficiency in the long-run and reduce the number of published reports.
    a. Respondents repeatedly embraced the notion of being able to develop one report that combines financial and sustainability disclosures. While this may not be feasible in the short term due to regulatory requirements and a potentially lengthy implementation process, companies would like the Framework to support the idea of an

integrated report not as an additional publication but rather as an enhancement of an existing financial report. The language on this issue in the Framework is not sufficiently clear [Section 1.18: "It is anticipated that a *stand-alone* integrated report will be prepared annually..."].

b. Respondents noted that synchronizing ESG data management with financial reporting cycles is critical to integrated reporting. However, some expressed concern about the difficulty of implementing this, when internal data management systems that track environmental and other indicators, collect information on a different timeframe from the financial reporting cycle. The Framework could be more flexible in acknowledging these practical challenges of synchronizing data management with financial reporting, at least in the short-term.

To address the feedback in 2b, a possible revision to Section 1.18 is: "It is anticipated that an integrated report will be prepared annually in line with the statutory financial reporting cycle, which may require companies to first make efforts to align internal data management systems with the financial reporting cycle."

4. **Greater Clarity on Meaning of Value:** Value creation over short-, medium-, and long-term is a core concept in the Draft <IR> Framework. However, the meaning of "value" could be clarified. Section 2.41 of the Draft states: "Value encompasses other forms of value [beyond financial] that the organization creates through the increase, decrease or transformation of the capitals, each of which may ultimately affect financial returns." This definition does not elaborate on the 'other forms of value' and how they relate to the capitals. For example, creation of value with respect to one capital (financial) could easily involve destruction of value in another. Respondents expressed the need for greater clarification on the meaning of value as it relates to other capitals and welcomes the forthcoming background paper on value later this year.
5. **Balancing Value Creation With Destruction, Inclusion of Long-Term Risks:** Some respondents expressed concern that value destruction and preservation are not adequately emphasized in the Draft Framework. Although Sections 2.37, 2.42, and 2.43 state that value destruction is implied each time value creation is mentioned, the risk of value destruction in the long-term is not afforded as much prominence. In addition, the

difficulty of calculating the price or cost of externalities could be used as justification to not consider an issue material.

One way to address this is to more explicitly state the time horizons of opportunities and risks in Section 4C (e.g., 4.17). This would help companies consider megatrends or long-term opportunities and risks, such as climate change, population growth, water shortage, etc. For those LEAD companies whose senior management teams already understand that long-term megatrends impact their business, systemic risks are more likely to be seen as material and included in an integrated report. However, the <IR> Draft could do more to help companies with less advanced understanding to identify these risks. That said, addressing specific risks should not be prescribed in the Framework. Respondents appreciate that the Framework allows them to identify "the issues that are most material to their own operations and strategy."

A suggested amendment to the text in Section 4.17 to address this concern is: "An integrated report identifies the organization's approach to any risks - *be they in the short, medium or long term* - that are fundamental to the ongoing ability of the organization to create value..."

6. **Time Horizons:** Duration of short, medium and long term varies by industry and even business cycle. A clearer definition of what these terms mean, or of how to determine them, would be helpful for applying the Framework and answering some of the questions raised in comment #5 above on materiality and value creation. The definition of short, medium and long term should take sector context into consideration.

July 14, 2013
IIRC Comment Committee for the Consultation Draft of the International <IR> Framework London

Dear IIRC <IR> Consultation Draft Comment Committee:

In response to the IIRC request for comments on the *Consultation Draft of the International <IR> Framework, Integrated Reporting*, we, the members of the <IR> Consultation Draft

Comment Committee of the International Association for Accounting Education & Research (IAAER) are pleased to offer our comments.

The views expressed are those of the authors and do not necessarily reflect a consensus view of the IAAER membership. However, all members of the Executive Committee (EC) and the Consult Council (CC) of the International

Appendix

Table 2. LEAD consultation participants

Company	Country	Industry
ARM Holdings Enel	United Kingdom Italy	Technology Hardware & Equipment Electricity
Eni Eskom	Italy South Africa	Oil & Gas Producers Electricity
Intel	United States of America	Technology Hardware & Equipment
KPMG	Germany	Professional Services
Novo Nordisk	Denmark	Pharmaceuticals & Biotechnology
Pirelli	Italy	Automobiles & Parts
SINOPEC	China	Oil & Gas Producers
Sumitomo Chemical Takeda Pharmaceutical	Japan Japan	Chemicals Pharmaceuticals & Biotechnology
Unilever Vale	United Kingdom Brazil	Food Producers Industrial Mining & Metals

Contributed to the submission via interview, webinar participation and written comments.

Association for Accounting Education & Research (IAAER) were requested to provide guidance to inform our comment letter.

The mission of the IAAER is to promote excellence in accounting education and research on a worldwide basis and to maximize the contribution of accounting academics to the development and maintenance of high quality, globally recognized standards of accounting practice.

Our comments are supportive of the IIRC's objective to develop an international framework for Integrated Reporting <IR>, and are delivered with the intent to enhance the acceptability of <IR> worldwide.

We thank you for considering our thoughts and suggestions.

Sincerely,

Joint Chairs <IR> Consultation Draft Comment Committee of IAAER:
Wendy Green
Associate Professor of Accounting
Australian School of Business
University of New South Wales
Sydney Australia
Mandy Cheng
Associate Professor of Accounting
Australian School of Business
University of New South Wales

Sydney Australia
Other Committee Members:
Pieter Conradie
Program Director: Integrated Reporting
The Albert Luthuli Centre for Responsible Leadership
Faculty of Economic and Management Sciences
University of Pretoria
Hatfield South Africa
Noriyuki Konishi
Professor of Accounting
Graduate School of Professional Accountancy
Aoyama Gakuin University
Shibuya-Ku, Tokyo Japan
Andrea Romi
Assistant Professor of Accounting
Rawls College of Business
Texas Tech University
Lubbock Texas USA

COMMENTS ON CONSULTATION DRAFT OF THE INTERNATIONAL <IR> FRAMEWORK

CHAPTER 1: OVERVIEW

Principles-Based Requirements

1. Should any additional principle-based requirements be added or should any be eliminated or changed? If so, please explain why.

Comment: As will be discussed in the rest of this submission, we have reservations with some of the key principles. We therefore propose IIRC to consider modifying or changing some of these principles to reflect our concerns.

Concern: The proposed framework takes the perspective of financial capital providers. Given that integrated thinking is best served (for all parties) when management answers to multiple stakeholders, rather than a 'silo' focus on the shareholder perspective; and given the extent that other capitals are deemed important enough to include as inputs and outputs of the business model, both creating value and somehow receiving value, the focus on financial capital providers may reduce the impact of <IR> as other stakeholder perspectives and interests are not embedded.

Suggestion: While we view this perspective as inevitable in producing a workable framework, this view may require further justification and clarification. For example, it may be useful to clarify that the <IR> framework is intended to provide guidance for better *external reporting*, rather than to prescribe the actual *processes* behind the report. Although the framework targets the financial capital provider as the primary audience, it does not suggest that the information gathering process should primarily focus on the perspective of financial capital providers.

Concern: In addition, we have some concerns with the three 'exclusion clauses' of 'unavailability of reliable data, specific legal prohibitions or competitive harms' (in particular, the last of the three). These clauses, combined with the stated key audience being the financial capital providers, can potentially result in approved rationalization for organizations to avoid disclosure of activities that are unfavorable to wider stakeholder groups. For example, organizations may argue that certain trade-off decisions between capitals (especially between non-financial capitals, say, appeasing unions by keeping an operation in an environmental sensitive area), may not require disclosure because of its potential to reveal their strategic intent and hence cause competitive harm. We note that 'strategic non-disclosure' may not always be intentional; prior research has alerted us to the fact that when managers are faced with difficult decisions, they will both intentionally and subconsciously seek ways to justify a course of action that is more desirable to themselves, especially if there is an easy justification or if the negative effect is indirect (e.g., Peters and Romi 2013a, 2013b; Moore, Tanlu and Bazerman 2010; Paharia, Kassam, Greene and Bazerman 2009; Festinger 1957). As managers are also known to focus more on short term results even if they are aware of the need for long term-thinking (e.g., Luft and Shields 2009; Farrell, Kadous and Towry 2008), these three exclusion clauses in paragraphs 1.11-1.12 can potentially facilitate undesirable non-disclosures.

Suggestion: One way IIRC can help overcome this concern is to provide additional guidance on what these three exclusion clauses mean: "legal prohibitions" is clear enough; but what is meant by "unavailability of reliable data" – what is deemed reliable? Is the concept consistent with the definition under IFRS? What is meant by "competitive harm"? What are examples of an acceptable "competitive harm" argument?

Integration With Other Reports and Communications

2. Do you agree with how paragraphs 1.18-1.20 characterize the interaction with other reports and communications?

Comment: We agree that interactions are necessary; a single integrated report is too limiting (again, especially if the intended audience is the financial capital providers). Further, this will assist in encouraging integrated thinking and holistic decision making.

Concern: Paragraph 1.20 suggests that one of the ways <IR> builds on other reporting is through the "combined emphasis on…..*and providers of financial capital as the primary audience*." [Italics added]. Given many existing reporting frameworks focus on financial capital providers, these italicized words do not assist in clearly distinguishing the difference between <IR> and other reports.

Suggestion: There needs to be sufficient emphasis placed on the fact that the integrated report is not intended to replace other reports but instead it should "build on" other reports.

3. If the IIRC were to create an online database of authoritative sources of indicators or measurement methods developed by established reporting standard setters and others, which references should be included?

Comment: Given that each industry, and indeed each organization, has a unique set of circumstances and strategy, it is not feasible to provide definitive suggestions of indicators or measurement methods. Indeed, it is often argued that indicators that uniquely reflect an organization's operation and strategy are potentially more informative than 'generic' indicators (e.g., Kaplan and Norton 1996). Furthermore, there is a risk of giving legitimacy to problematic indicators.

Suggestion: It may be useful to encourage specific industries to develop key performance areas of concern (rather than key indicators) and benchmarking exercises to aid their member organizations in their performance measurement. It would also be useful to provide guidance on desirable measurement attributes to consider when choosing key performance indicators. Expansion of the practical examples data on the IIRC web site should also be encouraged. For example, the SASB is developing industry norms in relation to materiality.

Other

4. Please provide any other comments you have about Chapter 1.

Suggestion: In explaining the importance of value creation in the short, medium and long term, it would be worthwhile to re-emphasize that even though financial capital holders are the key audience, organizations are encouraged to discuss how value is also created in other ways for other stakeholders. For example, value can be created when other capitals benefit (e.g. conservation), at the expense of financial capitals. Firms should be encouraged to disclose and explain how this type of value may provide social returns for stakeholders.

CHAPTER 2: FUNDAMENTAL CONCEPTS

The Capitals (Section 2B)

5. Do you agree with this approach to the capitals [The capitals – Section 2B]? Why/why not?

Comment: Overall, the capitals approach to the framework provides a good "completeness" check for the content of an integrated report.

Concern: Paragraph 2.18, suggests that in some cases organizations' interaction with some of the capitals may be "immaterial" for the purpose of <IR>. This paragraph introduces subjectivity and may lead to an organization ignoring certain capitals. As will be discussed further, the ambiguous concept of materiality (especially when defined from the perspective of financial capital providers) can result in inappropriate non-disclosure.

Suggestion: An "apply or otherwise explain why not" approach to the capitals would be beneficial in two ways: first it would force reporters to consider whether they have addressed all of the capitals in their reports; and second, it will reduce discretion with respect to "immaterial" items leading to non-disclosure.

6. Please provide any other comments you have about Section 2B?

Comment: The requirement to explain trade-offs that influence value creation over time, and the examples provided in paragraph 2.25 will be beneficial in increasing the likelihood of long term thinking. It also allows companies to justify difficult trade-offs.

Concern: With respect to 2.16, further clarifications with regard to "overall stock of capitals" would be helpful. Given that the target audience of an integrated report is financial capital providers, and that 2.16 acknowledges that "whether the net effect is an increase or decrease will depend on the perspective taken", the combined effect might be that "overall stock of capital" will primarily focus on financial capital. For example, from the perspective of financial capital providers, a trade-off between natural capital and financial capital can easily be interpreted as an "overall increase in capitals" if the positive impact on profit is significant. Further, some of the capitals are more difficult to measure, making it easier to justify an overall increase (e.g., it might be that only simple narrative is sufficient to justify an increase in social and relationship capital by referring to improved "shared norms, and common values and behaviors"). Evidence of such behavior can be found in the accounting literature describing the self-serving disclosure concerning legitimation tactics directed at aligning the firm's norms and values with that of the larger society (e.g., Patten, 1991, 1992, 1995, 2005; Cho and Patten 2007).

Suggestion: To avoid self-serving disclosure (see also comments to Question 1), further guidance on the concept of "overall stock of capital" is important.

Concern: With respect to paragraph 2.22, the concepts of "availability" and "affordability" require more clarification. Availability and affordability appear to be similar concepts: if a capital is low in availability, it is probably low in affordability, also. For example, consider the natural capital of old growth forests. They are not highly available (limited supplies), and therefore one would argue that the providers of this capital (the eco-system) will consider this resource not affordable. Unless you take the perspective of the primary audience, the financial capital provider, who can potentially consider this resource affordable if the organization can find a low cost way of harvesting.

Suggestion: One framework that has been used effectively for intangible assets is Sveiby's (1997) framework on intangible asset monitor. Sveiby suggests identifying measures on (i) growth and renewal, (ii) stability and (iii) efficiency. Applying these concepts to the current context, three useful aspects of measuring capitals might be growth (are there any actions taken to grow this capital?), availability/affordability, and quality (do these capitals enable value creation?).

Business Model (Section 2C)

7. Do you agree with this definition? [2.26] Why/why not?

Comment: Yes, this definition is reasonable.

Suggestion: It might be helpful to also include a statement of vision and value – the purpose of the organization. A statement of vision and value helps investors understand the rationale behind its subsequence choices (e.g., the trade-offs of various capitals over time). Disclosure of the reporting boundary may also be appropriate.

8. Do you agree with this definition? [2.35-2.36] Why/why not?

Comment: Yes, this definition is very inclusive, covering internal and external, positive and negative consequences. The discussions in paragraphs 2.28 (relating to how important it is to explain the security, availability, quality and affordability of the components of natural capital) and 2.35 (relating to the outcomes being defined as the internal and external consequences - positive and negative - for the capitals as a result of a firm's business activities and outputs) are particularly useful. Further, including externalities highlights the broader responsibilities of companies, and is an improvement over the narrow focus in past reporting frameworks.

9. Please provide any other comments you have about Section 2C or the disclosure requirements and related guidance regarding business models contained in the Content Elements Chapter of the Framework (see Section 4E)?

We do not have any additional comments.

Other

10. Please provide any other comments you have about Chapter 2 that are not already addressed by your responses above.

Concern: Overall, we reiterate our concern that, because the integrated report's primary audience is the financial capital providers, this may lead organizations to continue to place greater burdens on other stakeholders despite the claim in paragraph 2.9 that "the organization and society therefore share both the cost of the capital used as inputs and the value created by the organization." That is, oftentimes the cost of capital comes mainly from society but the value created is mostly restricted to financial capital providers.

With respect to paragraph 2.39, it is not clear how <IR> supports "broader societal interests by encouraging the allocation of financial capital to reward and support long term, as well as the short and medium term, value creation within planetary limits and societal expectations". This statement needs greater clarification. There is no clear provision to say that value is being created within any limits, unless management decides those "limits" are material, in an important capital that they choose to report on, and are willing to discuss negatives or risks associated with such limits.

Suggestion: Perhaps there is a need to improve clarity around these issues by tying the discussion back to the concepts of availability and affordability.

Concern: With respect to paragraph 2.40, although it indicates that <IR> is based on an understanding that future cash flows are dependent on a wider range of capitals, firms are not, at any point, asked to be truly accountable to those capitals.

Suggestion: If value creation is dependent on other capitals, as the framework claims, then paragraph 2.42 should more clearly explain why <IR> is not requiring value measurement for each capital.

Concern: Accounting research indicates users are not able to garner a true assessment of non-financial performance based on firm disclosures, which raises the question, what really is <IR> offering in the way of additional information to report (e.g. Gray et al., 1995; Guthrie and Parker, 1989; Cho and Patten, 2007; Patten, 1991, 1992, 1995, 2005; Walden and Schwartz, 1997; Brown and Deegan, 1998; O'Donovan, 2002; Deegan et al., 2002; Bansal and Clelland, 2004)

CHAPTER 3: GUIDING PRINCIPLES

Materiality and Conciseness (Section 3D)

11. Do you agree with this approach to materiality? If not, how would you change it?

Concern: The definition of materiality presented in paragraph 3.23 rests on an item being able to "substantively influence" the "primary intended report users", (which the first sections of the framework identify to be those supplying financial capital). We identify three concerns with this approach.

First, materiality should not be limited to financial capitals else the reporting will be skewed to items creating a financial return/impact on the financial capital. Materiality depends on both quantitative and qualitative factors: a matter may be material due to its nature or its size. Second, this is a report-driven rather reporting process materiality approach. In fact the framework does not address materiality in terms of the process of creating the report, but only in terms of the report itself. Even if the issues that the organization chooses to report are those that are material to investors, this should not mean that the underlying reporting processes should be unduly skewed to favor investors, since this would not be in the best interest of the organizations ability to create value in the short medium and longer term. Please also see comments to Question 1. Finally, although paragraph 3.26 notes a firm should include negative matters voluntarily in this report, accounting research has shown that firms will disregard reporting requirements if they feel the information may harm stock prices, thus they may be less inclined to follow such a mandate (Peters and Romi 2013a). Further, the audit function also does not fully support the completeness assertion of the disclosures.

Suggestion: During the integrated reporting process, the materiality of an item should be considered purely on its relevance to affect the organizations ability to create value in the short, medium and long term. At this point the source of the item is not relevant, it can come from any stakeholder group; the individual circumstances of the entity will dictate what is relevant in terms of the value creations process. It is recognized that it would be impossible to cater to the perspectives of all stakeholders, thus one group of intended users will take precedence. That said, if the intended users are short term investors, then changes to some of the capitals may not be seen as material. Thus we suggest that an additional clause be added to read: "substantively affect the assessment of a provider of capital of their intention to continue to provide capital to the company."

Concern: It is stated that materiality depends on both *relevance* and *importance*; and *importance* in turn refers to the *nature* and *magnitude* of the matter (see footnote 5 on p.21 of the Consultative Draft). However, in 5B, *importance* is more explicitly defined as a combination of the *magnitude* and *likelihood* (not nature) of the matter. This could potentially create some confusion. Further, it is not clear from the guidelines how one can assess the magnitude/nature of matters, especially in relation to social matters.

Suggestion: It will be useful for the <IR> Framework to provide guidance on the social indicators of importance (e.g. GRI guidelines and ISO26000). Either best practice consensus within industries may assist in this process, or a number of exemplar KPIs (KRIs) which combine quantitative information with qualitative information could be provided by the <IR> Framework. This will allow comparison of KPIs that are consistent over time and in a way that enables comparison with other organizations to the extent it is material to the organization's own value creation story.

12. Please provide any other comments you have about Section 3D or the Materiality determination process (Section 5B).

Concern: Paragraph 3.27 suggests that materiality assessment is to be integrated to "everyday management". This seems to suggest a need for continuous assessments which may be perceived as quite a burden.

Suggestion: The guidelines provided by GRI and ISO26000 may assist in prioritizing social indicators that may be considered material.

Reliability and Completeness (Section 3E)

13. How should the reliability of an integrated report be demonstrated?

Comment: A highly reliable integrated reporting process involves a circular process: the indicators that the organization uses to measure its strategic performance are subject to a robust materiality determination process; the information that is fed into the materiality determination process is subject to a robust stakeholder engagement process; and a robust stakeholder engagement process would be subject to a comprehensive understanding of the entities business model and its value chain, as well as the internal and external operating environment. The connectivity of these different elements of the integrated reporting process is thus compulsory to gauge reliability. The factual correctness of any piece of information in the integrated report is subject to the connectivity principle; otherwise the relevance thereof cannot be illustrated. Completeness is not addressed within this question, but remains a key element of report reliability.

Suggestion: The IASB and the FASB consider relevance to be more important than reliability, suggesting that reliability may not be the most critical consideration under <IR>. Further, the reliability of any report rests in the integrity of the report preparers. External assurance would provide the highest level of reliability for an integrated report. Some reliability may also be inferred via disclosure of processes used by management to ensure the report is reliable. The user can then decide if this process is reasonable.

Comment: Paragraph 5.21 mentions that "the framework provides reporting criteria against which organizations and assurance providers assess a reports adherence". This creates the impression that the framework will yield appropriate subject matter that can be subjected to criteria from assurance providers, however the framework is silent on what appropriate subject matter will look like. Industry norms and best practice are still being developed. It is thus a challenge to understand exactly what appropriate subject matter will look like.

Suggestion: The value of assurance and the nature of appropriate subject matter that is suitable for assurance could be further addressed in the framework. Report preparers should be encouraged to prepare reports as though it will be subject to external assurance. This will mean that an audit trail should be maintained for information that is being presented in the integrated report as far as possible. More importantly, where reporting organizations endeavor to develop disclosures that are not covered within an existing industry framework, the management assumptions that underlie these disclosures should be developed with an understanding of what appropriate subject matter looks like. Should this subject matter then be subject to assurance, the management assumptions will assist assurance providers to develop suitable criteria to assure these disclosures. It will thus greatly assist reporting organizations to understand what appropriate subject matter looks like, and what the attributes of suitable criteria looks like.

14. Please provide any other comments you have about Section 3E.

Comment: No guidance is provided to assist in assessing what an acceptably low level of freedom from material bias would be.

Other

15. Please provide any other comments you have about Chapter 3 that are not already addressed by your responses above

Comment: The discussion in paragraph 3.16 relating to the need to understand, incorporate, and respond to key stakeholders' legitimate needs, interests and expectations is useful. To the extent the framework is applied, at a minimum, <IR> will centralize information firms already report/misreport in a disaggregated fashion, however the extent to which <IR> enhances transparency and accountability will be a function of management integrity.

CHAPTER 4: CONTENT ELEMENTS

16. Please provide any comments you have about Chapter 4 that are not already addressed by your responses above (please include comments on the Content Element Business Model [Section 4E] in your answer to questions 7-9 above rather than here).

Comment: The principle based approach to reporting information about an organization's risks could result in a "boilerplate" disclosure tactic and potentially lead to a lack of completeness (see also comments to Question 5).

CHAPTER 5: PREPARATION AND PRESENTATION

Involvement of Those Charged With Governance (Section 5D)

17. Should there be a requirement for those charged with governance to include a statement acknowledging their responsibility for the integrated report? Why/why not?

Concern: The experience in South Africa suggests that without high-level buy-in integrated reporting can become a somewhat academic exercise (Deloitte 2012).

Suggestion: Buy-in may be enhanced by an alignment between executive remuneration and strategic objectives outlined in the <IR> framework.

Consider a requirement to include an acknowledgement that the processes employed in preparing the integrated report are reasonable, rather than focus only on the outcomes. In addition, since an internal audit may enhance/be perceived to enhance the integrated report reliability this process should also be disclosed.

18. Please provide any other comments you have about involvement of those charged with governance (Section 5D).

Comment: Research indicates that firm's with governance bodies assigned to particular reporting subjects (e.g. environmental) do render greater reporting quality about that information (Peters and Romi 2013b).

Credibility (Section 5E)

19. If assurance is to be obtained, should it cover the integrated report as a whole, or specific aspects of the report? Why?

Comment: Due to the amount of discretion allowed in this reporting framework we believe that external and independent assurance should be required to provide credibility to the integrated report.

This assurance should extend to the entire report given that whole <IR> concept is about connectivity. Also, report users may not distinguish between the information that is assured and the information that is not assured. It may be that investors will assume the whole report is already verified even if only one part is. It will also be difficult to assure the integrated report without assuring the underlying process.

The level of assurance is debatable. An alternative would be independent assurance of process compliance – i.e. that the company has a system in place that can ensure integrity (e.g. ISO 9000)

20. Please provide any other comments you have about Credibility (Section 5E). Assurance providers are particularly asked to comment on whether they consider the Framework provides suitable criteria for an assurance engagement.

No comments.

Other

21. Please provide any other comments you have about Chapter 5 that are not already addressed by your responses above (please include comments on the materiality determination process [Section 5B] in your answer to question 11 above rather than here).

Suggestions: In assessing importance, it may be beneficial to comment on the need to consider the company's risk appetite (i.e. its willingness to tolerate risks in pursuit of returns).

Also, the materiality assessment is geared towards future events (past and current events have 100% likelihood of occurrence since they have already occurred). Perhaps other dimensions can be discussed; e.g., current impact vs. length of impact (if current impact is small but it will have long term implications it may still be important; if high on both dimensions it is definitely important; if low on both dimensions it is not important).

Overall View

22. Recognizing that <IR> will evolve over time, please explain the extent to which you believe the content of the Framework overall is appropriate for use by organizations in preparing an integrated report and for providing report users with information about an organization's ability to create value in the short, medium and long term?

Comment: The overall approach to reporting is appropriate. The inclusion of capitals, the discussion of risks and opportunities associated with short, medium and long-term success, etc. are all commendable reporting practices.

Concern: The shortcoming of the <IR> framework is found in the principles-based approach that allows management significant discretion in reporting. More rules and specific requirements and examples would be a better approach in the initial stages of this reporting framework development. It is hoped that over time, as indicators, measurements, and societal expectations evolve, the reporting practices will follow.

Without clear guidelines and top executive buy-in, there is a risk that this framework will not provide any information to users about an organization's ability to create value in any term, beyond what is already available. This belief is not because the information requested is not valuable, it is based on the belief that organizations will not provide the information as requested.

Paragraph 1.8 suggests that long term investors' interests are aligned with other stakeholders as long term investors want long term value creation. This view can potentially be challenged by considering recent worldwide financial events and crises.

Development of <IR>

23. If the IIRC were to develop explanatory material on <IR> in addition to the Framework, which three topics would you recommend be given priority? Why?

    a. The audience; the capital inclusions; and materiality.
        i. **The Audience:** Per previous discussions, the primary audience being financial capital providers limits a firm's accountability, limits a firm's vantage point on what creates or destroys value, and does not render anything beyond what we presently have in public financial reports.
        ii. **The Capitals:** All firms should have to include information for all capitals. It is true that some will be more important for some firms than others, but firms should have to disclose why they are not considering a specific capital in relation to inputs, operations, and outputs.
        iii. **The Materiality:** The materiality section needs improvement. Materiality has traditionally been based on inclusion of information that may make a difference in the decisions made by users, and we still see management continuously (and predictably for negative information) not include items based on self-serving motives. The definition of materiality should consider ways of reflecting management's motivation to withhold harmful, but indeed important information.

Other

24. Please provide any other comments not already addressed by your responses to Questions 1-23.

About forty listed Japanese companies have already prepared integrated reports. Many companies state that integrated reporting will enhance corporate management through (1) better managerial training, (2) better risk management, and (3) improved accountability of management, investor protection and the meaningfulness of financial statements.

Consultation Questions

The IIRC welcomes comments on all aspects of the Draft International <IR> Framework (Draft Framework) from all stakeholders, whether to express agreement or to recommend changes.

The following questions are focused on areas where there has been significant discussion during the development process. Comments on any other aspect of the Draft Framework are also encouraged through the questions.

Please provide all comments in English.

All comments received will be considered a matter of public record and will be posted on the IIRC's website (www.theiirc.org).

Comments should be submitted by Monday 15th, July 2013.

Name: Melanie McLaren
Email: m.mclaren@frc.org.uk
Stakeholder group: Policy makers, regulators and standard setters If replying on behalf of an Organization please complete the following:
Organization name: The Financial Reporting Council
Industry sector: Not applicable
Geographical region: Western Europe

Key Points

If you wish to briefly express any key points, or to emphasize particular aspects of your submission, or add comments in the nature of a cover letter, then the following space can be used for this purpose. Please do not repeat large amounts of material appearing elsewhere in your comments.

This letter sets out the comments of the Financial Reporting Council (the 'FRC') on the Consultation Draft of the International Integrated Reporting Framework (the 'Framework').

We support the concept of Integrated Thinking (by which we mean thinking broadly about a range of issues such as those you encapsulate in the capitals) and the IIRC's efforts in encouraging businesses to report a holistic, longer-term view of their operations. We also agree with the qualities of good corporate communications described in the Guiding Principles, including the need to encourage more concise corporate reports containing connected information.

However, we have significant concerns that that the Framework, as set out in the Consultation Draft (the 'CD'), is unclear about the objectives and purpose of the Integrated Report. We believe that these need to be addressed before the Framework is suitable for practical application.

Objectives of the Framework

The CD is confusing the following issues:

- Promoting Integrated Thinking - a holistic, longer-term approach to an entity's management and corporate communications in general.
- Whether the Integrated Report is for the providers of financial capital or for a wider stakeholder group.
- Whether the Integrated Report is a new and additional form of corporate reporting or whether it builds on/ is aligned with existing reporting practices. This is causing considerable confusion in the UK.

Such confusion detracts from the usefulness and clarity of the Framework as a whole.

Purpose of the Integrated Report

We believe that the CD fails to make clear the purpose of an Integrated Report. The CD suggests that an Integrated Report is an additional form of corporate communication. If this is the case, then there is a need for the Framework to clarify the role of the report compared to existing forms of corporate communication such as the annual financial report and the corporate social responsibility report.

From a UK perspective, we have seen little appetite, in either the preparer or investor communities, for the Integrated Report to be introduced as an investor-focused corporate communication for a UK company in place of the annual report. This is because the Integrated Report is not very different from the narrative report already included by law in the annual reports of UK companies for which we produce guidance.

Who Is the Integrated Report for?

The IIRC needs to be very clear on who the users of an Integrated Report are. Although the Framework identifies the primary users of an Integrated Report as 'providers of financial capital', we believe that its underlying requirements, including the application of materiality, the concept of the capitals and value and the section on stakeholder responsiveness, would result in the content of the Integrated Report attempting to meet the needs of a wider group of stakeholders.

Our main concern is that the preparation of one document designed to meet the needs of all stakeholders would result in "clutter", increase the length of annual reports, and is likely to result in less relevant information for investors.

If the IIRC is firm in the objective to develop reporting for the providers of financial capital then much repositioning of the Framework needs to take place. Alternatively, if wider stakeholder reporting is the key then it should be stated as an explicit objective and it should be made clear that the current report and accounts process that is in place in many countries needs to be supplemented. It would of course be a significant debate to determine the most appropriate form of reporting to meet the information needs of the wider group of stakeholders.

Cost Benefit Analysis

The IIRC needs to undertake an analysis of the costs to preparers of an Integrated Report compared to the benefits for investors (or other stakeholders if they are indeed the intended audience). This should justify the introduction of an Integrated Report as an additional form of corporate communication or as an incremental improvement in reporting.

Materiality

We recommend that, if the Integrated Report is intended to be investor-focused corporate communication, where concepts have already been defined at international level by the IASB (e.g. materiality, primary users), consistent definitions should be used in the Framework.

Taking an inconsistent approach to materiality compared to that used in IFRSs is an unnecessary complexity for the preparers of an Integrated

Report which creates an increased risk of users misunderstanding the nature of information that is or is not included in it.

Practical Application and Implications

The structure of the Framework is confusing and the style of language used is unnecessarily complex in places. This is likely to make practical application of the guidance difficult.

Finally, we urge the IIRC to consider and report on the responses they receive to this consultation, and the findings of the pilot studies that are being conducted, before finalizing the Framework; re-consultation may be necessary to be certain that the confusions highlighted above have been fully addressed.

If you would like to discuss these comments, please contact me or Deepa Raval on 020 7492 2424.

Yours sincerely

Melanie McLaren
Executive Director, Codes and Standards
DDI: 020 7492 2406
Email: m.mclaren@frc.org.uk

Chapter 1: Overview

Principles-Based Requirements

To be in accordance with the Framework, an integrated report should comply with the principles-based requirements identified throughout the Framework in bold italic type (paragraphs 1.11-1.12).

1. *Should any additional principles-based requirements be added or should any be eliminated or changed? If so, please explain why.*

The phrase "taking account of the content of the Framework as a whole, including the fundamental concepts as explained in Chapter 2" (Paragraph 1.11) is unclear. We are concerned that the caveat suggests that compliance with each paragraph of the Framework is required by those preparing an Integrated Report. This would be inconsistent with a principles-based approach.

Whilst we are broadly supportive of the principles-based requirements identified in bold italic type, as discussed more fully in question 22, we are concerned that the principles in the Framework are often followed by detailed rules on how they should be applied.

We believe that this, coupled with a requirement to explain why a particular aspect of the Framework has not applied (e.g. in paragraph 4.5), could lead to clutter and the disclosure of immaterial information.

As noted in our response to question 12, we are also concerned about the application of materiality in the Framework. If the concept of materiality is extended beyond those matters that are of relevance to investors, we think that it might be difficult to identify all the matters requiring disclosure under paragraph 1.12.

Interaction With Other Reports and Communications

The <IR> process is intended to be applied continuously to all relevant reports and communications, in addition to the preparation of an integrated report. The integrated report may include links to other reports and communications, e.g., financial statements and sustainability reports. The IIRC aims to complement material developed by established reporting standard setters and others, and does not intend to develop duplicate content (paragraphs 1.18-1.20).

2. *Do you agree with how paragraphs 1.18-1.20 characterize the interaction with other reports and communications?*

We agree that all corporate communications should adhere to the Guiding Principles of connectivity of information; conciseness; and, reliability and completeness. However, the regulatory requirements and/or the intended purpose of a particular corporate communication may mean that the Guiding Principles of strategic focus and future orientation; stakeholder responsiveness; consistency and comparability; and, materiality may not be appropriate in all circumstances. The appropriateness of the Content Elements to particular corporate communication will also depend on the regulatory requirements and/or the intended purpose of a particular that communication.

Paragraph 1.6 indicates that the Integrated Report should be prepared primarily for the providers of financial capital. In the UK, we do not think that an Integrated Report is sufficiently different from the annual narrative report to warrant its preparation as a supplementary investor-focused document.

Most UK companies already prepare a narrative report (as part of their annual report) which enables the assessment of how the directors have performed their duty to promote the success of the company for the benefit of its shareholders. The content of this narrative report, which is governed by UK company law and regulations, includes information that is similar, but not identical, to that required in an Integrated Report. In addition, non-mandatory guidance on the application of the UK's statutory narrative reporting requirements already exists in the form of 'Reporting Statement: Operating and Financial Review' (the 'RS'), which will be updated following the finalization of recently proposed changes to UK company law. Whilst it is possible that the Framework could be used as an alternative to the RS in the preparation of a statutory narrative report, a company would need to undertake additional work to ensure that it takes into account the UK's specific statutory reporting requirements.

3. *If the IIRC were to create an online database of authoritative sources of indicators or measurement methods developed by established reporting standard setters and others, which references should be included?*

We agree in principle with the creation of an online database of indicators or measurement methods. We think it may be of benefit in two ways: (a) it might encourage a wider use of a particular indicator or measurement method and thereby enhance comparability between entities; and (b) a cross-reference to the database might allow an entity to focus on the key information in the communication without the risk of obscuring it with a detailed description of the indicator or measurement method. That said, we believe that the very wide range of indicators and measurement methods used in business may make the task of creating a comprehensive database impracticably large.

Other

4. *Please provide any other comments you have about Chapter 1.*

The objective of the Framework is confusing the following: (a) promoting a holistic, longer-term approach to an entity's management and corporate communications in general (Integrated Thinking); (b) describing and promoting the qualities of one particular form of corporate reporting (the Integrated Report); and (c) whether the Integrated Report is for the providers of financial capital or a wider stakeholder group.

It is unclear to us, however, which is considered to be the principal objective.

The information in the first (Overview), second (Fundamental Concepts) and fifth (Preparation and Presentation) chapters of the Framework seems, in general, to fit more clearly with the idea of promoting Integrated Thinking. By contrast, information in the third (Guiding Principles) and fourth (Content Elements) chapters seems to fit more clearly with a focus on the Integrated Report.

In our view, the lack of clarity regarding the Framework's principal objective has resulted in a merging of its elements which, in turn, has detracted from the usefulness and clarity of the guidance it provides in each area. We encourage the IIRC to provide more clarity over its principal objective and to differentiate more clearly between the elements of the Framework.

It is also unclear whether the Integrated Report is intended to be an investor-focused corporate communication or if it is intended to be addressed to a wider audience.

Although the Framework identifies the primary users of an Integrated Report as 'providers of financial capital', we consider that the underlying requirements of the Framework, including in particular the application of materiality (discussed in question 12), the concept of the capitals (discussed in question 5) and value (discussed in question 10) and stakeholder responsiveness (5G) means that the Integrated Report will be addressed to a wider range of stakeholders.

As noted in our response to question 2, we do not think there is a significant UK demand for the Integrated Report to be introduced as an investor-focused corporate communication. However there may be a role for the IIRC to start the debate on the most appropriate form of reporting to meet the information needs of the wider group of stakeholders. The information required by this group is different as it has a broader social purpose. If, however, the Integrated Report is intended to perform this broader role, the Framework needs to be clearer that this is its objective.

Chapter 2: Fundamental Concepts

The Capitals (Section 2B)

The Framework describes six categories of capital (paragraph 2.17). An organization is to use these categories as a benchmark when preparing an integrated report (paragraphs 2.19-2.21), and should disclose the reason if it considers any of the capitals as not material (paragraph 4.5).

5. *Do you agree with this approach to the capitals? Why/why not?*

We agree that the concept of capitals as one possible method of identifying, organizing and categorizing the source and nature of resources used in a business. We have, however, found that this has been one of the more difficult areas of the Framework to understand. In consequence, we recommend that the IIRC tries to simplify and condense its description of the concept of capitals in section 2B in order to improve its use in practice.

Our main concern with section 2B is that the model places the non-financial capitals on an equal level to financial capital. In our view, to the extent that an Integrated Report is intended to be an investor-focused corporate communication, they should be seen as supporting or contributory factors in assessing changes in and the quality of financial capital.

We understand that, particularly over the longer-term, there may be a strong relationship between many of the capitals and that objectives relating to them may overlap. Whilst it is important that investors are provided with this information where it is necessary for a full understanding of the issues affecting future cash flows and to assess the company's stewardship, we do not believe that it should be included in investor-focused corporate communications if it is not relevant for those purposes.

We are concerned that a lack of clarity regarding the intended audience for the Integrated Report, to which we think this approach to the capitals contributes, might result in a lengthy document that does not meet the needs of investors, or those of wider stakeholder groups. We would encourage the IIRC to ensure that the Framework is consistently clear about its intended audience.

The "bottom up" approach to the capitals adopted in the Framework, which tries to identify all possible issues faced by a company before then eliminating immaterial issues is, in our view, likely to result in the disclosure of information that is not relevant to investors. An alternative approach, which identifies the issues that are material to

investors and then drills down to the sources of those issues is likely to be both more efficient and result in more focused information. The "bottom up" approach to the capitals more likely to be appropriate if the purpose of the Integrated Report is to provide information to a wide range of stakeholders.

6. *Please provide any other comments you have about Section 2B?*

No further comments.

Business Model (Section 2C)

A business model is defined as an organization's chosen system of inputs, business activities, outputs and outcomes that aims to create value over the short, medium and long term (paragraph 2.26).

7. *Do you agree with this definition? Why/why not?*

We agree that the definition used in the Framework is one way of describing the concept of a business model. In our work on narrative reporting, we have heard that companies would like flexibility to describe their business model in their own way so we would caution against an overly prescriptive approach to the business model in the Framework.

Outcomes are defined as the internal and external consequences (positive and negative) for the capitals as a result of an organization's business activities and outputs (paragraphs 2.35-2.36).

8. *Do you agree with this definition? Why/why not?*

We agree with the definition of "outcomes" used in the Framework. However, we believe that there is a need to more clearly explain the distinction between the terms "outputs" and "outcomes".

9. *Please provide any other comments you have about Section 2C or the disclosure requirements and related guidance regarding business models contained in the Content Elements Chapter of the Framework (see Section 4E)?*

The purpose of section 2C is to describe the concept of a business model, however it appears to contain a number of embedded disclosure requirements (e.g. paragraphs 2.29, 2.33 and 2.34). These requirements are both difficult to identify and add unnecessary detail to this section. Any disclosure requirements relating to the business model should, in our view, be included only in section 4E.

Other

10. *Please provide any other comments you have about Chapter 2 that are not already addressed by your responses above.*

We have three main concerns about the description and application of the concept of value in the Framework.

Firstly, it is not wholly clear whether the Framework uses a single concept of value that encompasses all capitals (implied, for instance, in the second bullet of paragraph 2.35) or if each capital has its own value (implied, for instance, in paragraph 2.13). Given that the concept of value is core to the Integrated Report, we recommend that the IIRC clarifies this point.

Secondly, as acknowledged in paragraph 2.24 of the Framework, whereas the concept of financial capital value is normally easily understood and objectively measured, it is much more difficult to apply to the non-financial capitals. t will often be practical only to measure the effect of a business process on the non-financial capitals in qualitative terms. Further, as suggested in paragraph 2.16 of the Framework, the perception of the relative importance of changes in the capitals will differ depending on the perspective of the user of the Integrated Report. We are concerned about how the inherently more subjective and less reliable assessment of changes in non-financial capitals might affect the application of the Framework in practice.

Finally, many of the Content Elements described in chapter 4 of the Framework refer to the capitals and value in a more general sense. In a similar way to that described in question 5, we think that the use of a single net concept of value, or a combination of equally weighted individual capital values, might lead to the disclosure of information on

a fact or circumstance irrespective of its effect, or potential effect, on financial capital value. To the extent that an Integrated Report is intended to be an investor-focused corporate communication, we think that the application of the concept of value equally to all capitals might deflect the focus of the Integrated Report from being solely on the needs of investors. We are concerned that this might result in the Integrated Report being an unnecessarily lengthy document which does not efficiently meet the needs of investors, or those of wider stakeholder groups.

Chapter 3: Guiding Principles

Materiality and Conciseness (Section 3D)

Materiality is determined by reference to assessments made by the primary intended report users (paragraphs 3.23-3.24). The primary intended report users are providers of financial capital (paragraphs 1.6-1.8).

11. *Do you agree with this approach to materiality? If not, how would you change it?*

We are strongly supportive of the IIRC's encouragement of concise corporate communication and believe that an emphasis on including only the information that is material to investors is an important part of achieving that goal.

We are, however, concerned that the IIRC has adopted a different approach to materiality to that used in IFRSs.

We think that adopting a different approach to materiality to that used in IFRSs is an unnecessary complexity for the preparers and users of an Integrated Report which creates an increased risk of investors misunderstanding the nature of information that is or is not included in it. For this reason, to the extent that an Integrated Report is intended to be an investor-focused corporate communication, we think that it is important to use an approach to materiality that is consistent to that used under IFRSs.

We note that the IASB has recently announced a project on the application of materiality; we recommend that the IIRC considers working with the IASB to arrive at agreed position on the subject instead of adopting the approach currently included in the Framework.

12. *Please provide any other comments you have about Section 3D or the Materiality determination process (Section 5B).*

The definition of materiality, and the materiality determination process set out in Section 3D of the Framework, does not appear to limit the assessment of the materiality of a matter to its effect on financial capital value. Instead, the action of paragraphs 3.24 to 3.26 suggests that any substantive effect on any of the capitals could be considered material for an Integrated Report, irrespective of its effect, or potential effect, on financial capital value. This is another example of our concern regarding the lack of clarity regarding the intended audience for an Integrated Report raised in our response to questions 1, 4, 5 and 10.

Reliability and Completeness (Section 3E)

Reliability is enhanced by mechanisms such as robust internal reporting systems, appropriate stakeholder engagement, and independent, external assurance (paragraph 3.31).

13. *How should the reliability of an integrated report be demonstrated?*

We do not think that a Framework describing the nature and content of an Integrated Report should provide guidance or requirements on the mechanisms used to ensure the reliability of the information contained within it. It is the responsibility of the directors of a company to ensure that they have sufficient controls and procedures in place to ensure the reliability of the information in their corporate reporting. The nature of these controls and procedures may differ widely depending of the facts and circumstances of the company in question.

14. *Please provide any other comments you have about Section 3E.*

No further comments.

Other

15. *Please provide any other comments you have about Chapter 3 that are not already addressed by your responses above.*

Following on from the theme of the principal intended user of the Integrated Report discussed in our responses to questions 1, 4, 5, 10 and 12, to the extent that an Integrated Report is intended to be an investor-focused corporate communication, we do not think that the "stakeholder responsiveness" section, as currently drafted, is an appropriate principle to guide the content or presentation of an Integrated Report.

As noted above, we are of the view that an investor-focused corporate communication should be focused principally on the needs of shareholders.

Section 3C and, in particular paragraphs 3.20 and 3.21, seem to provide a further indication that the content of an Integrated Report should be driven by the needs of a wider stakeholder group.

In our view, a discussion of other stakeholder relationships should be included in an investor-focused corporate communication only to the extent they are relevant to the needs of shareholders. We also think this requirement would be better placed in the content elements chapter.

To the extent that an Integrated Report is intended to have a wider audience, we are concerned that the "stakeholder responsiveness" section might result in it being a very lengthy document, even if it does not attempt to meet all of the information needs of all of the stakeholders, due to the number of stakeholder groups that might claim to have a legitimate need, interest or expectation.

Chapter 4: Content Elements

16. *Please provide any comments you have about Chapter 4 that are not already addressed by your responses above (please include comments on the Content Element Business Model [Section 4E] in your answer to questions 7-9 above rather than here).*

We agree that the Content Elements identify the information that is important to investors. As noted in our responses to questions 10 and 12, however, we are concerned that, to the extent that an Integrated Report is intended to be an investor corporate communication, the lack of focus on financial capital value is compounded in the wording of any of the Content Elements in chapter 4, which refer to the capitals and value in a more general sense.

Chapter 5: Preparation and Presentation

Involvement of Those Charged With Governance (Section 5D)

Section 5D discusses the involvement of those charged with governance, and paragraph 4.5 requires organizations to disclose the governance body with oversight responsibility for <IR>.

17. *Should there be a requirement for those charged with governance to include a statement acknowledging their responsibility for the integrated report? Why/why not?*

We do not think this is necessary if respective responsibilities are made explicit either in the Framework or in the law or regulation requiring the preparation of an Integrated Report. In our experience such a requirement leads to boilerplate disclosure.

18. *Please provide any other comments you have about Involvement of those charged with governance (Section 5D).*

No further comments.

Credibility (Section 5E)

The Framework provides reporting criteria against which organizations and assurance providers assess a report's adherence (paragraph 5.21).

19. *If assurance is to be obtained, should it cover the integrated report as a whole, or specific aspects of the report? Why?*

As noted in our response to question 13, we do not think that a Framework describing the nature and content of an Integrated Report should provide guidance or requirements on the mechanisms used to ensure the reliability of the information contained within it. We agree that it is appropriate to begin to explore the need for assurance or other reporting that might provide credibility over an Integrated Report.

In our view, there will be significant questions to explore around the nature and extent of assurance or other eporting that may be either possible or desirable in relation to the information included in an Integrated Report.

These would include:

- Whether users would consider it desirable to have assurance or other reports addressing: the content of the Integrated Report; the processes and controls used in its production; or both or neither of these;
- If so, whether users would consider it desirable for such assurance or other reports to extend to all aspects of the content or processes or selectively;
- If so, what should be the nature of the assurance or other reports – attesting to explicit company assertions or direct reporting; assurance or other reporting (such as agreed upon procedures or exception

reporting by the auditor if, based on their audit work, they are aware of inconsistencies with their knowledge of the entity);

- If so, whether there are suitably qualified assurance providers with the range of skills and experience, both in relation to the wide range of subject matters and the provision of assurance, or whether these could be expected to develop;
- If so, whether there are suitable criteria, as the basis for the assurance or other reporting, either in the form of the Framework or otherwise, and what would constitute suitable criteria (see response to Q20);
- If so, to the extent the Integrated Report includes summarized information based on more detailed underlying information that has been subject to assurance or other reporting, what should be the relationship between the assurance over, and criteria applicable to, the summarized and more detailed information or related processes;
- If so, whether there are appropriate standards for such assurance or other reporting;
- What level of credibility would such assurance or other reporting be capable of providing;
- What would be the costs of obtaining such assurance or other reports and how would these compare with the benefits;
- Whether there would be any other (unintended) effects of requiring or voluntarily obtaining such assurance or other reporting;
- Whether any assurance or other reporting requirements should be established by laws or regulations or whether assurance or other reporting should be a matter for voluntary adoption by each entity.

We believe that these questions might be more effectively addressed with the International Auditing and Assurance Standards Board, and that answers may well need to be modified as the Framework is further developed in response to consultation feedback.

Extending the scope of information subject to assurance or other reporting would require further consultation with stakeholders, including in particular those who represent the principal addressees of an Integrated Report.

20. *Please provide any other comments you have about Credibility (Section 5E). Assurance providers are particularly asked to comment on whether they consider the Framework provides suitable criteria for an assurance engagement.*

The lack of clarity regarding the principal objective of the Framework makes it difficult to ascertain what exactly constitutes a Framework-compliant Integrated Report. This will, in turn, create challenges for those trying to assess objectively whether the Integrated Report, as a stand-alone document, has been prepared in accordance with the Framework. We would encourage the IIRC to consider how the structure of the Framework may be altered to make clearer the parts which address the Integrated Report specifically and those parts which deal with the more general approach to internal management and communications.

The Framework anticipates the Integrated Report including a wide range of different types of information, succinctly presented. As compared with developing suitable criteria for the preparation of a relatively narrowly scoped subject matter report (such as the financial report), developing suitable criteria for the Integrated Report will have additional challenges – such as consistency as to the extent and nature of the criteria that are appropriate in relation to each type of information, the need for criteria for summarization, and the need for criteria for balance between different types of information.

Other

21. *Please provide any other comments you have about Chapter 5 that are not already addressed by your responses above (please include comments on the materiality determination process [Section 5B] in your answer to question 11 above rather than here).*

Section 5G of the CD on the reporting boundary is confusing. Figure 7 implies that other stakeholders are part of the reporting boundary. The first bullet in 5.26 however, states that "providers of financial capital are the primary intended users of an Integrated Report. The third bullet in 5.30 goes on to say "the purpose is not to identify entities to be included in the reporting boundary…" but the second sentence says "the entities/stakeholders within this portion of the reporting boundary…". To the extent that the Integrated Report is intended to replace or supplement an existing part of UK corporate reporting, the uses of technology suggested in section 5I may be restricted by the current requirements in UK company law. Clearly, this position may change in time but we raise the point only highlight a potential obstacle that may be met in the initial implementation of the Framework.

Overall View

22. *Recognizing that <IR> will evolve over time, please explain the extent to which you believe the content of the Framework overall is appropriate for use by organizations in preparing an integrated report and for providing report users with information about an organization's ability to create value in the short, medium and long term?*

We make points below regarding the structure and style of the Framework with a view to improving the ease of its use in practice.

- Any principles-based guidance will normally need some more prescriptive requirements in order to ensure that all necessary information is disclosed, it is essential that these are made clear in the guidance. The Framework contains some disclosure requirements that are embedded in guidance paragraphs (e.g. paragraph 5.24: Disclosures relating to the reporting time frames), making them difficult to identify. There are also examples of lists of specific disclosures where it is unclear whether that information is a requirement or just an example of the sort of information that might be considered for inclusion in an Integrated Report (e.g. paragraph 4.20: "An integrated report describes…"). We encourage the IIRC to ensure that the Framework more clearly identifies disclosures that are required and those that are simply suggested as an example.
- The style of language used in the document seems to be unnecessarily complex in places. For example, the description of the theoretical model that underpins the Framework in chapter 2 stretches over more than seven pages. If this model is to be applied in practice, we think that it needs to be described more simply and concisely. By way of example, phrases such as "Catalyse a more cohesive and efficient approach" (paragraph 1.5) and "value creation within planetary limits and societal expectations" (paragraph 2.39) are complex and could be more simply expressed.

Development of <IR>

23. *If the IIRC were to develop explanatory material on <IR> in addition to the Framework, which three topics would you recommend be given priority? Why?*

No further comments.

Other

24. *Please provide any other comments not already addressed by your responses to Questions 1-23.*

Cost-benefit analysis is key to developing effective practice, however information on the cost of preparing an Integrated Report compared to the benefits it might bring to its intended audience has not been included in the CD. We believe that such an analysis, focusing on the benefit to investors in line with the Framework's expressed objectives, should be undertaken and published.

THE DRAFT FRAMEWORK FOR INTEGRATED REPORTING

A consultation draft issued by the International Integrated Reporting Council (IIRC)
Comments from ACCA
July 2013

ACCA (the Association of Chartered Certified Accountants) is the global body for professional accountants. We aim to offer business-relevant, first-choice qualifications to people of application, ability and ambition around the world who seek a rewarding career in accountancy, finance and management.

We support our 162,000 members and 426,000 students throughout their careers, providing services through a network of 89 offices and centers. Our global infrastructure means that exams and support are delivered – and reputation and influence developed – at a local level, directly benefiting stakeholders wherever they are based, or plan to move to, in pursuit of new career opportunities.

www.accaglobal.com

Further information about ACCA's comments on the matters discussed here can be obtained from:

Richard Martin
Head of Corporate Reporting, ACCA
Email: Richard.Martin@accaglobal.com 2 ACCA welcomes the opportunity to comment on the draft framework issued by the IIRC. We have consulted on the matters raised in the consultation draft (CD) very widely, and this submission benefits from input from ACCA's Council as well as our Global Forums for audit & assurance, business law, corporate reporting, governance, risk & performance and sustainability. We have been involved in roundtable discussions and events based on the CD in several countries, including the UK, Singapore, China and Russia. We have also benefitted from our own experience of participating in the IIRC's pilot programme and applying the developing concepts of integrated reporting in the production of our own integrated report.

KEY OBSERVATIONS

ACCA remains very supportive of the concept of integrated reporting (<IR>) and of the principles set out in the CD. Indeed, our own research has shown that many stakeholders would welcome the introduction of integrated reporting, seeing in it a number of benefits such as a focus on the long term, better understanding of risk, including long-term risks to the business model, and wider insights into how corporate value is created.

The <IR> initiative offers a significant opportunity for the quality of corporate reporting to be improved by giving to investors and others a more complete view of the entity and its prospects over a longer time frame than is usually covered in traditional corporate reporting. The process of reporting on this more complete basis also has great potential for influencing the way that companies approach their strategic planning and their operational management practices. Although we still find that there is a lack of detailed awareness of <IR> - this needs to be addressed by a campaign to promote awareness of the concept - we have found that support for the principles of <IR> is widespread when these are explained.

Having a non-statutory framework that can be used by companies and the wider market will help raise awareness, encourage adoption and help facilitate good practice. Experience of application will also help the IIRC to identify areas for further enhancements to the framework and help accumulate evidence of the benefits of <IR>, which in turn should help to drive market uptake.

The IIRC now has a significant opportunity to achieve progress on this project. The emphasis now should be on ensuring that the <IR> framework is as good, practical and well-founded as it can be. Unfortunately, in our experience, even where there is awareness of <IR> there is a significant degree of uncertainty about how it is meant to be applied in practice. In our view, what is needed at this stage is for the developing framework to be credibly grounded in the experience of the pilot programme and feedback from the investor network. The framework still needs to be thoroughly field-tested and there is also a need for the IIRC to provide compelling examples of best practice from a range of entities.

The relationship between the integrated report and other forms of reporting remains one of the areas where there is currently a lack of clarity. One of the IIRC's short term priorities should therefore be to liaise with other regulators and standard setters with a view to addressing potential barriers to the adoption of <IR>. In particular, steps need to be taken to ensure that <IR> can be made consistent with, and avoid duplication with, existing requirements and guidance relating to corporate reporting, for example the UK's new Strategic Report. Best practice examples are needed on how cohesion can be achieved with current requirements for annual reports, MD&A, sustainability reports and the like. The ideal should be to develop a framework which allows for the production of an integrated report which sets out a coherent and self-contained narrative, but which allows for greater detail to be provided either in appendices or by way of links.

Achieving the right balance between the wide ranging nature of the content guidance in the CD and the objective of 'conciseness' presents a particular challenge to prospective reporters. The way forward is, in our view, firstly to review and reduce the detailed content specified in the framework and place more emphasis on the principles. Secondly, there needs to be less emphasis on the objective of conciseness, given the complexity of the affairs of many reporting organizations and the range of information needs of many stakeholders, including providers of financial capital (who are the primary addressees of the integrated report). Furthermore, the materiality assessment process is an important factor in this regard and good examples of the application of this principle will be beneficial.

Informed guidance and good examples are needed to help with negotiating the interface between transparent reporting on the one hand and commercial sensitivity and exposure to risks in respect of forward-looking information on the other. The <IR> framework needs ultimately to take a realistic line on these issues. The 'boilerplate' issue is an existing problem for non-financial reporting in general, but that does not make it any the less applicable to <IR>, and new factors may emerge that drive boilerplate reporting in respect of integrated reports.

We recognize that there is a balance to be struck between maintaining momentum in this project and ensuring that the framework is sufficiently robust to facilitate the high quality of application that will enhance the reputation of <IR> among preparers and stakeholders. ACCA's own experience on the pilot programme has shown that the outline framework developed so far is sufficient for us to be able to produce a report which, in our own view, meets the core aspirations of <IR>. Our experience has also encouraged us to achieve a greater alignment of internal performance management and decision making with the external reporting process. We accept that the IIRC will continue to learn the lessons of the pilot exercise and learn from the experience of individual reporters and different countries. But in the best interests of the project it is important that any official iteration of the framework benefits from the widest possible experience of how it is applied in practice and is able to address satisfactorily the concerns and questions of many prospective preparers and users. If the various steps that we consider are necessary cannot be undertaken and completed within the existing project timetable, one option might be to issue something like an 'interim framework' that could provide guidance to preparers pending the preparation of a more definitive first version.

In conclusion, we can see that the IIRC framework has evolved quickly from the initial concept and has benefitted from contributions from many stakeholder groups. We welcome the direction of the project and are pleased to note that there appears to be broad support in many countries for the concept of <IR> as an idea whose time has come. However the outline framework as set out in the draft needs to be developed further and we have set out in this submission a number of general and technical points that we believe need to be effectively addressed. The two most pressing of these are:

- First and foremost, with a view to promoting adoption and aiding compliance, the framework needs to provide a range of compelling good examples of reporting which suggest themselves from the pilot programme and other comparable initiatives; and
- Second, with a view to promoting clarity and avoiding duplication of effort, the IIRC needs to establish, on as broad a basis as is practicable, how the voluntary <IR> is going to be accommodated within the suite of information that companies are currently required to disclose by law or standards.

SPECIFIC COMMENTS

Chapter 1: Overview

Principles-Based Requirements

To be in accordance with the Framework, an integrated report should comply with the principles-based requirements identified throughout the Framework in bold italic type (paragraphs 1.11-1.12).

Q1: Should any additional principles-based requirements be added or should any be eliminated or changed? If so, please explain why.

We support the idea of identified principles which would constitute the key elements for a company to claim compliance with the <IR> Framework. We note that the framework is referring to these as 'principles-based requirements', which appears to us to be an internally-contradictory phrase. Full compliance with the principles may be over-ambitious, for some organizations particularly, to begin with. We therefore think that a general 'comply or explain' provision might be helpful in encouraging adoption even when this cannot be complete.

In general we agree with the identification of those paragraphs. However, paragraph 4.5 requires more clarity and explanation.

Paragraph 4.5 requires compliance with 5.13 (the materiality determination process) – we think that the first bullet point in 5.13 covers all that is needed in this regard and that the requirements of the two other bullet points (identifying the key personnel involved and the role of those charged with governance) should not be needed to claim compliance.

In general the position of disclosures under the framework needs to be clarified as to what should be provided in order to claim compliance, which we think should be kept to a minimum. It would be better if paragraph 4.1 were included among the bold italic paragraphs because this would help to make clear how much of the disclosures in Chapter 4 are required via the phrase "In addition to the content elements …" in paragraph 4.5, and how much are simply recommended or desirable. 6 Interaction with other reports and communications

The <IR> process is intended to be applied continuously to all relevant reports and communications, in addition to the preparation of an integrated report. The integrated report may include links to other reports and communications, eg, financial statements and sustainability reports. The IIRC aims to complement material developed by established reporting standard setters and others, and does not intend to develop duplicate content (paragraphs 1.18-1.20).

Q2: Do you agree with how paragraphs 1.18-1.20 characterize the interaction with other reports and communications?

We have no problem with the text in the framework. However we observe that a number of parties seem to be very unclear how the integration of reporting is intended to work in practice and so IIRC needs to consider how best to address this lack of clarity.

In this and in many other regards, compelling examples from the pilot programme and elsewhere are needed to help answer these questions. At present there are insufficient such examples available. Arguably the finalisation of the framework should be informed by both the pilots' experience, feedback from the investor network and be able to refer to a variety of best practice examples.

In our view while integrated thinking can be applied to existing reporting, the best solution that should be encouraged is that companies produce an integrated report. For the foreseeable future this will not replace, for example, the financial statements or sustainability reports, but could form the basis of the other narrative report whether that is called a management commentary, strategic report, MD&A or some other title. In that context preparers and users of integrated reports need:

- Clarity on whether there are any obstacles in their jurisdictions to producing a compliant integrated report

- Guidance on how the integrated report can fit in with existing reporting frameworks.

We do not think that IIRC can do this on its own, but there is much that it could do to assist and encourage the process. As we have noted among our key observations above, they should be working with a number of other parties to ensure that <IR> is well embedded and consistent with other reporting frameworks. These should certainly include global frameworks such as GRI and IPSAs. For national non-financial reporting requirements, IIRC may start with guidance on the obstacles to adoption of <IR> and how it could fit (as noted above) in certain major jurisdictions. These might act as a starting point with others then following.

We would not encourage IIRC to promote mandatory application of <IR> by jurisdictions at this stage, given the lack of track record and examples, but rather promote this as a market-led initiative. We are aware of course that in some cases such best practice initiatives do not meet with much success, and that without mandation or strong endorsement from regulators that adoption of <IR> will make slow progress in those places. But we believe mandatory application is not appropriate at a time when IIRC will benefit more from allowing companies to experiment and evolve good practice, and develop the overall track record of application of the framework.

Q3: If the IIRC were to create an online database of authoritative sources of indicators or measurement methods developed by established reporting standard setters and others, which references should be included?

IIRC should be clearer on how other reporting frameworks and indicator sets are going to fit in with IIRC framework. It is not clear whether the IIRC's aim is to create a database that would essentially endorse indicator sets that are compatible with the IIRC framework or whether they are pulling the list together to serve as a resource to reporters, who could share experiences on which reporting standards would work best when looking to produce an integrated report.

When looking to compile a database of sources of indicator sets and measurement methods, the IIRC should not only look to international reporting frameworks such as the GRI, but should also consider regional and industry specific guidelines and regulations such as those issued by the SASB. Other potential references include financial accounting standards and stock exchange listing requirements. The recent KPMG / GRI Carrots and Sticks report would also serve as an excellent reference for this piece of work.

The needs of SMEs need also to be considered when undertaking this exercise, both in developed and developing nations.

The challenge of <IR> is to get companies to think in an integrated manner, therefore companies would benefit from guidance about what needs to be done from a cross-organisational perspective to produce an integrated report. This kind of approach has been applied by other standard setting bodies, such as the GRI, and provides a useful tool for companies.

Other

Q4: Please provide any other comments you have about Chapter 1.

Paragraph 1.6 states that the audience for the integrated report is, primarily, providers of financial capital, and the purpose of it is to support their capital allocation decisions. We agree with the identification of the primary audience, though we note this is seen as controversial and restrictive by many. We would suggest that the reference to the allocation decisions should be deleted. This would avoid the framework being perceived as being even more restricted than implied by the primary audience and <IR> being drawn into the debate around the distinction between decision-usefulness and stewardship/accountability, which is currently surrounding IFRS for example.

Paragraph 1.10 states that the framework is intended primarily for application by the for-profit private sector. We think that the principles of <IR> are applicable to the public sector and to the not-for-profit sector too, particularly because wider factors and measures of value beyond financial capital are at the heart of the concept. In those sectors the connection of the whole reporting system with profit is much reduced as compared to private sector financial reporting. The IIRC should therefore review the draft framework and consider where it would be inappropriate for these other entities – those elements are not obvious to us.

The current scope restriction may also create some uncertainty about the relevance of <IR> to state-owned enterprises.

We have set out in answer to Q24 below some of the relevant observations on <IR> from a public sector viewpoint.

Chapter 2: Fundamental Concepts

The Capitals (Section 2B)

The Framework describes six categories of capital (paragraph 2.17). An organization is to use these categories as a benchmark when preparing an integrated report (paragraphs 2.19-2.21), and should disclose the reason if it considers any of the capitals as not material (paragraph 4.5).

Q5: Do you agree with this approach to the capitals? Why/why not?

The approach to capitals is largely welcomed, and will be very beneficial. It will encourage entities to think about and then report on their business in the longer term and in a wider context than, for example, just financial performance.

The concept of the different capitals, and reporting on value changes in them, are among the least familiar elements of <IR>. As a result, significant difficulties are perceived in estimating value in some of the capitals – perhaps especially in developing nations. It would be beneficial to companies looking to apply <IR> to see examples from the pilot study on how to report on the capitals. Also guidance (not necessarily as part of the IIRC framework) would be welcomed on how value might be measured, however crudely, or simply how it might be discussed. In this context we noted that there was very little signposting in the framework to the five studies which the IIRC commissioned, including that on the capitals.

Another aspect of the capitals that would be helped by more examples is the trade-off between the capitals. ACCA will shortly publish a report with Carbon Tracker on the impact of possible future low carbon national policies on the reserves of carbon that energy companies are holding and reporting – the 'stranded assets' or 'unburnable carbon' issue as it is sometimes called.

IIRC also needs to ensure that a consistent message about the role of the capitals is given to those concerned. Though referred to in Chapter 4, other pronouncements have been interpreted as meaning that the capitals are a conceptual underpinning but should not be the basis of reporting.

In some countries around the world (e.g. Canada), much work has been done on how companies in a particular sector impact on the various capitals at a sector level. This may be helpful guidance for the IIRC to signpost.

A number of parties seem unsure how the six capitals model produced by the IIRC relates to the 5 capitals model produced by Forum for the Future, and what lessons could be learnt from earlier work.

The flexibility about reporting on the six identified capitals in paragraphs 2.18 to 2.20 is then lost with the approach in 2.21 and in the specific disclosures in 4.5. We would prefer that the flexibility is retained and the benchmark six are there for guidance but not as a compulsory element.

Q6: Please provide any other comments you have about Section 2B.

We have no further comments on Section 2B.

Business Model (Section 2C)

A business model is defined as an organization's chosen system of inputs, business activities, outputs and outcomes that aims to create value over the short, medium and long term (paragraph 2.26).

Q7: Do you agree with this definition? Why/why not?

This definition would benefit from a reference to the mission or objectives of the organisation, as indeed there is at paragraph 4.7.

Outcomes are defined as the internal and external consequences (positive and negative) for the capitals as a result of an organization's business activities and outputs (paragraphs 2.35-2.36).

Q8: Do you agree with this definition? Why/why not?

We agree with the definition.

Q9: Please provide any other comments you have about Section 2C or the disclosure requirements and related guidance regarding business models contained in the Contents Elements Chapter of the Framework (Section 4E).

The description of the business model could well be a difficult area for good reporting. The experience of the pilot programme and from the consultations with the investor network will be very useful in judging what are realistic and helpful disclosures. In paragraph 4.21, requiring an entity to report generally on the resilience of its business model is not likely to be very helpful and risks boiler-plate statements instead of meaningful information. Instead, what might be helpful is to supplement the discussion of risk and opportunities in 4C with any further information which might assist users of the report to make their own assessment of resilience.

That said, there should be some encouragement in the framework, in respect of the discussion of the connections between capitals, to consider how much a company's business model might be able to deal with potential future changes in the prices of energy or raw materials, or of the stranded assets issue noted above.

In paragraph 4.22, in the second bullet, the second sub-point (on revenue generation after the initial point of sale) looks an oddly detailed aspect to be including in a framework.

In paragraph 4.23, the fourth bullet point would be better included in 4.22. The other bullet points in 4.23 seem either repetitious or unnecessary, apart from the last one on connections to other elements.

Other

Q10: Please provide any other comments you have about Chapter 2 that are not already addressed by your responses above.

We have no further comments on Chapter 2. 1 2

Chapter 3: Guiding Principles

Materiality and Conciseness (Section 3D)

Materiality is determined by reference to assessments made by the primary intended report users (paragraphs 3.23-3.24). The primary intended report users are providers of financial capital (paragraphs 1.6-1.8).

Q11: Do you agree with this approach to materiality? If not, how would you change it?

We agree with the identification of providers of financial capital as the primary intended report users. This term will help with bringing in both debt providers and shareholders and can allow for application to the not-for-profit sector and public sectors by encompassing funders and taxpayers.

However there is a risk that the materiality judgement will tend towards an emphasis on financial capital and the subjects of existing financial statements and annual reports. These existing forms of reporting are also addressed primarily to the providers of financial capital. Therefore the risk is that <IR> will tend to report too little on environmental and social matters. Equally of course it is also possible that <IR> will steer entities towards a wider view of value and towards a longer term view and will deliver recognition of the materiality in that context and report adequately on those other capitals.

The assessment of materiality is always a difficult exercise of judgement. Where issues are capable of being expressed in financial terms or at least quantified there may at least be a numerical starting point for this judgement. A number of the capitals covered by <IR> will not be in this category at present and so the materiality assessment for an integrated report may be more difficult.

One of the key challenges for companies preparing integrated reports and for <IR> generally will be to try to increase the level of quantification of impacts on different capitals and to try to demonstrate in an unambiguous way the connections between value created/consumed in other capitals and the effect on financial capital. This will be needed both to give credibility to the reports with investors but also to determine materiality.

Materiality is clearly a concept relevant to other standard setters in financial reporting, regulation and in sustainability reporting. IIRC should be co-ordinating with these other interested parties to ensure the concept of materiality is consistent in all these related contexts. The concepts of materiality are very important and further research and guidance may well be needed as the experience from the pilot programme and others comes through, as noted in our key observations above.

Overall, we consider the IIRC's approach to materiality is a good starting point for companies. The experience from the pilot projects seems to be that the guidance provided worked well in identifying material issues, although the exercise required a significant investment of time and resource.

Q12: Please provide any other comments you have about Section 3D or the materiality determination process (Section 5B).

Conciseness is a desirable quality given that other forms of reporting will tend to continue in addition to <IR>. However proper coverage of material issues is the more important quality which should met.

We have noted among our key observations above that conciseness will be difficult to achieve given the wide range of content envisaged. The specified content is too detailed and should be reconsidered, as should the prominence given to conciseness as a guiding principle of <IR>.

Reliability and Completeness (Section 3E)

Reliability is enhanced by mechanisms such as robust internal reporting systems, appropriate stakeholder engagement, and independent, external assurance (paragraph 3.31).

Q13: How should the reliability of an integrated report be demonstrated?

We agree with most of what is included in Section 3E on the reliability of information.

Some of the matters to be included in <IR> will already be the subject of reporting and so the issues around their reliability are well understood. As noted in our response to Q11 above there will need to be continuing development of methodologies and benchmarks in reporting on a number of the new factors that <IR> is likely to entail. Management will have to make estimates and the basis of reporting disclosed for the material factors.

Robust reporting systems are a fundamental prerequisite for reliable reporting and for some issues which may need to be covered by <IR>. These systems may require some time to develop, even after benchmarks and methodologies are agreed. We have commented below on the helpfulness of a statement of responsibility for the report (Q17) and external assurance (Q19).

The relevance of appropriate stakeholder engagement to ensuring reliability of reports is not immediately obvious to us and so needs either removal or more explanation.

Q14: Please provide any other comments you have about Section 3E.

The Framework is using the term 'reliability' when the joint IASB/FASB framework has moved away from that term and towards 'faithful representation', with the enhancing qualitative characteristic of verifiability. It would be better if the two frameworks were harmonised in this respect.

As noted already in the Summary to this submission, many of the issues raised in this section are problems already experienced with existing forms of non-financial reporting in companies' annual reports – for example competitive disadvantage, future-oriented information etc. Many of these reports (whether called management commentary, business review or MD&A) have suffered from the problems of bland statements on the grounds of commercial disadvantage, a lack of forward looking material and a tendency to report more fully the positives rather than the negatives. These are likely risks for <IR> as well, and ultimately have the potential to engender scepticism in users and lead to a lack of credibility of the resulting reports.

This need not alter what is included in the framework in this section but it would be interesting for preparers and users to be alerted to any particular issues that arise from <IR> in this regard.

Other

Q15: Please provide any other comments you have about Chapter 3 that are not already addressed by your responses above.

While we support the consistency and comparability principle, we note that the "unique value creation story" and indeed the emphasis on the company's strategy will inevitably mean that comparability between integrated reports will only be achieved at the highest level. This is to some extent the experience from narrative reporting as well. On the other hand, drawing from the experience of existing annual reporting, we do accept that clear narrative explanations of an organisation's strategy and the impact that that strategy has had, have been useful nevertheless as tools for investors to differentiate between different entities. We note also that, for <IR>, a degree of innovation is seen as important during the initial stage. As benchmarks, methodologies and market expectations develop it is possible that greater comparability may be able to be achieved.

Even if comparability may be difficult for now, we agree with paragraph 3.49 that there should be consistency from period to period for an entity.

Chapter 4: Content Elements

Q16: Please provide any comments you have about Chapter 4 that are not already addressed by your responses above (please include comments on the Content Element Business Model [Section 4E] in your answer to questions 7-9 above rather than here).

The approach of using a question to indicate the objective of the different content elements is a helpful one.

In general, though, we think that this Chapter of the framework has been written at too detailed a level and risks becoming too prescriptive, with the contents of the section becoming seen as a checklist.

The text of Chapters 4 and 5 in particular needs to be scrutinised carefully to ensure that disclosure items are correctly described. For example, some seem to be identified as requirements, such as the time frame disclosures in paragraph 5.24 and the contents of paragraphs 4.15, 4.19 and 4.20. Other items are introduced with a variety of degrees of recommendation:

- "May include … "(paragraph 4.9)
- "This includes …" (paragraph 4.22)
- "Features that can enhance … include …" (paragraph 4.23)
- "Common characteristics … include …" (paragraph 4.31)

4B Governance

Paragraph 4.11 sets out a number of issues in the form of seven bullet points. We are not sure that bullet points 2, 3, 5 and 6 are very significant matters in terms of explaining the ability of the organisation to create value. The framework refers to "those charged with governance". This is a phrase from audit standards and it does not have a wide currency outside that context. It is not used in IFRS for example. At various points in the CD a distinction is made between those charged with governance and management. External stakeholders including providers of financial capital will generally not perceive or understand the difference if any between the two groups. The separation is also not relevant for most unlisted companies.

The framework would be better referring throughout to management only – for example in 4.31.

4D Strategy and Resource Allocation

Paragraph 4.20 includes items that should be addressed. We do not think that the third bullet should be included. Strategy and resource allocation is not always going to be formulated directly by stakeholder consultations.

4F Performance

In paragraph 4.31, some of the implied requirements are going significantly beyond what is currently provided, for example:

- The KPIs with forecasts for two or more future periods (5th bullet)
- Comparative KPIs for 3 or more prior periods (6th bullet)
- Comparison of outcomes with forecasts (7th bullet)

It is possible that there is a difference in the current approach of financial reporting (where direct forecasts would be rare) and sustainability reporting (where they may be more common practice). We think that existing common practice may be difficult to change in this regard, as has been the experience of some of the other narrative/non-financial frameworks. To achieve maximum take-up the framework may need to be less aspirational in this regard.

4G Future Outlook

The requirement for forecast information in paragraph 4.37 is again demanding when viewed from the current commonly provided information and raises the general issue about the ability and legality of providing such information.

Chapter 5: Preparation and Presentation

Involvement of Those Charged With Governance (Section 5D)

Section 5D discusses the involvement of those charged with governance, and paragraph 4.5 requires organizations to disclose the governance body with oversight responsibility for <IR>.

Q17: Should there be a requirement for those charged with governance to include a statement acknowledging their responsibility for the integrated report? Why/why not?

We agree with this idea, though as noted above we do not agree with the term ‘those charged with governance’ and would substitute ‘management’.

As noted above it is important to preparers and users of the reports to understand how an integrated report would fit into the regulatory or legal requirements in a jurisdiction. The responsibility for issuing reports varies between jurisdictions and so such a statement may clarify this for a particular case.

Q18: Please provide any other comments you have about involvement of those charged with governance (Section 5D).

We have no further comments on the section.

Credibility (Section 5E)

The Framework provides criteria against which organizations and assurance providers assess a report's adherence (paragraph 5.21).

Q19: If assurance is to be obtained, should it cover the integrated report as a whole, or specific aspects of the report? Why?

<IR> should be a market-led initiative and be for now an innovative one. In a similar way we think the question of assurance, the way it can be provided and by whom, should be left to market demand. There are some concerns with a development such as <IR> that assurance might inevitably reduce it to a series of requirements that must be ticked off in order that the assurer can support the claim of compliance with the framework.

On the other hand assurance could clearly assist with the credibility and reliability issues noted above. Reasonable assurance might be comparatively difficult and expensive to provide and so it should be left to users and the reporting companies to decide whether they want the extra credibility that assurance might bring.

If there is to be assurance of integrated reports then there should probably be some degree of innovation allowed as well. If, however, there is significant demand then standard setters such as IAASB must make sure that guidance to best practice is available and IIRC must liaise with them to help that and discuss relevant issues arising from <IR> (see examples in Q20 below).

In terms of whether there might be assurance of some aspects of the reports but not on the report as a whole, we note that without an overall assurance on the report then there will be no additional credibility provided over the balance of the report.

In the case of integrated reports that are issued with financial statements which have been audited, for example in accordance with international standards, the user can at least rely on a review for consistency with the financial statements.

Q20: Please provide any other comments you have about credibility (Section 5E). Assurance providers are particularly asked to comment on whether they consider the Framework provides suitable criteria for an assurance engagement.

The IIRC seem to have been too ready to equate credibility and reliability with assurance. Credibility is gained first and foremost by good transparent reporting against recognised frameworks, coherently and consistently across the piece – financial statements, sustainability reports, business review and integrated reports. External assurance can then follow and endorse that.

Turning to assurance, the framework provides suitable criteria in the same way that AA1000 does or COSO for control systems. We think that some assurers would be happy to provide an assessment as to whether the integrated report followed the principles. There will be a number of significant assurance issues including:

- To whom any report should be addressed
- Forward looking information
- Subjectivity of much of the qualitative content
- The training and skill sets for the assurance providers.

In some of these difficult and judgmental areas for example the assessment of materiality, there could be some place for assurance over the process rather than an opinion on the outcome. Other

Q21: Please provide any other comments you have about Chapter 5 that are not already addressed by your responses above (please include comments on the materiality determination process [Section 5B] in your answer to question 11 above rather than here).

Section 5B on materiality discusses the magnitude of effects and the likelihood of occurrence. It is important that in doing so the effects of ranges of outcomes are considered: the emerging concept of 'confidence accounting' may be relevant here.

Overall View

Q22: Recognizing that <IR> will evolve over time, please explain the extent to which you believe the content of the Framework overall is appropriate for use by organizations in preparing an integrated report and for providing report users with information about an organization's ability to create value in the short, medium and long term?

One aspect to which the framework does not give sufficient emphasis concerns the link between <IR> and changes in the way that strategy is devised and implemented through organisational structures. Perhaps those changes, which will invariably include changes to the way that information is collected, need to be achieved before reporting can be properly undertaken on an integrated basis. So far, successfully achieving this transformation seems to have been both the biggest challenge in implementation and also its biggest reward.

We agree that <IR> will evolve. As noted already, it is important that the framework benefits from the experience derived from the pilot programmes, investor networks and from other early adopters such as listed companies in South Africa. We do not think that, to date, this combined experience has been authoritatively collated and communicated so as to inform the practice of prospective reporters.

But if a finalized framework is produced at this early stage, so as to help encourage adoption and innovation, then presumably there may well be a further version produced in a few years' time. Greater clarity on what the intentions are in this regard and how the IIRC views this framework, would be helpful for those considering applying it. Development of <IR>

Q23: If the IIRC were to develop explanatory material on <IR> in addition to the Framework, which three topics would you recommend be given priority? Why?

Our three priorities for extra material that <IR> would benefit from are:

- First and foremost a range of compelling good examples of reporting to highlight best practice.
- Guidance on how <IR> might fit in with annual reporting requirements in different jurisdictions.

- Research and guidance on how value changes in different capitals can be represented whether by quantitative indices or qualitatively, for the reasons given in Q11 above.

Other

Q24: Please provide any other comments not already addressed by your responses to Questions 1-23.

Languages and Translation

For global systems of standards, even of non-mandatory guidance, the development of a key number of official languages and the quality of translations are important for encouraging the take-up and for the proper application in different countries. The IIRC will need to monitor both the demands for different language versions and the standard of the translations.

Comments on Application of <IR> to the Public Sector

<IR> seems very applicable to the public sector and we would be generally supportive of the development of a global integrated reporting framework for the sector on a principles based approach.

Currently there is a myriad of reporting practices across the sector between national, regional and local governments and via country, and there is considerable inconsistency in reporting. Some coherence around an international framework would be helpful.

There is much already developing in the sector on which <IR> could build.

At an international level the IPSASB recently published a draft exposure draft on non- financial reporting information that puts forward the principle that reporting on service performance provides a key indicator to the recipients of those services. In ACCA's publication 'Sustainability reporting: what are governments doing about it?' we found that it most cases where governments were reporting on sustainability the focus was on the environmental aspects as opposed to social and economic factors.

Reporting on non-financial performance will improve comparability between public sector entities, but comparing service performance is not any more straightforward in the public sector than elsewhere. A KPI can only be used as a starting point for understanding difference and drawing conclusions about performance, and a particular valuation creation story applies here as well.

Although we agree with the principles contained within the IIR framework, it would need to be reviewed considering what is fundamentally different about the public sector. The contextual factors are different, for example, the political dimension, accountability imperative and multiple users of financial statements and reports. The primary stakeholder group for financial reports would be the legislature and the taxpayers. Are they the providers of capital for the public sector? Perhaps, but they will not be the only ones.

A key development particularly in developed countries is the transparency agenda, where governments are making available to the public vast amounts of data (financial and non-financial) for them to analyse and draw their own conclusions about service performance. The development of an IIRC framework would have to take account of this changing context, in particular, how such reports would add value to this agenda.

The principles of <IR> may well be very transferable to the public sector, but the problems and shortcomings of this narrative/non-financial reporting are also comparable to the experience in the private sector. For example in a review of UK government department annual reports included the following issues:

- In most cases reports were not 'forward looking' beyond the political cycle.
- Performance reporting was used as an exercise to showcase what was good and where positive progress had been made and hid what was bad.

THE DRAFT FRAMEWORK FOR INTEGRATED REPORTING

A consultation draft issued by the International Integrated Reporting Council (IIRC)
Comments from ACCA
July 2013

ACCA (the Association of Chartered Certified Accountants) is the global body for professional accountants. We aim to offer business-relevant, first-choice qualifications to people of application, ability and ambition around the world who seek a rewarding career in accountancy, finance and management.

We support our 162,000 members and 426,000 students throughout their careers, providing services through a network of 89 offices and centres. Our global infrastructure means that exams and support are delivered – and reputation and influence developed – at a local level, directly benefiting stakeholders wherever they are based, or plan to move to, in pursuit of new career opportunities.

www.accaglobal.com

Further information about ACCA's comments on the matters discussed here can be obtained from:

Richard Martin
Head of Corporate Reporting, ACCA
Email: Richard.Martin@accaglobal.com 2

ACCA welcomes the opportunity to comment on the draft framework issued by the IIRC. We have consulted on the matters raised in the consultation draft (CD) very widely, and this submission benefits from input from ACCA's Council as well as our Global Forums for audit & assurance, business law, corporate reporting, governance, risk & performance and sustainability. We have been involved in roundtable discussions and events based on the CD in several countries, including the UK, Singapore, China and Russia. We have also benefitted from our own experience of participating in the IIRC's pilot programme and applying the developing concepts of integrated reporting in the production of our own integrated report.

KEY OBSERVATIONS

ACCA remains very supportive of the concept of integrated reporting (<IR>) and of the principles set out in the CD. Indeed, our own research has shown that many stakeholders would welcome the introduction of integrated reporting, seeing in it a number of benefits such as a focus on the long term, better understanding of risk, including long-term risks to the business model, and wider insights into how corporate value is created.

The <IR> initiative offers a significant opportunity for the quality of corporate reporting to be improved by giving to investors and others a more complete view of the entity and its prospects over a longer time frame than is usually covered in traditional corporate reporting. The process of reporting on this more complete basis also has great potential for influencing the way that companies approach their strategic planning and their operational management practices. Although we still find that there is a lack of detailed awareness of <IR> - this needs to be addressed by a campaign to promote awareness of the concept - we have found that support for the principles of <IR> is widespread when these are explained.

Having a non-statutory framework that can be used by companies and the wider market will help raise awareness, encourage adoption and help facilitate good practice. Experience of application will also help the IIRC to identify areas for further enhancements to the framework and help accumulate evidence of the benefits of <IR>, which in turn should help to drive market uptake.

The IIRC now has a significant opportunity to achieve progress on this project. The emphasis now should be on ensuring that the <IR> framework is as good, practical and well-founded as it can be. Unfortunately, in our experience, even where there is awareness of <IR> there is a significant degree of uncertainty about how it is meant to be applied in practice. In our view, what is needed at this stage is for the developing framework to be credibly grounded in the experience of the pilot programme and feedback from the investor network. The framework still needs to be thoroughly field-tested and there is also a need for the IIRC to provide compelling examples of best practice from a range of entities.

The relationship between the integrated report and other forms of reporting remains one of the areas where there is currently a lack of clarity. One of the IIRC's short term priorities should therefore be to liaise with other regulators and standard setters with a view to addressing potential barriers to the adoption of <IR>. In particular, steps need to be taken to ensure that <IR> can be made consistent with, and avoid duplication with, existing requirements and guidance relating to corporate reporting, for example the UK's new Strategic Report. Best practice examples are needed on how cohesion can be achieved with current requirements for annual reports, MD&A, sustainability reports and the like. The ideal should be to develop a framework which allows for the production of an integrated report which sets out a coherent and self-contained narrative, but which allows for greater detail to be provided either in appendices or by way of links.

Achieving the right balance between the wide ranging nature of the content guidance in the CD and the objective of 'conciseness' presents a particular challenge to prospective reporters. The way forward is, in our view, firstly to review and reduce the detailed content specified in the framework and place more emphasis on the principles. Secondly, there needs to be less emphasis on the objective of conciseness, given the complexity of the affairs of many reporting organisations and the range of information needs of many stakeholders, including providers of financial capital (who are the primary addressees of the integrated report). Furthermore, the materiality assessment process is an important factor in this regard and good examples of the application of this principle will be beneficial.

Informed guidance and good examples are needed to help with negotiating the interface between transparent reporting on the one hand and commercial sensitivity and exposure to risks in respect of forward-looking information on the other. The <IR> framework needs ultimately to take a realistic line on these issues. The 'boilerplate' issue is an existing problem for non-financial reporting in general, but that does not make it any the less applicable to <IR>, and new factors may emerge that drive boilerplate reporting in respect of integrated reports.

We recognise that there is a balance to be struck between maintaining momentum in this project and ensuring that the framework is sufficiently robust to facilitate the high quality of application that will enhance the reputation of <IR> among preparers and stakeholders. ACCA's own experience on the pilot programme has shown that the outline framework developed so far is sufficient for us to be able to produce a report which, in our own view, meets the core aspirations of <IR>. Our experience has also encouraged us to achieve a greater alignment of internal performance management and decision making with the external reporting process. We accept that the IIRC will continue to learn the lessons of the pilot exercise and learn from the experience of individual reporters and different countries. But in the best interests of the project it is important that any official iteration of the framework benefits from the widest possible experience of how it is applied in practice and is able to address satisfactorily the concerns and questions of many prospective preparers and users. If the various steps that we consider are necessary cannot be undertaken and completed within the existing project timetable, one option might be to issue something like an 'interim framework' that could provide guidance to preparers pending the preparation of a more definitive first version.

In conclusion, we can see that the IIRC framework has evolved quickly from the initial concept and has benefitted from contributions from many stakeholder groups. We welcome the direction of the project and are pleased to note that there appears to be broad support in many countries for the concept of <IR> as an idea whose time has come. However the outline framework as set out in the draft needs to be developed further and we have set out in this submission a number of general and technical points that we believe need to be effectively addressed. The two most pressing of these are:

- First and foremost, with a view to promoting adoption and aiding compliance, the framework needs to provide a range of compelling good examples of reporting which suggest themselves from the pilot programme and other comparable initiatives; and
- Second, with a view to promoting clarity and avoiding duplication of effort, the IIRC needs to establish, on as broad a basis as is practicable, how the voluntary <IR> is going to be accommodated within the suite of information that companies are currently required to disclose by law or standards.

SPECIFIC COMMENTS

Chapter 1: Overview

Principles-Based Requirements

To be in accordance with the Framework, an integrated report should comply with the principles-based requirements identified throughout the Framework in bold italic type (paragraphs 1.11-1.12).

Q1: Should any additional principles-based requirements be added or should any be eliminated or changed? If so, please explain why.

We support the idea of identified principles which would constitute the key elements for a company to claim compliance with the <IR> Framework. We note that the framework is referring to these as 'principles-based requirements', which appears to us to be an internally-contradictory phrase. Full compliance with the principles may be over-ambitious, for some organisations particularly, to begin with. We therefore think that a general 'comply or explain' provision might be helpful in encouraging adoption even when this cannot be complete.

In general we agree with the identification of those paragraphs. However, paragraph 4.5 requires more clarity and explanation.

Paragraph 4.5 requires compliance with 5.13 (the materiality determination process) – we think that the first bullet point in 5.13 covers all that is needed in this regard and that the requirements of the two other bullet points (identifying the key personnel involved and the role of those charged with governance) should not be needed to claim compliance.

In general the position of disclosures under the framework needs to be clarified as to what should be provided in order to claim compliance, which we think should be kept to a minimum. It would be better if paragraph 4.1 were included among the bold italic paragraphs because this would help to make clear how much of the disclosures in Chapter 4 are required via the phrase "In addition to the content elements …" in paragraph 4.5, and how much are simply recommended or desirable. Interaction with other reports and communications

The <IR> process is intended to be applied continuously to all relevant reports and communications, in addition to the preparation of an integrated report. The integrated report may include links to other reports and communications, eg, financial statements and sustainability reports. The IIRC aims to complement material developed by established reporting standard setters and others, and does not intend to develop duplicate content (paragraphs 1.18-1.20).

Q2: Do you agree with how paragraphs 1.18-1.20 characterize the interaction with other reports and communications?

We have no problem with the text in the framework. However we observe that a number of parties seem to be very unclear how the integration of reporting is intended to work in practice and so IIRC needs to consider how best to address this lack of clarity.

In this and in many other regards, compelling examples from the pilot programme and elsewhere are needed to help answer these questions. At present there are insufficient such examples available. Arguably the finalisation of the framework should be informed by both the pilots' experience, feedback from the investor network and be able to refer to a variety of best practice examples.

In our view while integrated thinking can be applied to existing reporting, the best solution that should be encouraged is that companies produce an integrated report. For the foreseeable future this will not replace, for example, the financial statements or sustainability reports, but could form the basis of the other narrative report whether that is called a management commentary, strategic report, MD&A or some other title. In that context preparers and users of integrated reports need:

- Clarity on whether there are any obstacles in their jurisdictions to producing a compliant integrated report
- Guidance on how the integrated report can fit in with existing reporting frameworks.

We do not think that IIRC can do this on its own, but there is much that it could do to assist and encourage the process. As we have noted among our key observations above, they should be working with a number of other parties to ensure that <IR> is well embedded and consistent with other reporting frameworks. These should certainly include global frameworks such as GRI and ISAs. For national non-financial reporting requirements, IIRC may start with guidance on the obstacles to adoption of <IR> and how it could fit (as noted above) in certain major jurisdictions. These might act as a starting point with others then following.

We would not encourage IIRC to promote mandatory application of <IR> by jurisdictions at this stage, given the lack of track record and examples, but rather promote this as a market-led initiative. We are aware of course that in some cases such best practice initiatives do not meet with much success, and that without mandation or strong endorsement from regulators that adoption of <IR> will make slow progress in those places. But we believe mandatory application is not appropriate at a time when IIRC will benefit more from allowing companies to experiment and evolve good practice, and develop the overall track record of application of the framework.

Q3: If the IIRC were to create an online database of authoritative sources of indicators or measurement methods developed by established reporting standard setters and others, which references should be included?

IIRC should be clearer on how other reporting frameworks and indicator sets are going to fit in with IIRC framework. It is not clear whether the IIRC's aim is to create a database that would essentially endorse indicator sets that are compatible with the IIRC framework or whether they are pulling the list together to serve as a resource to reporters, who could share experiences on which reporting standards would work best when looking to produce an integrated report.

When looking to compile a database of sources of indicator sets and measurement methods, the IIRC should not only look to international reporting frameworks such as the GRI, but should also consider regional and industry specific guidelines and regulations such as those issued by the SASB. Other potential references include financial accounting standards and stock exchange listing requirements. The recent KPMG / GRI Carrots and Sticks report would also serve as an excellent reference for this piece of work.

The needs of SMEs need also to be considered when undertaking this exercise, both in developed and developing nations.

The challenge of <IR> is to get companies to think in an integrated manner, therefore companies would benefit from guidance about what needs to be done from a cross-organisational perspective to produce an integrated report. This kind of approach has been applied by other standard setting bodies, such as the GRI, and provides a useful tool for companies.

Other

Q4: Please provide any other comments you have about Chapter 1.

Paragraph 1.6 states that the audience for the integrated report is, primarily, providers of financial capital, and the purpose of it is to support their capital allocation decisions. We agree with the identification of the primary audience, though we note this is seen as controversial and restrictive by many. We would suggest that the reference to the allocation decisions should be deleted. This would avoid the framework being perceived as being even more restricted than implied by the primary audience and <IR> being drawn into the debate around the distinction between decision-usefulness and stewardship/accountability, which is currently surrounding IFRS for example.

Paragraph 1.10 states that the framework is intended primarily for application by the for-profit private sector. We think that the principles of <IR> are applicable to the public sector and to the not-for-profit sector too, particularly because wider factors and measures of value beyond financial capital are at the heart of the concept. In those sectors the connection of the whole reporting system with profit is much reduced as compared to private sector financial reporting. The IIRC should therefore review the draft framework and consider where it would be inappropriate for these other entities – those elements are not obvious to us.

The current scope restriction may also create some uncertainty about the relevance of <IR> to state-owned enterprises.

We have set out in answer to Q24 below some of the relevant observations on <IR> from a public sector viewpoint.

Chapter 2: Fundamental Concepts

The Capitals (Section 2B)

The Framework describes six categories of capital (paragraph 2.17). An organization is to use these categories as a benchmark when preparing an integrated report (paragraphs 2.19-2.21), and should disclose the reason if it considers any of the capitals as not material (paragraph 4.5).

Q5: Do you agree with this approach to the capitals? Why/why not?

The approach to capitals is largely welcomed, and will be very beneficial. It will encourage entities to think about and then report on their business in the longer term and in a wider context than, for example, just financial performance.

The concept of the different capitals, and reporting on value changes in them, are among the least familiar elements of <IR>. As a result, significant difficulties are perceived in estimating value in some of the capitals – perhaps especially in developing nations. It would be beneficial to companies looking to apply <IR> to see examples from the pilot study on how to report on the capitals. Also guidance (not necessarily as part of the IIRC framework) would be welcomed on how value might be measured, however crudely, or simply how it might be discussed. In this context we noted that there was very little signposting in the framework to the five studies which the IIRC commissioned, including that on the capitals.

Another aspect of the capitals that would be helped by more examples is the trade-off between the capitals. ACCA will shortly publish a report with Carbon Tracker on the impact of possible future low carbon national policies on the reserves of carbon that energy companies are holding and reporting – the 'stranded assets' or 'unburnable carbon' issue as it is sometimes called.

IIRC also needs to ensure that a consistent message about the role of the capitals is given to those concerned. Though referred to in Chapter 4, other pronouncements have been interpreted as meaning that the capitals are a conceptual underpinning but should not be the basis of reporting.

In some countries around the world (e.g. Canada), much work has been done on how companies in a particular sector impact on the various capitals at a sector level. This may be helpful guidance for the IIRC to signpost.

A number of parties seem unsure how the six capitals model produced by the IIRC relates to the 5 capitals model produced by Forum for the Future, and what lessons could be learnt from earlier work.

The flexibility about reporting on the six identified capitals in paragraphs 2.18 to 2.20 is then lost with the approach in 2.21 and in the specific disclosures in 4.5. We would prefer that the flexibility is retained and the benchmark six are there for guidance but not as a compulsory element.

Q6: Please provide any other comments you have about Section 2B.

We have no further comments on Section 2B.

Business Model (Section 2C)

A business model is defined as an organization's chosen system of inputs, business activities, outputs and outcomes that aims to create value over the short, medium and long term (paragraph 2.26).

Q7: Do you agree with this definition? Why/why not?

This definition would benefit from a reference to the mission or objectives of the organisation, as indeed there is at paragraph 4.7.

Outcomes are defined as the internal and external consequences (positive and negative) for the capitals as a result of an organization's business activities and outputs (paragraphs 2.35-2.36).

Q8: Do you agree with this definition? Why/why not?

We agree with the definition.

Q9: Please provide any other comments you have about Section 2C or the disclosure requirements and related guidance regarding business models contained in the Contents Elements Chapter of the Framework (Section 4E).

The description of the business model could well be a difficult area for good reporting. The experience of the pilot programme and from the consultations with the investor network will be very useful in judging what are realistic and helpful disclosures. In paragraph 4.21, requiring an entity to report generally on the resilience of its business model is not likely to be very helpful and risks boiler-plate statements instead of meaningful information. Instead, what might be helpful is to supplement the discussion of risk and opportunities in 4C with any further information which might assist users of the report to make their own assessment of resilience.

That said, there should be some encouragement in the framework, in respect of the discussion of the connections between capitals, to consider how much a company's business model might be able to deal with potential future changes in the prices of energy or raw materials, or of the stranded assets issue noted above.

In paragraph 4.22, in the second bullet, the second sub-point (on revenue generation after the initial point of sale) looks an oddly detailed aspect to be including in a framework.

In paragraph 4.23, the fourth bullet point would be better included in 4.22. The other bullet points in 4.23 seem either repetitious or unnecessary, apart from the last one on connections to other elements.

Other

Q10: Please provide any other comments you have about Chapter 2 that are not already addressed by your responses above.

We have no further comments on Chapter 2.

Chapter 3: Guiding Principles

Materiality and Conciseness (Section 3D)

Materiality is determined by reference to assessments made by the primary intended report users (paragraphs 3.23-3.24). The primary intended report users are providers of financial capital (paragraphs 1.6-1.8).

Q11: Do you agree with this approach to materiality? If not, how would you change it?

We agree with the identification of providers of financial capital as the primary intended report users. This term will help with bringing in both debt providers and shareholders and can allow for application to the not-for-profit sector and public sectors by encompassing funders and taxpayers.

However there is a risk that the materiality judgement will tend towards an emphasis on financial capital and the subjects of existing financial statements and annual reports. These existing forms of reporting are also addressed primarily to the providers of financial capital. Therefore the risk is that <IR> will tend to report too little on environmental and social matters. Equally of course it is also possible that <IR> will steer entities towards a wider view of value and towards a longer term view and will deliver recognition of the materiality in that context and report adequately on those other capitals.

The assessment of materiality is always a difficult exercise of judgement. Where issues are capable of being expressed in financial terms or at least quantified there may at least be a numerical starting point for this judgement. A number of the capitals covered by <IR> will not be in this category at present and so the materiality assessment for an integrated report may be more difficult.

One of the key challenges for companies preparing integrated reports and for <IR> generally will be to try to increase the level of quantification of impacts on different capitals and to try to demonstrate in an unambiguous way the connections between value created/consumed in other capitals and the effect on financial capital. This will be needed both to give credibility to the reports with investors but also to determine materiality.

Materiality is clearly a concept relevant to other standard setters in financial reporting, regulation and in sustainability reporting. IIRC should be co-ordinating with these other interested parties to ensure the concept of materiality is consistent in all these related contexts. The concepts of materiality are very important and further research and guidance may well be needed as the experience from the pilot programme and others comes through, as noted in our key observations above.

Overall, we consider the IIRC's approach to materiality is a good starting point for companies. The experience from the pilot projects seems to be that the guidance provided worked well in identifying material issues, although the exercise required a significant investment of time and resource.

Q12: Please provide any other comments you have about Section 3D or the materiality determination process (Section 5B).

Conciseness is a desirable quality given that other forms of reporting will tend to continue in addition to <IR>. However proper coverage of material issues is the more important quality which should met.

We have noted among our key observations above that conciseness will be difficult to achieve given the wide range of content envisaged. The specified content is too detailed and should be reconsidered, as should the prominence given to conciseness as a guiding principle of <IR>.

Reliability and Completeness (Section 3E)

Reliability is enhanced by mechanisms such as robust internal reporting systems, appropriate stakeholder engagement, and independent, external assurance (paragraph 3.31).

Q13: How should the reliability of an integrated report be demonstrated?

We agree with most of what is included in Section 3E on the reliability of information.

Some of the matters to be included in <IR> will already be the subject of reporting and so the issues around their reliability are well understood. As noted in our response to Q11 above there will need to be continuing development of methodologies and benchmarks in reporting on a number of the new factors that <IR> is likely to entail. Management will have to make estimates and the basis of reporting disclosed for the material factors.

Robust reporting systems are a fundamental prerequisite for reliable reporting and for some issues which may need to be covered by <IR>. These systems may require some time to develop, even after benchmarks and methodologies are agreed. We have commented below on the helpfulness of a statement of responsibility for the report (Q17) and external assurance (Q19).

The relevance of appropriate stakeholder engagement to ensuring reliability of reports is not immediately obvious to us and so needs either removal or more explanation.

Q14: Please provide any other comments you have about Section 3E.

The Framework is using the term 'reliability' when the joint IASB/FASB framework has moved away from that term and towards 'faithful representation', with the enhancing qualitative characteristic of verifiability. It would be better if the two frameworks were harmonised in this respect.

As noted already in the Summary to this submission, many of the issues raised in this section are problems already experienced with existing forms of non-financial reporting in companies' annual reports – for example competitive disadvantage, future-oriented information etc. Many of these reports (whether called management commentary, business review or MD&A) have suffered from the problems of bland statements on the grounds of commercial disadvantage, a lack of forward looking material and a tendency to report more fully the positives rather than the negatives. These are likely risks for <IR> as well, and ultimately have the potential to engender scepticism in users and lead to a lack of credibility of the resulting reports.

This need not alter what is included in the framework in this section but it would be interesting for preparers and users to be alerted to any particular issues that arise from <IR> in this regard.

Other

Q15: Please provide any other comments you have about Chapter 3 that are not already addressed by your responses above.

While we support the consistency and comparability principle, we note that the "unique value creation story" and indeed the emphasis on the company's strategy will inevitably mean that comparability between integrated reports will only be achieved at the highest level. This is to some extent the experience from narrative reporting as well. On the other hand, drawing from the experience of existing annual reporting, we do accept that clear narrative explanations of an organisation's strategy and the impact that that strategy has had, have been useful nevertheless as tools for investors to differentiate between different entities. We note also that, for <IR>, a degree of innovation is seen as important during the initial stage. As benchmarks, methodologies and market expectations develop it is possible that greater comparability may be able to be achieved.

Even if comparability may be difficult for now, we agree with paragraph 3.49 that there should be consistency from period to period for an entity.

Chapter 4: Content Elements

Q16: Please provide any comments you have about Chapter 4 that are not already addressed by your responses above (please include comments on the Content Element Business Model [Section 4E] in your answer to questions 7-9 above rather than here).

The approach of using a question to indicate the objective of the different content elements is a helpful one.

In general, though, we think that this Chapter of the framework has been written at too detailed a level and risks becoming too prescriptive, with the contents of the section becoming seen as a checklist.

The text of Chapters 4 and 5 in particular needs to be scrutinised carefully to ensure that disclosure items are correctly described. For example, some seem to be identified as requirements, such as the time frame disclosures in paragraph 5.24 and the contents of paragraphs 4.15, 4.19 and 4.20. Other items are introduced with a variety of degrees of recommendation:

- "May include … "(paragraph 4.9)
- "This includes …" (paragraph 4.22)
- "Features that can enhance … include …" (paragraph 4.23)
- "Common characteristics … include …" (paragraph 4.31)

4B Governance

Paragraph 4.11 sets out a number of issues in the form of seven bullet points. We are not sure that bullet points 2, 3, 5 and 6 are very significant matters in terms of explaining the ability of the organisation to create value. The framework refers to "those charged with governance". This is a phrase from audit standards and it does not have a wide currency outside that context. It is not used in IFRS for example. At various points in the CD a distinction is made between those charged with governance and management. External stakeholders including providers of financial capital will generally not perceive or understand the difference if any between the two groups. The separation is also not relevant for most unlisted companies.

The framework would be better referring throughout to management only – for example in 4.31.

4D Strategy and Resource Allocation

Paragraph 4.20 includes items that should be addressed. We do not think that the third bullet should be included. Strategy and resource allocation is not always going to be formulated directly by stakeholder consultations.

4F Performance

In paragraph 4.31, some of the implied requirements are going significantly beyond what is currently provided, for example:

- The KPIs with forecasts for two or more future periods (5th bullet)
- Comparative KPIs for 3 or more prior periods (6th bullet)
- Comparison of outcomes with forecasts (7th bullet)

It is possible that there is a difference in the current approach of financial reporting (where direct forecasts would be rare) and sustainability reporting (where they may be more common practice). We think that existing common practice may be difficult to change in this regard, as has been the experience of some of the other narrative/non-financial frameworks. To achieve maximum take-up the framework may need to be less aspirational in this regard.

4G Future Outlook

The requirement for forecast information in paragraph 4.37 is again demanding when viewed from the current commonly provided information and raises the general issue about the ability and legality of providing such information.

Chapter 5: Preparation and Presentation

Involvement of Those Charged With Governance (Section 5D)

Section 5D discusses the involvement of those charged with governance, and paragraph 4.5 requires organizations to disclose the governance body with oversight responsibility for <IR>.

Q17: Should there be a requirement for those charged with governance to include a statement acknowledging their responsibility for the integrated report? Why/why not?

We agree with this idea, though as noted above we do not agree with the term 'those charged with governance' and would substitute 'management'.

As noted above it is important to preparers and users of the reports to understand how an integrated report would fit into the regulatory or legal requirements in a jurisdiction. The responsibility for issuing reports varies between jurisdictions and so such a statement may clarify this for a particular case.

Q18: Please provide any other comments you have about involvement of those charged with governance (Section 5D).

We have no further comments on the section.

Credibility (Section 5E)

The Framework provides criteria against which organizations and assurance providers assess a report's adherence (paragraph 5.21).

Q19: If assurance is to be obtained, should it cover the integrated report as a whole, or specific aspects of the report? Why?

<IR> should be a market-led initiative and be for now an innovative one. In a similar way we think the question of assurance, the way it can be provided and by whom, should be left to market demand. There are some concerns with a development such as <IR> that assurance might inevitably reduce it to a series of requirements that must be ticked off in order that the assurer can support the claim of compliance with the framework.

On the other hand assurance could clearly assist with the credibility and reliability issues noted above. Reasonable assurance might be comparatively difficult and expensive to provide and so it should be left to users and the reporting companies to decide whether they want the extra credibility that assurance might bring.

If there is to be assurance of integrated reports then there should probably be some degree of innovation allowed as well. If, however, there is significant demand then standard setters such as IAASB must make sure that guidance to best practice is available and IIRC must liaise with them to help that and discuss relevant issues arising from <IR> (see examples in Q20 below).

In terms of whether there might be assurance of some aspects of the reports but not on the report as a whole, we note that without an overall assurance on the report then there will be no additional credibility provided over the balance of the report.

In the case of integrated reports that are issued with financial statements which have been audited, for example in accordance with international standards, the user can at least rely on a review for consistency with the financial statements.

Q20: Please provide any other comments you have about credibility (Section 5E). Assurance providers are particularly asked to comment on whether they consider the Framework provides suitable criteria for an assurance engagement.

The IIRC seem to have been too ready to equate credibility and reliability with assurance. Credibility is gained first and foremost by good transparent reporting against recognised frameworks, coherently and consistently across the piece – financial statements, sustainability reports, business review and integrated reports. External assurance can then follow and endorse that.

Turning to assurance, the framework provides suitable criteria in the same way that AA1000 does or COSO for control systems. We think that some assurers would be happy to provide an assessment as to whether the integrated report followed the principles. There will be a number of significant assurance issues including:

- To whom any report should be addressed
- Forward looking information
- Subjectivity of much of the qualitative content
- The training and skill sets for the assurance providers.

In some of these difficult and judgmental areas for example the assessment of materiality, there could be some place for assurance over the process rather than an opinion on the outcome.

Other

Q21: Please provide any other comments you have about Chapter 5 that are not already addressed by your responses above (please include comments on the materiality determination process [Section 5B] in your answer to question 11 above rather than here).

Section 5B on materiality discusses the magnitude of effects and the likelihood of occurrence. It is important that in doing so the effects of ranges of outcomes are considered: the emerging concept of 'confidence accounting' may be relevant here.

Overall View

Q22: Recognizing that <IR> will evolve over time, please explain the extent to which you believe the content of the Framework overall is appropriate for use by organizations in preparing an integrated report and for providing report users with information about an organization's ability to create value in the short, medium and long term?

One aspect to which the framework does not give sufficient emphasis concerns the link between <IR> and changes in the way that strategy is devised and implemented through organisational structures. Perhaps those changes, which will invariably include changes to the way that information is collected, need to be achieved before reporting can be properly undertaken on an integrated basis. So far, successfully achieving this transformation seems to have been both the biggest challenge in implementation and also its biggest reward.

We agree that <IR> will evolve. As noted already, it is important that the framework benefits from the experience derived from the pilot programmes, investor networks and from other early adopters such as listed companies in South Africa. We do not think that, to date, this combined experience has been authoritatively collated and communicated so as to inform the practice of prospective reporters.

But if a finalised framework is produced at this early stage, so as to help encourage adoption and innovation, then presumably there may well be a further version produced in a few years' time. Greater clarity on what the intentions are in this regard and how the IIRC views this framework, would be helpful for those considering applying it. Development of <IR>

Q23: If the IIRC were to develop explanatory material on <IR> in addition to the Framework, which three topics would you recommend be given priority? Why?

Our three priorities for extra material that <IR> would benefit from are:

- First and foremost a range of compelling good examples of reporting to highlight best practice.
- Guidance on how <IR> might fit in with annual reporting requirements in different jurisdictions.

- Research and guidance on how value changes in different capitals can be represented whether by quantitative indices or qualitatively, for the reasons given in Q11 above.

Other

Q24: Please provide any other comments not already addressed by your responses to Questions 1-23.

Languages and Translation

For global systems of standards, even of non-mandatory guidance, the development of a key number of official languages and the quality of translations are important for encouraging the take-up and for the proper application in different countries. The IIRC will need to monitor both the demands for different language versions and the standard of the translations.

Comments on Application of <IR> to the Public Sector

<IR> seems very applicable to the public sector and we would be generally supportive of the development of a global integrated reporting framework for the sector on a principles based approach.

Currently there is a myriad of reporting practices across the sector between national, regional and local governments and via country, and there is considerable inconsistency in reporting. Some coherence around an international framework would be helpful.

There is much already developing in the sector on which <IR> could build.

At an international level the IPSASB recently published a draft exposure draft on non- financial reporting information that puts forward the principle that reporting on service performance provides a key indicator to the recipients of those services. In ACCA's publication 'Sustainability reporting: what are governments doing about it?' we found that it most cases where governments were reporting on sustainability the focus was on the environmental aspects as opposed to social and economic factors.

Reporting on non-financial performance will improve comparability between public sector entities, but comparing service performance is not any more straightforward in the public sector than elsewhere. A KPI can only be used as a starting point for understanding difference and drawing conclusions about performance, and a particular valuation creation story applies here as well.

Although we agree with the principles contained within the IIR framework, it would need to be reviewed considering what is fundamentally different about the public sector. The contextual factors are different, for example, the political dimension, accountability imperative and multiple users of financial statements and reports. The primary stakeholder group for financial reports would be the legislature and the taxpayers. Are they the providers of capital for the public sector? Perhaps, but they will not be the only ones.

A key development particularly in developed countries is the transparency agenda, where governments are making available to the public vast amounts of data (financial and non-financial) for them to analyse and draw their own conclusions about service performance. The development of an IIRC framework would have to take account of this changing context, in particular, how such reports would add value to this agenda.

The principles of <IR> may well be very transferable to the public sector, but the problems and shortcomings of this narrative/non-financial reporting are also comparable to the experience in the private sector. For example in a review of UK government department annual reports included the following issues:

- In most cases reports were not 'forward looking' beyond the political cycle.
- Performance reporting was used as an exercise to showcase what was good and where positive progress had been made and hid what was bad.
- Reporting against performance outcomes was the least well done, inputs were satisfactory and to a more limited extent outputs too.

Consultation Questions

The IIRC welcomes comments on all aspects of the Draft International <IR> Framework (Draft Framework) from all stakeholders, whether to express agreement or to recommend changes.

The following questions are focused on areas where there has been significant discussion during the development process. Comments on any other aspect of the Draft Framework are also encouraged through the questions.

Please provide all comments in English.

All comments received will be considered a matter of public record and will be posted on the IIRC's website (www.theiirc.org).

Comments should be submitted by Monday 15th, July 2013.

Name:
Email:
Stakeholder group:

If replying on behalf of an Organization please complete the following:

Industry sector:
Geographical region:

Key Points

If you wish to briefly express any key points, or to emphasize particular aspects of your submission, or add comments in the nature of a cover letter, then the following space can be used for this purpose. Please do not repeat large amounts of material appearing elsewhere in your comments.

Professor Mervyn King
mervyn@mervynking.co.za; leighr@saica.co.za

Other

Integrated Reporting Committee
Not applicable
Africa

Key Points

The Integrated Reporting Committee of South Africa (IRC) supports the Framework. It is a clear and well written document offering a sound balance between providing guidance to assist preparers of integrated reports and flexibility for innovation in reporting. We strongly support the principles-based approach, as well as the principles-based requirements although we do have some suggestions in this regard which are set out in our comments below and include our recommendation for the "apply or explain" approach to be adopted

The IRC comprises a number of organisational bodies from diverse sectors of the economy (for a full list of members see www.sustainabilitysa.org). While the bulk of comments provided in this submission reflect the consensus view of the IRC members there are divergent views on certain key aspects of the Framework; these have been stated, with cogent motivations for the different views, under the relevant questions in this online submission.

The two main areas prompting the divergent views within the IRC are the primary audience of the report and the definition of materiality. While some members support the view of the primary audience being the providers of financial capital (1.6), other members have significant reservations about this proposal. The divergent views carried through to the related area of materiality.

Chapter 1: Overview

Principles-Based Requirements

To be in accordance with the Framework, an integrated report should comply with the principles-based requirements identified throughout the Framework in bold italic type (paragraphs 1.11-1.12).

1. *Should any additional principles-based requirements be added or should any be eliminated or changed? If so, please explain why.*

Interaction With Other Reports and Communications

The <IR> process is intended to be applied continuously to all relevant reports and communications, in addition to the preparation of an integrated report. The integrated report may include links to other reports and communications, e.g., financial statements and sustainability reports. The IIRC aims to complement material developed by established reporting standard setters and others, and does not intend to develop duplicate content (paragraphs 1.18-1.20).

2. *Do you agree with how paragraphs 1.18-1.20 characterize the interaction with other reports and communications?*
3. *If the IIRC were to create an online database of authoritative sources of indicators or measurement methods developed by established reporting standard setters and others, which references should be included?*

While we agree with the approach of principles-based requirements we would like to point out the inconsistent use of imperative and bold type lettering in the Framework. Several of the bold type sentences/ paragraphs include examples of a context likely to be encountered or of explanatory guidance, rather than a clear statement of what is required (also see Question 24 in this regard).

Given that many companies are still in the early stage of their integrated reporting journey we suggest that the "apply or explain" approach be adopted for the principles-based requirements set out in the Framework.

We suggest the following additional requirements:

- Chapter 3 Guiding Principles: As we have stated under Question 15, we suggest two additional separately listed guiding principles, namely transparency and accessibility of information. If these are accepted as new guiding principles they should accordingly be stated in bold type as requirements in line with the other guiding principles.
- Remuneration: The last bullet point of 4.11 should be stated as a requirement given the importance of remuneration, namely: "How remuneration and incentives are linked to value creation in the short, medium and long term, including how they are linked to the organisation's use of and effects on the capitals."
- Statement from the governance body: It is widely accepted that a company's board is responsible for corporate reporting. Accordingly, the integrated report should, as a requirement, carry such a statement from the governance body (per 5.18). This is a matter of credibility and reassurance, and it's important to know that when a judgement call is being made about materiality and the content of the report that it is done so at the highest level of authority, accountability and responsibility. Further, any future assurance of the report will be premised on the basis that the highest governance body accepts and acknowledges its responsibility for the report. Further, we suggest that the important role of leadership in the organisation's value creation over time receive more prominence in the Framework and consideration be given to addressing this in the chapter on fundamental concepts (see further comments in this regard under Question 10).
- Reporting time frame: The first sentence of 5.24 should be a requirement given the importance to a particular organisation and industry, namely:

"The length of each reporting time frame and the reason for such length are disclosed in an integrated report, and may affect the nature of the information disclosed."

- We agree and have no further comment.
- A source of accepted and authoritative indicators and measurement methods could be extremely useful to report preparers and could assist assurance providers as it will offer 'frameworks' for topic-specific information. Deciding on which sources to include in the database, however, could be subjective and hence controversial for the IIRC. Moreover, such a list would need to be kept current and regularly updated. Perhaps the question the IIRC should be publicly asking here is what are the principles that such authoritative sources should be based on? If such a list of reference sources is provided it is suggested that the list carry a disclaimer to the effect that the reference sources are not endorsed by the IIRC.
- Possible reference sources to include in such a list are:
    - ISO 26000 International Standard on Social Responsibility - This guidance standard, although not freely available, provides a detailed set of expectations and 'international norms of behaviour'; these expectations can be used as part of a structured process by organisations to inform the development of indicators. The ISO 26000 bibliography gives a comprehensive listing of the authoritative international instruments used to inform the guidance and Annex 1 provides reference to a useful set of additional information sources.
    - Other sources include the Global Reporting Initiative, the International Accounting Standards Board, Carbon Disclosure Project, AccountAbility and the World Business Council for Sustainable Development. Some sources relate mainly to one or more of the capitals (as opposed to a comprehensive approach), but could be useful in promoting understanding of the impacts and interdependencies within and among the different capitals.

Other

4. *Please provide any other comments you have about Chapter 1.*

Chapter 2: Fundamental Concepts

The Capitals (Section 2B)

The Framework describes six categories of capital (paragraph 2.17). An organization is to use these categories as a benchmark when preparing an integrated report (paragraphs 2.19-2.21), and should disclose the reason if it considers any of the capitals as not material (paragraph 4.5).

5. *Do you agree with this approach to the capitals? Why/why not?*
6. *Please provide any other comments you have about Section 2B?*

Business Model (Section 2C)

A business model is defined as an organization's chosen system of inputs, business activities, outputs and outcomes that aims to create value over the short, medium and long term (paragraph 2.26).

7. *Do you agree with this definition? Why/why not?*

The primary audience of the report (1.6 – 1.8)

As mentioned in the Key Points section, while some members support the wording of 1.6 others disagreed with the primary audience of the report being providers of financial capital. The points raised under both views are stated below.

It must be noted that both views agree on certain fundamental issues. These include the stakeholder inclusive approach as elucidated in the King Code of Governance for South Africa 2009 (King III), the concept of the co-creation of value involving all forms of capital, and that an organisation should be directed and managed on an integrated thinking basis.

On the stakeholder inclusive approach, it is acknowledged by all that an organisation's highest governing body considers, as stated in King III, "… the legitimate interests and expectations of stakeholders on the basis that this is in the best interests of the company, and not merely as an instrument to serve the interests of the shareholder". A truly stakeholder inclusive approach means that in acting in the best interests of the company the legitimate interests of all stakeholders must be taken into account and appropriate trade-offs be made based on what is in the best interests of the company in the particular circumstances, realising that not all interests may be accommodated. This understanding of the stakeholder inclusive approach is supported by all as the appropriate way for an organisation to make decisions, with the divergent aspect being on how that should be reported. In other words, the main point of departure of the two views is the difference in the 'lens' used in compiling the integrated report, namely providers of financial capital versus all key stakeholders of the organisation.

The points raised in support of providers of financial capital as the primary audience of the report are:

- An effective annual report (that addresses many of the shortcomings with of traditional annual reports) should be responsive to the material interests of its particular target audience. Seeking to meet the information requests of all stakeholders in one report
- We agree with this approach and welcome that it is one of the "fundamental concepts" that underpins integrated reporting.

Experience in South Africa has shown that this approach to the capitals is a compelling means for fostering a deeper and more integrated understanding of value creation, and for developing an appreciation within organizations of the important contribution of societal (human, social and natural capital) and environmental issues on organizational value.

- We support the aim of encouraging organizations to use the categories of capital as defined as a benchmark when preparing a report, and to disclose the reasons as to why it might consider any of the capitals as not material. And suggest that consideration be given for companies to disclose how they define their capitals.
- Figure 4's explanatory caption: The goal of this diagram is to increase understanding of the relationship and interdependencies between the various capital stocks, and in particular to emphasize that manufactured and financial capital stocks are products of, and dependent on, human, social and intellectual capital stocks, which in turn are products of, and dependent on, natural capital. Financial and manufactured capital stocks cannot be built systematically at the expense of human, social and natural capital. The current caption does not adequately reflect the interrelationships and dependencies between the capitals at an organizational level as described above.

- We support the definition of business model as stated. The following matters, however, could be considered for inclusion in the business model section: first, not all business models aim to create long-term value as some explicitly aim to create short-term value and hence are viable in the short term; second, the presentation of a linear set of inputs and outputs fails to convey the other essential dynamics that make business models work, namely the value proposition and the profit formula.
- There is an argument for saying that any business model aims primarily to create financial value in the short term, but must take into account the impact it has on other value capitals in order to prosper in the medium and long term.

Business Model (Section 2C) Continued

Outcomes are defined as the internal and external consequences (positive and negative) for the capitals as a result of an organization's business activities and outputs (paragraphs 2.35-2.36).

8. *Do you agree with this definition? Why/why not?*
9. *Please provide any other comments you have about Section 2C or the disclosure requirements and related guidance regarding business models contained in the Content Elements Chapter of the Framework (see Section 4E)?*

Other

10. *Please provide any other comments you have about Chapter 2 that are not already addressed by your responses above.*

Chapter 3: Guiding Principles

Materiality and Conciseness (Section 3D)

Materiality is determined by reference to assessments made by the primary intended report users (paragraphs 3.23-3.24). The primary intended report users are providers of financial capital (paragraphs 1.6-1.8).

11. *Do you agree with this approach to materiality? If not, how would you change it?*

We agree with the definition as stated. It offers a useful approach and is a vital component in the value chain as it connects processes with the impact on capitals.

There should be greater emphasis that strategy flows from business model; this will serve to increase understanding of the differences. Accordingly, in section 4E the order should be first business model and then strategy.

In 2.30 - 2.33, the description of "business activities" should emphasize that the value drivers are to be communicated here. Paragraph 2.45 - which explains value drivers - may be better placed in the section on business activities.

In 4.23 the first bullet point, clarity is needed on what "elements" are being referred to.

Greater clarity is needed on the disclosure requirements for organizations with multiple business models, such as those with diverse businesses or those that operate across geographic regions.

Paragraph 4.25 covers the instance of an investment holding company. Guidance should be provided as to the boundary to be applied in order to ensure there is a still a good understanding of the underlying operations of the entity and its investments. Further, this boundary should be clearly disclosed in the report of the holding company.

We suggest that a requirement is made for the organization to define in the report what it understands by the short, medium and long term as these timescales will different for different industries. This should be briefly explained with reference to the business model.

The section on value creation is thorough and better defines value more broadly than in the past. We note that there is no stated definition of value in the Framework, however, the second bullet point in 2.37 more or less defines value. This implied definition should be explicitly stated in the Framework. For instance: "Value is the increase, decrease or transformation of the capitals the organization uses or affects through its activities or outputs". Again, it is implied, but not explicitly stated, that the consequential outcomes affected by the organization is the value created by the organization.

The two divergent views on the primary audience for the report being the providers of financial capital, as set out under Question 4, have direct relevance for the questions on materiality and should be read with the comments below. The two divergent views on materiality are stated below.

Agree with the approach to materiality:

The materiality principle and approach, as currently worded, underpins the underlying objective of integrated reporting and, if appropriately adopted, will result in integrated reports that address many of the shortcomings with existing annual reports. The principle recognizes and supports the reasoning as to why "an integrated report should be prepared primarily for providers of financial capital". This view is supported by the following points:

An effective corporate report should be responsive to the material interests of its target audience and seeking to meet the information requests of all stakeholders in one report may detract from the ability to distil true materiality. The aim of the organization's other detailed reports is to provide information of material interest to different stakeholders in a medium and using language appropriate to those stakeholders.

Responsible and informed providers of financial capital are seen to have an interest in the organization's ability to create value in the short, medium and long term and as such serve as a useful proxy for individuals and organizations from other stakeholder groups similarly interested in the organisation's capacity to create value over time.

In following the requirements of the Framework the report will necessarily reflect on the extent to which key resources and stakeholder relationships materially impact on value, and will provide insight into the quality of relationships with key stakeholders and how the organisation responds to their legitimate interests and expectations (in so far as these impact on value creation). An effective report will thus be responsive to key stakeholder interests and critical societal issues over the short, medium and long term even though it is targeted primarily at providers of financial capital.

In preparing the report for the primary financial audience the organisation will do so informed by the guiding principles and content elements of the Framework - even when this would result in disclosure of information not currently requested by the target audience. The fact that the organisation might have providers of financial capital who, for instance, are interested only in short-term value creation or who fail to appreciate the organisation's dependency on certain capitals, does not take precedence over the principles-based requirements of the Framework.

12. *Please provide any other comments you have about Section 3D or the Materiality determination process (Section 5B).*

Reliability and Completeness (Section 3E)

Reliability is enhanced by mechanisms such as robust internal reporting systems, appropriate stakeholder engagement, and independent, external assurance (paragraph 3.31).

13. *How should the reliability of an integrated report be demonstrated?*
14. *Please provide any other comments you have about Section 3E.*

Other

15. *Please provide any other comments you have about Chapter 3 that are not already addressed by your responses above.*

It is suggested that consideration be given to the guidance on materiality focusing on identifying the minimum factors that need to be taken into account in the process, such as the value drivers, the organisation's affects on the capitals, the risks and opportunities arising in context, and stakeholder perspectives.

We fully support the disclosure of the organisation's materiality determination process. This will help in fostering greater accountability and engagement in the process by "senior management and those charged with governance." By being held to account, it is hoped they will be incentivised to apply their minds appropriately.

The role of those charged with governance is crucial in addressing reliability and completeness. This body should take responsibility for the report and its content and be seen to be doing so by its 'responsibility statement' included in the report.

The reliability of nonfinancial data should be assessed in the same way as that of financial data, and this includes internal controls and assurance.

In seeking to demonstrate reliability, the following aspects could be included in the report: an account of the internal information and data gathering systems and control measures; a balanced account of the outcomes of key stakeholder engagement processes; a description of the materiality determination process; details on the external verification process (scope and findings); and information on the role of senior management in the report process and their accountability for the outcome of the process.

There is a concern that organisations omit or downplay negative matters and inflate positive information in their reports, thus achieving balance is an area that requires research and more guidance.

No further comments.

Transparency and accessibility of information should be separately listed as guiding principles: While both of these principles are already mentioned in the Framework, or at least alluded to, it is submitted that these are higher order principles and should thus be separately listed as guiding principles in chapter 3. It is noted that "conciseness" and "completeness" are already stated as guiding principles, but that these are the means to achieve transparency and accessibility of information.

Future-orientated information: Future-oriented information provides important information to report users. We suggest that the Framework encourage a statement in the report by management/ governance body, as follows: "An integrated report contains future orientated or forward looking information that is inherently subject to uncertainty and the assumptions and outcomes may differ from those portrayed in the report".

Competitive advantage: There is a concern that some organisations may choose to hide behind the mask of competitive advantage. It is suggested that those charged with governance (possibly through the audit committee if appropriate) should be required to interrogate these matters.

Chapter 4: Content Elements

16. *Please provide any comments you have about Chapter 4 that are not already addressed by your responses above (please include comments on the Content Element Business Model [Section 4E] in your answer to questions 7-9 above rather than here).*

Chapter 5: Preparation and Presentation

Involvement of Those Charged With Governance (Section 5D)

Section 5D discusses the involvement of those charged with governance, and paragraph 4.5 requires organizations to disclose the governance body with oversight responsibility for <IR>.

17. *Should there be a requirement for those charged with governance to include a statement acknowledging their responsibility for the integrated report? Why/why not?*
18. *Please provide any other comments you have about involvement of those charged with governance (Section 5D).*

The content elements are comprehensive and appropriate. We support the overall approach of not prescribing a proposed order and applaud framing the principles-based requirements in the form of a question for each content element.

The requirement included in 4.5 for the disclosure of "The nature and magnitude of material trade-offs that influence value creation over time" may not be practical as the trade-offs may not always be quantifiable.

In the "Governance" content element, we suggest that this include the influence and review by directors of the internal controls of the organisation.

Opportunities and risks: In paragraph 4.16, the word "boilerplate" is used. It is suggested that this is better phrased in the positive, for instance as: "Information on risks and opportunities must be specific to the organisation. Lists of general industry risks and opportunities should be avoided. The aim is to enable the user of the report to apply the information in order to assess the organisation's current and future exposure and the suitability of actions whether proactive or reactive."

We advocate that there should be a requirement for those charged with governance to include in the report a statement acknowledging its collective responsibility for the report. The following reasons are given in support:

- This body has ultimate responsibility for the information in the integrated report, and in many jurisdictions directors are legally responsible for corporate reporting. Further, this body may not knowingly portray incorrect information or incomplete information in the report regardless of whether or not there is a statement in the report.
- Evidence of the acknowledgement of the collective responsibility of the body adds to the "credibility" of a report and provides reassurance to users. It is important for users to know that when a judgment call is being made about materiality and the content of the report, that it is done so at the highest possible level of authority, accountability and responsibility.

- The unwillingness of this body to expressly acknowledge its responsibility for the report could raise questions and be negatively perceived.
- Future external assurance of the report, or any part of it, will be premised on the basis that the highest governing body first accept and acknowledge its responsibility for the report before a provider will express assurance.

We are aware that there may be some reluctance by those charged with governance to acknowledge responsibility through such a statement in the report because the potential legal implications of the content of the report are still unclear. Other concerns include the reliability of the information presented and whether the information has been internally assured. Requiring this body to acknowledge responsibility may thus prove to be an evolutionary process in some jurisdictions, but there are numerous benefits to be had. For instance, it will ensure there are better controls over the information flowing into the report, it will add to the robustness of the disclosure provided, and it will give the governing body itself greater comfort not only from an external reporting perspective but also from an internal decision-making one.

In the statement per paragraph 5.18, we suggest the deletion of the word "conclusion" in the third bullet point as the governance body would always give an opinion, rather than a conclusion, as to whether the integrated report is presented in accordance with the Framework.

No further comments.

Credibility (Section 5E)

The Framework provides reporting criteria against which organizations and assurance providers assess a report's adherence (paragraph 5.21).

19. *If assurance is to be obtained, should it cover the integrated report as a whole, or specific aspects of the report? Why?*
20. *Please provide any other comments you have about Credibility (Section 5E). Assurance providers are particularly asked to comment on whether they consider the Framework provides suitable criteria for an assurance engagement.*

Other

21. *Please provide any other comments you have about Chapter 5 that are not already addressed by your responses above (please include comments on the materiality determination process [Section 5B] in your answer to question 11 above rather than here).*

It must be acknowledged that it is the board's role to ensure that a system of internal controls exists allowing the organization to report information in a credible manner. The board has the responsibility for determining whether internal or external assurance obtained by them fulfils this objective. To the extent that full external assurance on the integrated report is requested by a board, the board will need to assess who the assurance report will be directed at and who the audience is, the level of external assurance required (reasonable or limited assurance), by whom the assurance will be provided, and what frameworks will be used.

We see the need for independent external assurance on the entire report as this will enhance credibility and increase reliability.

Obtaining assurance over the report in its entirety requires the development of new guidance and processes to support assurance providers in the application of existing standards. One approach to assurance may involve a multi-disciplinary team of assurance providers, each having the requisite knowledge and skills in frameworks applicable to specific subject matter information. This approach may develop over time to allow for one assurance provider to act as a facilitator of the assurance over the entire report, which is based on the reports issued by the multi-disciplinary team of assurance providers (with the responsibility being that of the collective of assurance providers). There are many other approaches currently being considered.

We realize achievement of assurance on the entire report will be a journey given the current lack of theoretical know-how. Right now, it will prove difficult to obtain reasonable assurance over the entire report, and for certain sections of the report even limited assurance may prove to be a challenge.

It is acknowledged that assurance can currently be sought on specific aspects of the report, such as: selected areas, specific financial data and clearly identified nonfinancial data, and the accuracy of information extracted from other reports. This approach is building the extent of assurance coverage from the bottom up. Another approach would be to consider assurance from the top down, i.e. begin with assurance over the entire integrated report and exclude specific areas that may still pose a challenge to assurance providers.

An area that could concern assurance providers is that of future-oriented information.

We fully support the work of the international research project looking at the assurance of the integrated report, under the leadership of the IRBA's Sustainability Standing Committee, and look forward to their ground-breaking research report.

It is noted that chapter 5 does not contain any specific bold type requirements. It may thus be inferred that there are no clear 'principle disclosures required' which might provide "suitable criteria" for an assurance provider to report against. This may mitigate against attempts for the chapter to provide a basis for an independent external assurance provider to express an opinion on the integrated report as a whole, or on aspect of it. The IAASB Framework defines an assurance engagement as: "An engagement in which a practitioner expresses a conclusion designed to enhance the degree of confidence of the intended users other than the responsible party about the outcome of the evaluation or measurement of a subject matter against criteria. The outcome of the evaluation or measurement of a subject matter is the information that results from applying the criteria".

We note the importance of achieving a Framework that meets the needs of reporting criteria suitable for assurance, namely relevance, completeness, neutrality, understandability and reliability. While it is important that the Framework is considered in detail for suitability, a significant determining factor of whether the Framework provides suitable criteria for an assurance engagement is the actual process followed during exposure and the responsible and transparent consideration of comments received before the Framework is finalized.

The Framework suggests that where relevant information is contained on the organization's website that this be cross-referenced in the integrated report. We suggest that where such other information has been assured, that the related assurance report also be presented on the website.

Overall View

22. *Recognizing that <IR> will evolve over time, please explain the extent to which you believe the content of the Framework overall is appropriate for use by organizations in preparing an integrated report and for providing*

report users with information about an organization's ability to create value in the short, medium and long term?

Development of <IR>

23. *If the IIRC were to develop explanatory material on <IR> in addition to the Framework, which three topics would you recommend be given priority? Why?*

Other

24. *Please provide any other comments not already addressed by your responses to Questions 1-23.*

Please save the completed PDF form to your computer and submit via the IIRC website at www.theiirc.org/consultationdraft2013

The Framework has the potential to prompt a much needed shift in the corporate and investor understanding of value creation. It provides a very useful outline and set of principles for use by preparers but still allows flexibility to innovate.

For the Framework to achieve its aims, an effective communication and awareness raising campaign, including engagement with the business media and increased engagement with the financial sector, is needed.

It is suggested that clear guidance be given by the IIRC to clarify the role of the integrated report and that of the sustainability report. There is a need to explain the commonality and the differences, and to lessen the apparent confusion particularly after the release of the GRI's G4 Guidelines.

The process of determining materiality and the matter prioritization process. This is a difficult judgment area and it would be helpful to have a set of tools to assist preparers and reviewers in exercising judgment.

Content Elements – more practical guidance is needed specifically on the "Business model". For instance, on outcomes and how they relate to the organization's reporting boundary, with specific guidance on the information to be sought from suppliers particularly outlying tier 3 suppliers; the disclosure requirements relating to the business model and particularly for diverse businesses/ conglomerates that operate across geographic regions or industry sectors. In this regard there may be merit for offering fictitious worked examples similar to those provided in A4S's Connected Reporting: A practical guide with worked examples (http://www.accountingforsustainability.org/connected-reporting/connected-reporting-a-how-to-guide. More practical guidance is also needed on possible content for "Future outlook".

The capitals model - There are many nuances and aspects to consider. More guidance is sought on how capitals are transformed, how they interact, and how the causes and effects should be articulated. Further, there should be additional separate guidance on the financial materiality of human, social and natural capital (see ACCA's Is Natural Capital a Material Issue http://www.accaglobal.com/en/research-insights/environmental-accountability/natural-capital.html)

More guidance on the role of leadership in the organization's short, medium and long term viability is needed.

The drafting convention applied in the Framework needs to be consistent in the manner in which the "bold type requirements" are presented. The bold type text should be clearly phrased as matters that should be included in an integrated report that claims to have been prepared in accordance with this Framework. There needs to be clearer identification between a principle-based requirement and explanatory guidance. Further, there needs to be consistent application of the words "should", "must" and "shall".

15 July 2013
International Integrated Reporting Council
10 Lincoln's Inn Fields
Holborn
London
WC 2A 3BP
United Kingdom
Dear Sir/Madam,

SAICA SUBMISSION ON THE CONSULTATION DRAFT OF THE INTERNATIONAL INTEGRATED REPORTING (IR) FRAMEWORK

In response to your request for comments on the *Consultation Draft of the International Integrated Reporting (IR) Framework*, attached is the comment letter which has resulted from the deliberations of many members of our CFO Forum (top 40 Listed companies and top 5 State Owned Enterprises) in a variety of industries and the Accounting Practices Committee (APC) of The South African Institute of Chartered Accountants (SAICA), which comprises members from reporting organisations, regulators, auditors, IFRS specialists and academics.

We thank you for the opportunity to provide comments on this document.

Please do not hesitate to contact us should you wish to discuss any of our comments.

Yours faithfully,

Sue Ludolph
Project Director – Financial Reporting
cc: Paul O'Flaherty (Chairman of the Accounting Practices Committee)
Danie Coetsee (Deputy Chairman of the Accounting Practices Committee)

SAICA SUBMISSION ON THE CONSULTATION DRAFT OF THE INTERNATIONAL INTEGRATED REPORTING (IR) FRAMEWORK GENERAL COMMENTS

We welcome the Consultation Draft of the International Integrated Reporting Framework *(Consultation Draft)*. We are supportive of the Consultation Draft and we believe that it will be a useful document for organizations when embarking on the journey of preparing an Integrated Report.

Despite having reviewed the website, we are still concerned about how the International Integrated Reporting Council (IIRC) plans to legitimize the Integrated Reporting (IR) process globally and intends driving this process forward. We believe this is an essential part of global acceptance of IR and should be clearly communicated.

Many listed companies in South Africa have been preparing an Integrated Report for a few years and we are of the view that this is a journey and that IR will be enhanced over time, as long as the Framework remains principle-based. We therefore encourage the IIRC to continue along this path.

We reiterate the comments we made in our previous comment letter that there was also concern amongst our constituents that smaller listed companies, pension funds and medical schemes would struggle to produce an Integrated Report initially due to resource and experience constraints and recommended that, although the Framework is principle based, additional prescriptive guidance should be provided.

We have a concern regarding the achievability of comparability and this will include the lack of a standardized set of Key Performance Indicators and a core set of material issues by industry.

We also suggest that guidance is needed on how the Global Reporting Initiatives G4 guidelines will fit in with the Framework's Integrated Annual Report.

Chapter 1: Overview

Principles-Based Requirements

1. *Should any additional principles-based requirements be added or should any be eliminated or changed? If so, please explain why.*

We agree that there should be a list of principle-based requirements.

Our constituents had strong views against the proposals that the primary audience of the integrated report should be the "*providers of financial capital*". While it is mentioned in paragraph 1.7 that an Integrated Report is likely to benefit all stakeholders interested in an organization's ability to create value over time, it does not follow that such benefit will be achieved from the Integrated Report if the primary audience is limited to the "*providers of financial capital*". Furthermore limiting the scope of IR also has implications for the determination of materiality and what is €included in the integrated report. IR is meant to be the product of a process of integrated thinking, so limiting the audience of the Integrated Report to primarily those "*providers of financial capital*" is inappropriate in our view.

Furthermore IR should tell a story of an organisation, its performance, how it has created value for its stakeholders and its impact on the society in which it operates. The impact would be relevant to all stakeholders.

In South Africa we have seen a distinct evolution from the "enlightened shareholder" approach to the "stakeholder inclusive" approach. The King III Report on Corporate Governance in South Africa (King III) states clearly that in the former approach "stakeholders are only considered in as far as it would be in the interests of shareholders to do so", while in the more inclusive approach, the legitimate interests and expectations of stakeholders are considered "on the basis that this is in the best interests of the organisation, and not merely as an instrument to serve the interests of the shareholder".

Based on our experience in South Africa with King III, we are of the view that the more inclusive approach is more appropriate to follow for IR too.

Expectations of sound corporate governance in an organisation is equally appropriate for providers of other capitals beyond only financial capital.

Our constituents had concerns about the proposal that organisations should apply all the principle-based requirements identified in bold italic type in order to comply with the Framework as mentioned in paragraph 1.11. This principle is inappropriate given that Integrated Reporting is a journey and smaller listed companies would struggle to apply all the principle-based requirements. We propose to the IIRC that paragraph 1.11 should be re-worded to indicate that organisations should state which sections of the Framework they have complied with as opposed to a prohibition on partial compliance.

There are no bold type principles in the fundamental concepts and preparation and presentation sections. We propose that the IIRC consider cross referencing appropriate principles in the fundamental concepts and preparation and presentation section as mentioned in paragraph 1.11 to Chapters 3 and 4.

We consider the 'forward orientation' guiding principal requirement and the 'not disclosing if considered an issue regarding competitive advantage' clause challenging or conflicting concepts. Further guidance should be provided on how this is governed to ensure that non-disclosure of material information is not placed under the banner of 'not disclosed due to competitive advantage'. Further consideration should also be made on whether future oriented information (e.g. financial forecasting) is allowed to be provided with regards to certain stock exchange listing requirements.

Interaction With Other Reports and Communications

2. *Do you agree with how paragraphs 1.18-1.20 characterize the interaction with other reports and communications?*

The Consultation Draft indicates that the Integrated Report should be a stand-alone document with links to the other reports and communications that the organisation prepares. While there is reference in paragraph 1.18 to the fact that the IR process is intended to be applied to all relevant reports and communications, the focus on an entire integrated process is not coming across strongly enough and should be emphasised more in our opinion.

Paragraph 1.18 also states that "*it is anticipated that a stand-alone integrated report will be prepared annually in line with the statutory financial reporting cycle*", we would like the IIRC to clarify the period to which the financial reporting cycle relates to, whether it is the current year, previous year etc. In addition, some constituents who have interim and quarterly reporting requirements raised the issue as to how integrated reporting should be applied; if the intent is that integrated reporting is a "way of doing business" then it would be appropriate to apply the principles for these reporting cycles as well.

3. *If the IIRC were to create an online database of authoritative sources of indicators or measurement methods developed by established reporting standard setters and others, which references should be included?*

In our view, the IIRC should not create an online database of authoritative sources of indicators or measurement methods developed by established reporting standard setters and others. Authoritative sources differ per industry and the guidance could be seen as prescriptive and an endorsement of what is credible or not, leading to too much subjectivity. In addition it would also impose a burden on the IIRC to keep the list up-to-date.

Other

4. *Please provide any other comments you have about Chapter 1.*

There was much debate between our constituents on the need to have the "competitive harm" out clause in paragraph 1.12. The majority were of the view that it was good to have such a clause and that it would rely on the maturity of management and their integrity. A minority of our constituents were of the view that that such a clause could have unintended consequences. This is one of the areas where the constituents felt more explanatory material could be developed.

Chapter 2: Fundamental Concepts

The Capitals (Section 2B)

5. *Do you agree with this approach to the capitals? Why/why not?*

As noted in our response to question 1, there are no bold type principles in the fundamental concepts section. We propose that the IIRC consider cross referencing appropriate principles in the fundamentals concepts and presentation and preparation section as mentioned in paragraph 1.11 to Chapters 3 and 4.

Constituents from the financial services industry raised concerns with the manner in which the approach to capitals was expressed. They were of the view that care should be exercised in ensuring that the capitals approach does not give rise to prescriptive guidance as to how a business model should be presented (Figures 2 and 3 in chapter 2) and it should be emphasised that these figures are generic and should be viewed broadly.

6. *Please provide any other comments you have about Section 2B?*

We have no further comments.

Business Model (Section 2C)

7. *Do you agree with this definition? Why/why not?*

We agree with the definition of a business model.

8. *Do you agree with this definition? Why/why not?*

We agree with the definition of outcomes.

We propose that the IIRC provide guidance on how the outcomes of the organisation's business activities and outputs link to the value over the short, medium and long term. This is a further area where the constituents felt more explanatory material could be developed.

9. *Please provide any other comments you have about Section 2C or the disclosure requirements and related guidance regarding business models contained in the Content Elements Chapter of the Framework (Section 4E).*

Our constituents raised concerns that it will be challenging in practice to explain how an organisation creates value over time to all the stakeholders. They were also of the view that if the primary audience for IR was defined (and it would not necessarily be only providers of financial capital), organisations would be able to better explain the value over time to their primary stakeholders.

Other

10. *Please provide any other comments you have about Chapter 2 that are not already addressed by your responses above.*

We have no further comments.

Chapter 3: Guiding Principles

Materiality and Conciseness (Section 3D)

11. *Do you agree with this approach to materiality? If not, how would you change it?*

We agree with this approach to materiality.

12. *Please provide any other comments you have about Section 3D or the Materiality determination process (Section 5B).*

We propose that the IIRC include a requirement on the materiality determination process in paragraph 3.25 of the Consultation Draft to consider individual matters which are immaterial, but when they are combined they will be material.

We also propose that the IIRC change the first word of the first bullet of paragraph 3.25 from "*identifying*" to "*consider*" as part of the materiality determination process.

We further propose the IIRC link paragraph 3.25 to 5.13. In addition, Paragraph 3.28 links to paragraph 4.5, but should also link to paragraph 5.13. As materiality is discussed in the various sections of this Framework the references to materiality in the various sections could be structured more clearly and they should be linked together so as not to cause confusion of what is required or not.

Reliability and Completeness (Section 3E)

13. *How should the reliability of an integrated report be demonstrated?*

An Integrated Report should be drafted in such a way that the stakeholders will be able to understand the internal governance process that was undertaken to produce the report, as this will enhance the reliability of the information presented.

14. *Please provide any other comments you have about Section 3E.*

In terms of paragraph 3.42, where the banner of commercial sensitivity is not to be used inappropriately to avoid disclosure, consideration should be given as to how this is to be defined and governed.

Other

15. *Please provide any other comments you have about Chapter 3 that are not already addressed by your responses above.*

Some constituents from reporting organisations raised concerns about the manner in which consistency and comparability are expressed in the Consultation Draft. They are of the view that requiring comparability across organisations would limit the information that should be included in the Integrated Report; it should rather be a choice to help explain how an organisation measures its success. However, requiring comparability within an organisation and from period to period would be acceptable.

Chapter 4: Content Elements

16. *Please provide any comments you have about Chapter 4 that are not already addressed by your responses above (please include comments on the Content Element Business Model [Section 4E] in your answer to questions 7-9 above rather than here).*

The content elements in the Consultation Draft are appropriate. We do however have a few suggestions below. We propose that the IIRC include additional guidance under the "*Performance*" element that will assist entities to increase their comparability across periods by reporting against their targets. The additional guidance should not be prescriptive.

Paragraph 4.5 in our view is out of place and the layout is difficult to read and comprehend. Chapter 3 indicates that materiality is a principle, chapter

4 discusses the content elements and paragraph 4.5 says "*in addition to the Content Elements, an integrated report should disclose:*

- *The organisation's materiality determination process*"

and chapter 5 contains the presentation section. Paragraph 5.13 refers again to disclosing the organisation's materiality determination process. We reiterate our view that as materiality is discussed in the various sections of this framework, the references to materiality in the various sections could be structured more clearly and they should be linked together so as not to cause confusion of what is required or not.

We also propose that the IIRC consider swapping around chapter 3 and chapter 4, as it appears that certain of our constituents better understood the Guiding Principles in chapter 3 after they had read the Content Elements in chapter 4.

Furthermore, in our view the "Summary of Principles-Based Requirements" could be further enhanced as to how the chapters are related and an introductory sentence under each chapter and each content element linking it to the others would be useful.

We also propose that the IIRC include the additional disclosures in paragraph 4.5 should be grouped under their own heading entitled "Reporting Structure" (which should also be referred to in paragraph 4.1). This should be called 4A, and the other elements should be renumbered.

We also propose that the IIRC include "Remuneration" to the heading on 4B "*Governance*" as remuneration is a principle as explained in paragraph 4.12 and is such a relevant and pertinent matter.

Chapter 5: Preparation and Presentation

Involvement of Those Charged With Governance (Section 5D)

17. *Should there be a requirement for those charged with governance to include a statement acknowledging their responsibility for the integrated report? Why/why not?*

It is our view that there should be a requirement for those charged with governance to include a statement acknowledging their responsibility and to ensure the integrity of their Integrated Report (for example the Board and/or the Audit and Risk Committee should sign off the Integrated Report)

18. *Please provide any other comments you have about involvement of those charged with governance (Section 5D).*

We refer to our response to question 13, where we stated that an Integrated Report should be drafted in such a way that the stakeholders will be able to understand the internal governance process that was undertaken to produce the report, as this will enhance the reliability of the information presented.

Credibility (Section 5E)

19. *If assurance is to be obtained, should it cover the integrated report as a whole, or specific aspects of the report? Why?*

We are of the view that the Integrated Report should not be prescriptive on the issue of assurance. The manner in which that paragraph 5.20 is worded "organisations may seek independent, external assurance" is in line with a principled Integrated Report and the organisation can then decide how it would wish to deal with the issue of assurance on any part of the Integrated Report, if at all.

20. *Please provide any other comments you have about Credibility (Section 5E). Assurance providers are particularly asked to comment on whether they consider the Framework provides suitable criteria for an assurance engagement.*

The concept of combined assurance is defined in King III and was referred to in the previous IRC of South Africa discussion paper, but it has not been described in the Consultation Draft. It is our view that a brief description of what combined assurance is, be provided.

The majority of the constituents felt that the Consultation Draft does not provide suitable criteria for an assurance engagement that will be consistent across organisations. This is a further area where the constituents felt more explanatory material could be developed.

Other

21. *Please provide any other comments you have about Chapter 5 that are not already addressed by your responses above (please include comments*

on the materiality determination process [Section 5B] in your answer to question 11 above rather than here).

There are no bold type principles in Chapter 5. We propose that the IIRC consider the need to bold any pertinent sections in Chapter 5.

Integrated reporting can only be achieved if organisations have proper governance processes in place. We propose that the IIRC consider encouraging the organisations to have a concise Integrated Report and include all the other information as supplementary information by means of reference (for example information on how to determine materiality, etc.)

Overall View

22. *Recognizing that IR will evolve over time, please explain the extent to which you believe the content of the Framework overall is appropriate for use by organizations in preparing an integrated report and for providing report users with information about an organization's ability to create value in the short, medium and long term?*

We are supportive of the Integrated Reporting Framework and believe that it will evolve over time. We have already seen this evolution process in South Africa in the few years that our listed companies have been preparing them. We also believe that only by keeping the content of the Framework principle-based will it continue to evolve over time and would be useful for providing IR users with information about an organisation's ability to create value in the short, medium and long term.

Development of IR

23. *If the IIRC were to develop explanatory material on IR in addition to the Framework, which three topics would you recommend be given priority? Why?*

If the IIRC were to develop explanatory material on IR we would suggest the following:

- Guidance on how the outcomes of the organisation's business activities and outputs link to the value over the short, medium and long term (also linked to value chain across the capitals) ;

- Guidance on items which could be excluded due to commercial sensitivity; and
- Guidance on what information and/or elements of the integrated report could be assured and by whom.

Other

24. *Please provide any other comments not already addressed by your responses to Questions 1-23.*

We have no further comments.

#430952

Consultation Questions

The IIRC welcomes comments on all aspects of the Draft International <IR> Framework (Draft Framework) from all stakeholders, whether to express agreement or to recommend changes.

The following questions are focused on areas where there has been significant discussion during the development process. Comments on any other aspect of the Draft Framework are also encouraged through the questions.

Please provide all comments in English.

All comments received will be considered a matter of public record and will be posted on the IIRC's website (www.theiirc.org).

Comments should be submitted by Monday 15th, July 2013.

Name:
Email:
Stakeholder group:

If replying on behalf of an Organization please complete the following:

Industry sector:
Geographical region:

Key Points

If you wish to briefly express any key points, or to emphasize particular aspects of your submission, or add comments in the nature of a cover letter, then the following space can be used for this purpose. Please do not repeat large amounts of material appearing elsewhere in your comments.

Amy Pawlicki
wici-global-questions@wici-global.com
Other
World Intellectual Capital Initiative (WICI)
Not applicable
Global

Chapter 1: Overview

Principles-Based Requirements

To be in accordance with the Framework, an integrated report should comply with the principles-based requirements identified throughout the Framework in bold italic type (paragraphs 1.11-1.12).

1. *Should any additional principles-based requirements be added or should any be eliminated or changed? If so, please explain why.*

Interaction With Other Reports and Communications

The <IR> process is intended to be applied continuously to all relevant reports and communications, in addition to the preparation of an integrated report. The integrated report may include links to other reports and communications, e.g., financial statements and sustainability reports. The IIRC aims to complement material developed by established reporting standard setters and others, and does not intend to develop duplicate content (paragraphs 1.18-1.20).

2. *Do you agree with how paragraphs 1.18-1.20 characterize the interaction with other reports and communications?*

3. *If the IIRC were to create an online database of authoritative sources of indicators or measurement methods developed by established reporting standard setters and others, which references should be included?*

We support the contents, however we question the inclusion of item 4.5 as part of the requirements (please see our response to question 17 for further explanation of this point).

Yes, but we believe there is ongoing market confusion with respect to whether the IIRC is advocating for a separate, stand-alone integrated report, or whether it is acceptable for companies to incorporate <IR> into their existing reporting structures, and if the latter is acceptable, what companies should consider in doing so, for example to avoid duplication and to connect related information. Given that practice is likely to vary by jurisdiction, we believe that it is very important for the IIRC to clearly articulate that there is flexibility in terms of how a company might approach <IR> vis a vis their other reporting processes and channels.

Indicators suggested by METI (Japanese Ministry of Economy, Trade and Industry) and WICI serve as a useful reference, however, these are just examples as there are many sources of high-quality KPIs.

Instead of providing a set of KPIs, IIRC should recommend a set of common criteria for desirable attributes of KPIs to drive quality and consistency in the KPIs that companies choose to report on. The IIRC may wish to consult the

WICI Concept paper as a helpful example of such criteria, accessible at http://www.wici-global.com/kpis.

Other

4. *Please provide any other comments you have about Chapter 1.*

Chapter 2: Fundamental Concepts

The Capitals (Section 2B)

The Framework describes six categories of capital (paragraph 2.17). An organization is to use these categories as a benchmark when preparing an integrated report (paragraphs 2.19-2.21), and should disclose the reason if it considers any of the capitals as not material (paragraph 4.5).

5. *Do you agree with this approach to the capitals? Why/why not?*
6. *Please provide any other comments you have about Section 2B?*

Business Model (Section 2C)

A business model is defined as an organization's chosen system of inputs, business activities, outputs and outcomes that aims to create value over the short, medium and long term (paragraph 2.26).

7. *Do you agree with this definition? Why/why not?*

We agree with the approach as it is important to build a common understanding that capitals other than just financial and manufactured can contribute to the organization's unique value creation potential. Additional illustrative examples may be helpful in explaining the approach to the capitals, as may a reference to the more detailed IIRC background paper on the capitals.

Most of the social capitals in the draft framework are considered to be the organization's relationship capitals. There is already consensus among academics and practitioners around the definition of intellectual capital, and the expression of intellectual capital in the <IR> framework should reflect this accepted definition under which intellectual capital refers to human capital, relationship capital and organizational capital as a whole. Therefore, in our view the categorization of the capitals should be financial capital, manufactured capital, intellectual capital and natural capital.

It may be beneficial to further clarify in the framework that companies are not required to address each of the capitals, rather to consider each of the capitals and then to determine what to disclose following the materiality determination process.

It would also be beneficial to include in the <IR> framework a comparison between the traditional accounting definition of capital, and the concept of capital presented in the <IR> framework.

Yes we agree as the approach reflects the realities of business and the individual characteristics of each organization. The definition of outcomes could, however, be revised for clarity as explained in our response to question 8.

Business Model (Section 2C) Continued

Outcomes are defined as the internal and external consequences (positive and negative) for the capitals as a result of an organization's business activities and outputs (paragraphs 2.35-2.36).

8. *Do you agree with this definition? Why/why not?*
9. *Please provide any other comments you have about Section 2C or the disclosure requirements and related guidance regarding business models contained in the Content Elements Chapter of the Framework (see Section 4E)?*

Other

10. *Please provide any other comments you have about Chapter 2 that are not already addressed by your responses above.*

Chapter 3: Guiding Principles

Materiality and Conciseness (Section 3D)

Materiality is determined by reference to assessments made by the primary intended report users (paragraphs 3.23-3.24). The primary intended report users are providers of financial capital (paragraphs 1.6-1.8).

11. *Do you agree with this approach to materiality? If not, how would you change it?*

We do not disagree, however, the idea to regard 'outcome' as the impact on capitals may be improved. Output creates value, which has influence on society as well as the allocation of capitals for future value creation strategy.

It would be more clear if the framework were to provide a comparison between the traditional definition of value (corporate value=total market value), and the concept of value reflected in the consultation draft.

The explanation covering the fact that business models can change over time is not sufficient. The context of 4E can be misleading since it can be perceived to be required to disclose how the past business model is resilient for the future. Instead, it is desirable to require disclosure related to the resilience of the business model from the future perspective based on the recognition of risks and opportunities.

It would be clearer if the business model diagram were to articulate where the value is created. The concept of value can be included in the definition of outcome.

It would also be clearer if the framework were to provide a comparison between the traditional definition of business model (earning model with the focus on profit) and the concept of business model presented in the framework (value creation model with the focus on outcome).

Yes we agree.

12. *Please provide any other comments you have about Section 3D or the Materiality determination process (Section 5B).*

Reliability and Completeness (Section 3E)

Reliability is enhanced by mechanisms such as robust internal reporting systems, appropriate stakeholder engagement, and independent, external assurance (paragraph 3.31).

13. *How should the reliability of an integrated report be demonstrated?*
14. *Please provide any other comments you have about Section 3E.*

Other

15. *Please provide any other comments you have about Chapter 3 that are not already addressed by your responses above.*

It would be more beneficial if the materiality determination processes were to articulate assessing the importance of those matters in terms of potential effect on future value creation.

We agree with the articulation of the connectivity concept, and believe that this concept is critical in helping preparers to articulate their value creation story in an integrated and effective manner.

Chapter 4: Content Elements

16. *Please provide any comments you have about Chapter 4 that are not already addressed by your responses above (please include comments*

on the Content Element Business Model [Section 4E] in your answer to questions 7-9 above rather than here).

Chapter 5: Preparation and Presentation

Involvement of Those Charged With Governance (Section 5D)

Section 5D discusses the involvement of those charged with governance, and paragraph 4.5 requires organizations to disclose the governance body with oversight responsibility for <IR>.

17. *Should there be a requirement for those charged with governance to include a statement acknowledging their responsibility for the integrated report? Why/why not?*
18. *Please provide any other comments you have about involvement of those charged with governance (Section 5D).*

We do not view paragraph 4.5 as being on the same level as the other content elements, and therefore we do not believe it should be included in chapter 4 alongside the other content elements.

We believe it would be helpful for the framework to provide further clarification around Future Outlook. As already

mentioned, we believe it is important for companies to disclose information about business model, strategy and performance based on opportunities and risks and available capitals both in the past-to-present period and the present- to- future period.

Credibility (Section 5E)

The Framework provides reporting criteria against which organizations and assurance providers assess a report's adherence (paragraph 5.21).

19. *If assurance is to be obtained, should it cover the integrated report as a whole, or specific aspects of the report? Why?*
20. *Please provide any other comments you have about Credibility (Section 5E). Assurance providers are particularly asked to comment on whether they consider the Framework provides suitable criteria for an assurance engagement.*

Other

21. *Please provide any other comments you have about Chapter 5 that are not already addressed by your responses above (please include comments on the materiality determination process [Section 5B] in your answer to question 11 above rather than here).*

It is important to undertake a social collaborative process to ensure continuous improvement of the framework over time. As integrated reporting gains momentum, a feedback loop will develop between the investors who use integrated reports and the companies who prepare integrated reports, thereby improving the reporting process and informing ongoing framework development and maintenance.

Furthermore, if the reporting cycle is annual, it could be perceived that the organization is only expected to update the report on an annual basis. The IIRC might consider suggesting that organizations report major changes related to integrated reporting concepts through mid-term reports.

Overall View

22. *Recognizing that <IR> will evolve over time, please explain the extent to which you believe the content of the Framework overall is appropriate for use by organizations in preparing an integrated report and for providing report users with information about an organization's ability to create value in the short, medium and long term?*

Development of <IR>

23. *If the IIRC were to develop explanatory material on <IR> in addition to the Framework, which three topics would you recommend be given priority? Why?*

Other

24. *Please provide any other comments not already addressed by your responses to Questions 1-23.*

Please save the completed PDF form to your computer and submit via the IIRC website at www.theiirc.org/consultationdraft2013 "Evolve over time" is a core concept of the integrated reporting framework.

As long as the focus on this concept is maintained, the proposal of the draft framework serves as the appropriate starting point.

- Further explanation around each organization's freedom of choice about what to disclose
- Articulation of the attributes of high-quality KPIs (please see our response to question 3 for further clarification)
- Further explanation around the connectivity between the time horizons of past-to-present and present-to-future
- Further explanation to address the concept of comparability in the context of a principles-based framework, including a discussion of the need for transparency in disclosure where the traditional notion of comparability is not practical due to company-specific and industry-specific differences.
- Further explanation around the concept of "integrated thinking," which is introduced on page 9 of the draft framework.
- Further explanation/clarification on setting the scope of the reporting boundary, including consideration of where to set boundaries in addressing outcomes.

It could be further emphasized that it is important to disclose the total picture of value creation in a concise and integrated manner In addition, it is important to articulate the point that long-term investors value convincing evidence that informs future outlook, to support an understanding of what has changed vis a vis the past-to-present period.

It is desirable to encourage the use of a standard format (such as XBRL) to support the reusability of company disclosures from any source. Further, references between disclosures and referential sources can be expressed in the XBRL Taxonomies and reused by companies and analysts.

Internet web service/RSS (or 'broadcasting') distribution of company disclosures from disparate enterprise communities enable consumer/analyst assembly of concepts deemed relevant for their specific analysis. This standardized supply chain approach reflects a 'consumer' centric approach to 'reporting' wherein consumers integrate disclosures deemed relevant to their analysis. This consumer centric or 'pull' approach enables more cost effective processes while placing responsibility for transparency and relevance on producers and consumers respectively.

Furthermore, the recent EC Transparency Directive guidance includes 2020 incorporation of regulatory requirements for a harmonized electronic reporting format such as XBRL. This mandatory reporting requirement may enhance the demand for a comprehensive IIRC styled framework and related XBRL taxonomy to facilitate the desired enhancements in accessibility, analysis

and comparability. It may be useful for IIRC and WICI to enhance their collaboration and accelerate development and testing of XBRL taxonomies relevant for the EC Transparency Directive.

July 15, 2013
Mervyn King
Chairman
International Integrated Reporting Council
Submitted via www.theiirc.org/consultationdraft2013
Re: Consultation Draft of the International Integrated Reporting Framework

Dear Professor King,

The International Federation of Accountants (IFAC) values the opportunity to comment on the International Integrated Reporting Council (IIRC)'s *Consultation Draft of the International Integrated Reporting Framework* (the Framework) and seeks to provide the perspective of the global accountancy profession.

We highlight key matters before responding to the various questions in the addendum. Both our Professional Accountants in Business (PAIB) and our Small and Medium Practices (SMP) Committees played a central role in the development of our response, as a large part of their constituencies is involved in the planning, implementation, execution, evaluation, or improvement of integrated business reporting provided internally as a professional accountant in business or externally as a professional service delivered by an accountancy firm.

General Comments on the Framework

IFAC believes that high-quality reporting lies at the heart of strong and sustainable organizations, financial markets, and economies, as the disclosure of useful information is crucial for the various internal and external stakeholders who need to make informed decisions regarding an organization's capacity to create and preserve value. As organizations depend on their stakeholders for their sustainable success, it is in their interest to provide high-quality reports. In addition, high-quality reports are integral to the successful management of the business, as they promote better internal decision making and are one of the major drivers of sustainable organizational success.

Effective reporting should ensure that all internal and external stakeholders receive appropriate high-quality organizational reports in a timely fashion. In that light, IFAC welcomes the publication of the draft Framework, which can be truly called a landmark step forward in the evolution of organizational reporting, as it provides direction for how integrated reporting might look. We offer the following suggestions for further improvement of the Framework.

Stimulate Professional Judgment Through Principles-Based Application of the Framework

IFAC strongly supports the principles-based approach to integrated reporting that the IIRC takes and notes that taking this approach is more likely to result in a Framework that will be capable of application in a manner proportionate with the size of an entity. However, various sections the draft Framework use language that is difficult to reconcile with such a principles-based approach. For example, "to be in accordance with the Framework, an integrated report should *comply* with the principles-based *requirements*" (see the Overview section of Summary of Principles-Based Requirements). By referencing compliance with requirements, the Framework implies that there is only one prescribed way for integrated reporting. Throughout the document, these sentences could be rephrased from "*complying with the requirements*" to "*properly applying the principles*" to better capture the spirit of principles-based *application* of the Framework, thus stimulating professional judgment.

Organizations Should Determine the Intended Audience

IFAC believes the reason an integrated report should be prepared "primarily for providers of financial capital in order to support their financial capital allocation assessments" is not sufficiently explained (paragraph 1.6 and other sections).2 Paragraph 1.7 indicates that other stakeholders will also benefit from integrated reporting. Furthermore, it seems that a focus on providers of financial capital might be inconsistent with the wording in other parts of the Framework—such as in section 3.C, Stakeholder Responsiveness—where the broader concept of "key stakeholders" is used. Therefore, IFAC recommends the IIRC adopt a position whereby it suggests that each individual organization should determine its intended users of an integrated report based on its own particular circumstances, especially as the various stakeholders' interests are "likely to align over time" (see wording in paragraph 1.8). This would allow organizations to identify for themselves the primary stakeholder groups they would like to communicate/engage with through integrated reporting.

Providers of financial capital are not a homogeneous group and the various sections may have very different information needs.

Implementation

IFAC commends the IIRC on conducting a pilot program for integrated reporting. Clearly, the IIRC will learn a great deal from these pilots to assist in advancing the Framework and guiding future implementation. However, there are two areas where IFAC believes improvements could be made to the Framework that will assist in its implementation.

- Clearly defining and explaining some of the key concepts outlined in the Framework (examples provided in responses to some of the specific questions below)
- Streamlining, and better coordinating, figures used to help describe the Framework (see responses to question 9 below)

Ideally, many of the lessons learned from the pilot program, including the suitability of the Framework for the various types and sizes of organizations, could be taken into account when the IIRC finalizes the Framework. In addition, IFAC encourages the IIRC to consider developing guidance on how the Framework might be applied to smaller entities (e.g., via case studies, illustrative examples, etc.).

Suitable Criteria and Assurance

IFAC believes it is imperative that the Framework promotes reporting that provides suitable criteria against which preparers can consistently determine the appropriate content of an integrated report *and* assurance can be provided. The main characteristics of reported information that are generally considered suitable encompass relevance, completeness, reliability, neutrality, and level of understanding.

Assurance enhances the degree of confidence of intended users in the information being provided. Assurance on the integrated report should be provided in accordance with high-quality, internationally-accepted assurance standards. To achieve this end, IFAC believes it is important for the IIRC to liaise with the International Auditing and Assurance Standards Board in the development of the Framework.

Comments on Specific Questions

For the convenience of the development team, we have included our comments on the specific questions outlined in the IIRC Consultation Questions in the addendum to this response. We hope you find our recommendations useful and constructive as you finalize the Framework.

Please do not hesitate to contact me should you wish to discuss any of the matters raised in this submission. We also welcome further discussions on how IFAC can continue supporting the work of the IIRC.

Yours sincerely,

Fayezul Choudhury
Chief Executive Officer About IFAC

Through its membership, currently 173 professional accountancy organizations in 129 countries and jurisdictions, IFAC represents approximately 2.5 million accountants in public practice, industry and commerce, government, and education. As the global organization for the accountancy profession, IFAC is committed to contributing to the highest-quality professional services by the accountancy profession around the world.

Chartered Professional Accountants of Canada 277 Wellington Street West Toronto ON CANADA M5V 3H2 T. 416 977.3222 F. 416 977.8585 www.cpacanada.ca Comptables professionnels agréés du Canada 277, rue Wellington Ouest Toronto (ON) CANADA M5V 3H2 T. 416 204.3222 Téléc. 416 977.8585 www.cpacanada.ca

July 15, 2013
Mr. Paul Druckman, FCA
Chief Executive Officer
The International Integrated Reporting Council
By e-mail via website
www.theiirc.org/consultationdraft 2013

Dear Mr. Druckman:

Re: Consultation Draft of the International Framework – Integrated Reporting

Chartered Professional Accountants of Canada (CPA Canada) is pleased to comment on the Consultation Draft of the International Integrated Reporting Framework. CPA Canada is the national organization representing the Chartered Professional Accountant (CPA) profession in Canada. The Canadian Institute of Chartered Accountants (CICA) and The Society of Management Accountants of Canada (CMA Canada) created the organization on January 1, 2013, to support unification of the Canadian accounting profession under the CPA banner. CPA Canada is responsible for providing services to CAs and CMAs on behalf of CICA and CMA Canada as well as to CPAs and CGAs participating in the unification effort. CPAs will serve the public interest across all sectors of the economy with integrity, sound ethical practices, disciplined regulation and proven strategic management and financial expertise. Accounting bodies representing almost 90 per cent of Canada's professional accountants are committed to unification or have already merged under the CPA banner.

Our comments on the Consultation Draft have been formulated after promoting and reviewing it with primary stakeholders in Canada's performance reporting community. This included sponsoring the Canadian launch event for the Consultation Draft and explaining the proposals in a CPA Canada webinar attended by over 1,000 participants. The proposals were also reviewed with CPA Canada's Canadian Performance Reporting Board (CPRB) and Sustainability Advisory Board (SAB), the volunteer boards established to enhance the quality of organizations' external performance reporting and provide critical insight on priority sustainability issues. A working group was then established that reviewed the proposals in detail and developed this response, in consultation with the CPRB and SAB.

Our responses to the consultation questions are set out in the attachment to this letter. In addition, however, we have some general comments about an organization's ability to prepare an integrated report, the current demand for such a report, and the process to develop an integrated reporting framework.

CPA Canada agrees with the concept of an integrated report that would provide a concise report about how an organization's strategy, governance, performance and prospects lead to the creation of value. In today's business environment, there is general agreement that various aspects of the current business reporting framework need to be streamlined. As well, there is increased demand for environmental, social and governance information that has the potential to affect investment decisions to be better integrated and connected in one external report, instead of using today's separate reporting strands. In our view, however, few organizations currently have sufficiently integrated and robust systems and processes or an integrated thinking mindset necessary to generate a reliable integrated report.

While we agree there should be benefits to an integrated approach to reporting, we see little evidence, at least in Canada, that providers of financial capital are demanding an integrated report. In our view, there will need to be clearly demonstrated capital allocation benefits to encourage widespread voluntary adoption. In the meantime, however, we note over 90 companies have participated in the pilot program, and others may join them. These companies no doubt decided to participate in anticipation of reaping benefits from an integrated approach to reporting.

The concept of an integrated report as proposed by the IIRC is both new and complex. Accordingly, we are pleased that the IIRC has established a pilot program for both preparers and investors. The current workplan, however, calls for version 1 of the Framework to be published in December 2013, and for the pilot program to conclude in September 2014. There is much to be learned from the pilot program about issues with the Framework and how it can best be applied. Therefore, to maximize these insights, we believe the pilot program should be extended beyond September 2014. As well, we believe version 1 of the Framework should not be published until the pilot program is complete, to enable revisions to the draft Framework to consider everything learned from the pilot.

With the above points in mind, we provide our detailed comments on the Consultation Draft to foster the evolution of relevant integrated reporting. We hope they are useful. Should you wish to discuss them in greater detail, please contact Pamela Campagnoni, CPA, CA, CPA (Illinois) at pcampagnoni@cpacanada.ca, or Chris Hicks, CPA, CA at chicks@cpacanada.ca.

Yours truly,

Kevin J. Dancey, FCPA, FCA

President and CEO Chartered Professional Accountants of Canada 277 Wellington Street West Toronto ON CANADA M5V 3H2 T. 416 977.3222 F. 416 977.8585 www.cpacanada.ca Comptables professionnels agréés du Canada 277, rue Wellington Ouest Toronto (ON) CANADA M5V 3H2 T. 416 204.3222 Téléc. 416 977.8585 www.cpacanada.ca

RESPONSES TO IIRC CONSULTATION QUESTIONS

Chapter 1: Overview

Principles-Based Requirements

To be in accordance with the Framework, an integrated report should comply with the principles-based requirements identified throughout the Framework in bold italic type (paragraphs 1.11-1.12).

1. *Should any additional principles-based requirements be added or should any be eliminated or changed? If so, please explain why.*

Response: We do not think any additional principle-based requirements should be added to the Framework. However, some paragraphs in the Consultation Draft (CD) use prescriptive terminology that we find inconsistent with a principles-based framework, for example 4.12. We believe prescriptive terminology should be removed or altered to rectify this concern.

As well, the consistency and comparability principle would benefit from additional guidance about how to develop useful qualitative discussions that can help users draw comparisons between organizations.

Interaction With Other Reports and Communications

The <IR> process is intended to be applied continuously to all relevant reports and communications, in addition to the preparation of an integrated report. The integrated report may include links to other reports and communications, e.g., financial statements and sustainability reports. The IIRC aims to complement material developed by established reporting standard setters and others, and does not intend to develop duplicate content (paragraph 1.18-1.20).

2. *Do you agree with how paragraphs 1.18-1.20 characterize the interaction with other reports and communications?*

Response: No comment.

3. *If the IIRC were to create an online database of authoritative sources of indicators or measurement methods developed by established reporting standard setters and others, which references should be included?*

Response: Some examples of decision models to assist organizations determine appropriate measures would be useful. One such example would be CPA Canada's publication series *Future Value Drivers*.

Other

4. *Please provide any other comments you have about Chapter 1.*

Response:

Placement of Content

We believe the Overview section would be improved if the "audience" and "application of the framework" discussions were to be relocated to the Fundamental Concepts and Guiding Principles sections, respectively.

Extent of Detail Contemplated in an Integrated Report

The extent of detail anticipated in an integrated report is not clear. On the one hand, the CD notes it should be a concise communication about how strategy, governance, performance and prospects lead to the creation of value in the short, medium and long term. The idea of a concise report is further reinforced by the CD's reference to the need for additional reports such as financial statements to satisfy compliance needs. Accordingly, it seems that a report outside those required by the statutory reporting cycle is contemplated, which, for some information, would cross-reference such reports. On the other hand, all material matters are expected to be reported in an integrated report and this should include discussions such as a description of the business model and management processes such as materiality determination.

Further discussion of the level of detail contemplated would be useful. In Canada, for example, much of the information contemplated in the CD would seem to be captured by following CPA Canada's guide *Management's Discussion And Analysis – Guidance on Preparation and Disclosure*. As well, we note that in various areas, such as business model, risk, and materiality determination, investors who are familiar with an organization are not interested in the entire discussion, but rather focus on the changes from the last reporting period. In areas such as these, restricting the integrated report to a discussion of the changes and providing more information by cross-referencing to other publicly-filed documents could be a useful way of contributing to a concise report.

Timing of Integrated Report Preparation

There is significant concern about the proposal to prepare an integrated report at the same time as annual statutory reports. We believe this would create significant resource issues and that the CD should discuss the resource implications arising as a result of the proposed timing of an integrated report. At the same time, we recognize that if the integrated report is not prepared on a timely basis with all the statutory reporting it loses its value for investors.

Chapter 2: Fundamental Concepts

The Capitals (Section 2B)

The Framework describes six categories of capital (paragraph 2.17). An organization is to use these categories as a benchmark when preparing an integrated report (paragraphs 2.19-2.21), and should disclose the reason if it considers any of the capitals as not material (paragraph 4.5).

5. *Do you agree with this approach to the capitals? Why/why not?*

Response: We found the CD confusing as to the extent of compliance expected around reporting the six capitals in an integrated report. While the concept of the capitals set out in the CD provides useful guidance for organizations in determining whether they have considered all matters that are significant to performance, many organizations will find that the capitals in the CD are inconsistent with their approach to managing the business. As well, the capitals discussion focuses on the effects of each capital in isolation, whereas we believe a much more integrated discussion of capitals is needed. In addition, we believe the CD should be clear that there is no necessity for an integrated report to report in conformity with the six capitals discussed in the CD.

6. Please provide any other comments you have about Section 2B?

Response: No further comments.

Business Model (Section 2C)

A business model is defined as an organization's chosen system of inputs, business activities, outputs and outcomes that aims to create value over the short, medium and long term (paragraph 2.26).

7. Do you agree with this definition? Why/why not?

Response: While we agree that a discussion of an organization's business model will help users understand the organization, we believe the defined business model is oversimplified and incomplete. We do not believe that the Framework should define a business model or its components. It should be for organizations to communicate their business model in their own terms rather than be forced to comply with components established by the IIRC. Many organizations would summarize their business model in terms of matters that are driving change in the business. In this regard, we note that the CD places very little emphasis on technology in the Framework's discussion of business model, yet this is often the single most important factor for change in an organization.

8. Outcomes are defined as the internal and external consequences (positive and negative) for the capitals as a result of an organization's business activities and outputs (paragraphs 2.35-2.36). Do you agree with this definition? Why/why not?

Response: Refer to responses to questions 5 and 7.

9. Please provide any other comments you have about Section 2C or the disclosure requirements and related guidance regarding business models contained in the Content Elements Chapter of the Framework (Section 4E).

Response: No further comments.

Other

10. Please provide any other comments you have about Chapter 2 that are not already addressed by your responses above. 5

Response: The CD notes that an integrated report explains how an organization creates value over time. The value creation section of the CD notes that value encompasses not only the present value of future cash flows but other forms of value that the organization creates through the increase, decrease or transformation of the capitals. Meanwhile, the capitals section of the CD notes that some of the capitals would have different values depending on the perspective taken. As well, that section acknowledges that it would not be practical to expect organizations to attempt to quantify all uses of and effects on the capitals, apparently recognizing that in some circumstances there may be no reasonable way to value a capital.

These statements result in a confusing image of what is meant by creating value over time. We believe the value creation and capitals discussions need to be better integrated and focus on what would be a useful representation for a provider of financial capital. This part of the CD might be enhanced if it were to concentrate on the traditional idea of value creation for the organization, measured in discounted future cash flows, and discuss how other capitals enhance or jeopardize the organization's ability to continue creating value. This seems to be the essence of the CD statement that the purpose of an integrated report is *to provide information that enables the intended report users to assess the ability of the organization to provide value over time*. In that event, the material should discuss how to incorporate a useful objective qualitative discussion of those capitals not subject to a quantitative assessment. As well, perhaps it should be up to an organization to provide its definition of value for each of the capitals it discusses.

Chapter 3: Guiding Principles

Materiality and Conciseness (Section 3D)

Materiality is determined by reference to assessments made by the primary intended report users (paragraphs 3.23- 3.24). The primary intended report users are providers of financial capital (paragraphs 1.6-1.8).

11. Do you agree with this approach to materiality? If not, how would you change it?

Response: We agree with the focus on providers of financial capital as the audience for an integrated report. Any other approach would not result in a concise report due to the disparate demands for information among the various stakeholder groups. The CD's definition of materiality differs from that which is generally accepted in traditional financial reporting, as defined by the International Accounting Standards Board and Canadian securities regulators. The proposed definition that considers whether a matter will have the potential to substantively affect strategy, business model or any of the capitals in the short, medium or long term will result in an extremely large number of material items. This will particularly be the case for matters that have a potentially large affect but a low likelihood of occurrence. The definition will result in confusion, especially when considering that much of the information for an integrated report will likely have been drawn from an organization's traditional financial reports.

The concept of materiality discussed in the CD is further complicated by the prioritization process it contemplates that includes a potential to reassess the materiality threshold. The described process suggests that when applying the Framework, the quantum of material matters found by an organization could be larger than they should be. If that is the case, the materiality approach is not working.

In our view, the CD focuses too much on materiality whereas identifying, assessing and prioritizing are probably the more relevant concepts. We found the Framework did not provide enough information to help differentiate and prioritize items. We believe this section needs to be reframed in terms of prioritization and more guidance should be provided to help an organization determine the key items to report in an integrated report.

12. Please provide any other comments you have about Section 3D or the Materiality determination process (Section 5B).

Response: We recommend the Framework consider suggesting alternate modes for providing detailed information – perhaps, some of the information could be disclosed on the website or a hyperlink could be provided in the online integrated report. There needs to be more discussion in the Framework about these disclosure alternatives for organizations. This is a key discussion area as it helps ensure the integrated report is concise.

Reliability and Completeness (Section 3E)

Reliability is enhanced by mechanisms such as robust internal reporting systems, appropriate stakeholder engagement, and independent, external assurance (paragraph 3.31).

13. How should the reliability of an integrated report be demonstrated?

Response: In our view, most organizations strive to provide reliable information in their external reporting. Given the developmental stage of the Framework, it is too soon to be contemplating reliability enhancement mechanisms beyond the extent to which they are already addressed in the CD. Our comments on external assurance are set out in the response to question 20.

14. Please provide any other comments you have about Section 3E.

Response: No further comments.

Other

15. Please provide any other comments you have about Chapter 3 that are not already addressed by your responses above.

Response: *Chapter 3, Section 3C - Stakeholder Responsiveness*

The CD notes that an integrated report should provide insight into the quality of an organization's relationships with its key stakeholders and how and to what extent it understands, takes into account and responds to their legitimate needs, interests and expectations. We agree that it is important for organizations to understand the needs of their stakeholders. As well, we agree that providers of financial capital want to understand the measures an organization takes to obtain an understanding of its stakeholders.

We find it unlikely, however, that an organization would be able to report the quality of the relationships with its various stakeholders, who in any event are likely changing fairly frequently. Furthermore, it would be very difficult for organizations to discuss the quality of the relationships in an objective manner. In our view, it would be better for organizations to discuss their approach and/or process for stakeholder engagement, rather than the quality of the relationship. Accordingly, we believe this aspect of the Guiding

Principles should be reframed in terms of the approach taken to understand stakeholder needs.

Chapter 4: Content Elements

16. Please provide any comments you have about Chapter 4 that are not already addressed by your responses above (please include comments on the Content Element Business Model [Section 4E] in your answer to questions 7-9 above rather than here).

Response: *Chapter 4, Sections 4F and 4G – Performance and Future Outlook*

We agree that an integrated report should have a future orientation. The performance and future outlook sections of the CD, however, place far too much emphasis on quantitative future-oriented information, for example paragraphs 4.31 and 4.37. In the Canadian environment, there are various securities regulatory compliance requirements that must be observed when reporting quantitative future-oriented information and these requirements result in significant monitoring and maintenance costs. Furthermore, organizations are reluctant to include certain forward-looking information that may result in compromising their competitive position in the marketplace.

Accordingly, we believe the forward-looking information section of the CD should focus on qualitative discussions about progress towards specific goals. The CD should also encourage quantitative discussions, but it should frame this discussion in the context of the reliability of the information and its cost/benefit in light of the costs to monitor and update the information. In addition, it would be useful to stress the importance of reporting actual performance against targets when quantitative forward-looking information is presented to enable readers to gain an understanding of the organization's ability to predict future outcomes.

Chapter 5: Preparation and Presentation

Involvement of Those Charged With Governance (Section 5D)

Section 5D discusses the involvement of those charged with governance, and paragraph 4.5 requires organizations to disclose the governance body with oversight responsibility for <IR>.

17. Should there be a requirement for those charged with governance to include a statement acknowledging their responsibility for the integrated report? Why/why not?

Response: We do not believe that those charged with governance, an oversight function, should provide a statement acknowledging their responsibility for the integrated report. Identifying the governance body responsible for the oversight of integrated reporting in the report, as advocated in the CD, should be sufficient.

18. Please provide any other comments you have about involvement of those charged with governance (Section 5D).

Response: No further comments.

Credibility (Section 5E)

The Framework provides reporting criteria against which organizations and assurance providers assess a report's adherence (paragraph 5.21).

19. If assurance is to be obtained, should it cover the integrated report as a whole, or specific aspects of the report? Why?

Response: Refer to our response to Question 20.

20. Please provide any other comments you have about Credibility (Section 5E). Assurance providers are particularly asked to comment on whether they consider the Framework provides suitable criteria for an assurance engagement.

Response: While we believe that assurance over an integrated report would add to its credibility, there are significant hurdles to overcome before assurance services on integrated reports could become commonplace. For example, the Guiding Principles in the Framework are quite broad, and therefore do not have the characteristics of suitable criteria on which an assurance service, performed in accordance with standards for such engagements, would need to be based.

Other

21. Please provide any other comments you have about Chapter 5 that are not already addressed by your responses above (please include comments on the materiality determination process [Section 5B] in your answer to question 11 above rather than here).

Response: No further comments.

Overall View

22. Recognizing that <IR> will evolve over time, please explain the extent to which you believe the content of the Framework overall is appropriate for use by organizations in preparing an integrated report and for providing report users with information about an organization's ability to create value in the short, medium and long term?

Response: We agree with the concept of an integrated report that would provide a concise report about how an organization's strategy, governance, performance and prospects lead to the creation of value. In today's business environment, there is general agreement that various aspects of the current business reporting framework need to be streamlined. As well, there is increased demand for environmental, social and governance information that has the potential to affect investment decisions to be better integrated and connected in one external report, instead of using today's separate reporting strands. In our view, however, few organizations currently have sufficiently integrated and robust systems and processes or an integrated thinking mindset necessary to generate a reliable integrated report.

While we agree there should be benefits to an integrated approach to reporting, we see little evidence, at least in Canada, that providers of financial capital are demanding an integrated report. In our view, there will need to be clearly demonstrated capital allocation benefits to encourage widespread voluntary adoption. In the meantime, however, we note over 90 companies have participated in the pilot program, and others may join them. These companies no doubt decided to participate in anticipation of reaping benefits from an integrated approach to reporting.

The concept of an integrated report as proposed by the IIRC is both new and complex. Accordingly, we are pleased that the IIRC has established a pilot program for both preparers and investors. The current workplan, however, calls for version 1 of the Framework to be published in December 2013, and for the pilot program to conclude in September 2014. There is much to be learned from the pilot program about issues with the Framework and how it can best be applied. Therefore, to maximize these insights, we believe the pilot program should be extended beyond September 2014. As well, we believe version 1 of the Framework should not be published until the pilot program is complete, to enable revisions to the draft Framework to consider everything learned from the pilot.

Development of <IR>

23. If the IIRC were to develop explanatory material on <IR> in addition to the Framework, which three topics would you recommend be given priority? Why?

Response: No comment.

Other

24. Please provide any other comments not already addressed by your responses to Questions 1-23.

Response: *Separate integrated report or a MD&A incorporating integrated reporting requirements*

Even though the CD suggests a stand-alone integrated report in addition to statutory reporting, we found there is significant discussion around whether to prepare a separate integrated report or prepare an MD&A incorporating the integrated reporting requirements. If the integrated report were to be a more comprehensive MD&A that contained an executive summary, some of the concern around an additional report might be mitigated, although in that event there would be regulatory compliance matters to be considered. Options for what could constitute an integrated report need more clarification.

Detailed Comments

- We found there is a lack of cohesiveness between the chapters of the Framework. For example, the significance of the various capitals as fundamental concepts does not seem to be reflected in the content elements that contain relatively little information describing how these capitals should be reported.

- In several places there are requirements to discuss management processes that are not consistent with a concise report.
- The unavailability of reliable data at 1.12 would benefit by being accompanied by a cost/benefit discussion.
- The improved system discussion in 3.41 would benefit from a cost/benefit discussion.
- An organization's value drivers are described as those over which it has some control, which will not always be the case, for example in some organizations raw material prices are the most significant value driver.
- In various places, the CD views the decision making process as a collaborative effort of senior management and those charged with governance, which is inconsistent with the Canadian perspective on governance as an oversight function, not management.
- The CD believes that for quantitative indicators to be reported they need to be used by the organization. In our view, knowledgeable investor demand could also drive this.

Consultation Questions

The IIRC welcomes comments on all aspects of the Draft International <IR> Framework(Draft Framework) from all stakeholders, whether to express agreement or to recommend changes.

The following questions are focused on areas where there has been significant discussion during the development process. Comments on any other aspect of the Draft Framework are also encouraged through the questions. Please provide all comments in English. All comments received will be considered a matter of public record and will be posted on the IIRC's website (www.theiirc.org).

Comments should be submitted by Monday 15th, July 2013.

Name: Nelmara Arbex
Email: arbex@globalreporting.org
Stakeholder group: Policy makers, regulators and standard setters
If replying on behalf of an Organization please complete the following:
Organization name: Global Reporting Initiative
Industry sector: Not applicable
Geographical region: Global

Key Points

If you wish to briefly express any key points, or to emphasize particular aspects of your submission, or add comments in the nature of a cover letter, then the following space can be used for this purpose. Please do not repeat large amounts of material appearing elsewhere in your comments.

The Global Reporting Initiative (GRI) congratulates the IIRC for offering for public comment the first proposal for an Integrated Reporting framework, and values the opportunity to comment on the consultation draft. In responding to the consultation draft, GRI seeks to provide the perspective of the provider of the most widely-used sustainability reporting framework globally.

This submission represents the views of the GRI Secretariat, and also reflects the main points for clarification identified by GRI's network in various forums in the last year.

GRI hopes that this feedback will provide valuable input for the finalization of the <IR> Framework (IRF). Please do not hesitate to contact us should you have any questions or wish to discuss any of the issues raised in this submission.

General Observations

GRI would like to share the following high-level observations about the consultation draft.

1. IIRC framework-based reports as a 'summary' The consultation draft states that a report prepared based on the <IR> framework (IRF) is a 'stand-alone' report, with details or indicators to be found in other reports such as financial statements and sustainability reports (paragraphs 1.18, 1.19, 1.20 in the consultation draft). Considering this, GRI recommends:
    a. The text positions an <IR> report as an extra report, potentially as a strategic summary. As such its value, scope and remit has to be discussed and precisely defined by reporters and the main report audience (providers of financial capital, as mentioned in 1.7). Otherwise, the preparation of an IRF-based <IR> report will represent an unjustified extra burden for reporters, and might be difficult to combine with the current reporting needs and with new regulations on reporting in several countries around the world.

b. In this respect, it is particularly important to describe what a 'concise communication' is (as mentioned, e.g., on page 6 – Content Elements)
c. Some explanation should also be offered on how this <IR> concept aligns with, or relates to, the 'one report' concept: For instance, if considering its future evolution an IRF-based report is intended to become a comprehensive corporate report (One Report) that integrates all material information and will replace – perhaps over time – other types of reports and disclosure frameworks. On this point GRI has noticed that even reporting entities that are familiar with the IRF consultation draft are not entirely clear on this question.

2. Relation between the IRF, other frameworks, and other reporting requirements. The consultation draft states that <IR> should offer insights about the elements of reporting organizations which are summarized in 2.2 and further presented in section 4. Considering this, GRI recommends:
   a. Many of these content elements ('Strategy and resource allocation', 'Opportunities and risks', 'Organization overview and external environment', 'Governance', 'Performance') suggested in the IRF are already covered by other types of reports and disclosure frameworks (i.e., financial and sustainability) and regional legislation. As part of the IRF, GRI recommends to develop explanatory narrative on the linkages between these content elements and the disclosures from other established frameworks, to avoid duplication and lack of conceptual harmonization.
   b. The same recommendation would apply to Section 3 (The Guiding Principles) 3C, 3D, 3E and 3F, related to existing and in-use reporting principles ('Stakeholder responsiveness', 'Materiality and conciseness', 'Reliability and completeness', 'Consistency and comparability'). Here it is also recommended to develop explanatory narrative as part of the IRF, on the linkages between these Principles and those from other established frameworks, to avoid duplication and lack of conceptual harmonization.
3. Relation between <IR> and Sustainability Reporting On the IIRC website there are two statements about IIRC and <IR>:

THE NEED FOR <IR>

At the heart of <IR> is the growing realization that a wide range of factors determine the value of an organization – some of these are financial or tangible in nature and are easy to account for in financial statements (e.g. property, cash), while many are not (e.g. people, natural resources, intellectual capital, market and regulatory context, competition, energy security). <IR> reflects the broad and longer-term consequences of the decisions organizations make, based on a wide range of factors, in order to create and sustain value. <IR> enables an organization to communicate in a clear, articulate way how it is drawing on all the resources and relationships it utilizes to create and preserve value in the short, medium and long term, helping investors to manage risks and allocate resources most efficiently.

THE CURRENT CORPORATE REPORTING FRAMEWORK

The current corporate reporting framework needs to evolve to reflect the wide range of factors that affect corporate performance. The current focus on an organization's financial statements is insufficient to answer the question: what is the value of the organization? Financial reporting covers both financial performance and risk, and this will remain an important part of the reporting universe; it is, however, insufficient by itself to provide all the information than users now need for rational and high quality decision-making. In a scenario where the majority of the information available to investors is historic, they are required to navigate a course around the next corner with reference only to a rear view mirror as if there were no road ahead. <IR> is the route map that supports investment decision-making, reflective of the integrated thinking and decision-making within organizations.

"In these statements (and many others on its website), the IIRC refers to areas covered by GRI sustainability reporting framework and other sustainability disclosure standards – e.g., non-financial factors that influence value creation – and the fact that financial statements are insufficient to express the entire value creation, or destruction, of an organization. These two elements were the foundation on which GRI's Sustainability Reporting Framework, and other sustainability disclosure standards, were developed in the last 10 years. These standards have become part of the 'corporate reporting universe' and today thousands of companies rely on them to prepare non-financial disclosures in various formats.

But the statements on the IIRC website do not clarify the relationship between the IRF, sustainability, sustainable triple bottom line development, and sustainability reporting frameworks.

'Sustainability Reporting' is also mentioned in paragraphs 1.18, 1.19, 1.20 in the consultation draft but, again the draft do not clarify the relationship between the IRF, sustainability, sustainable triple bottom line development and sustainability reporting frameworks.

Considering this, GRI recommends:

a. The IRF includes a section containing explanations of how it relates to the concept of sustainability and sustainability reporting/sustainability disclosure standards.
b. The IRF makes explicit the necessity of having sustainability reporting processes in place to develop an IRF-based report.
c. The IRF provides a narrative on the relation of <IR> and sustainability reporting processes, including related synergies and benefits, as part of paragraphs 1.18-1.20.
d. The IRF clarifies the relationship – now and in the future – of the IRF with financial and sustainability reporting.
    4. On the link between 'materiality' and the <IR> content elements The application of the 'Materiality and conciseness' Principle (3D) is not clearly linked to the report elements in 2.2 and Section 4 (Report Elements).

More explanation is needed on how the proposed 'materiality' analysis is expected to be used when defining specific parts of the content for the report elements 4A ('Organizational overview and external environment'), 4B ('Governance'), 4C ('Opportunities and risks'), 4D ('Strategy and resource allocation'), 4E ('Business model'), 4F ('Performance') and 4G ('Future outlook').

5. Audience for <IR> Paragraphs 1.6, 1.7 and 1.8 explain the <IR> audience. The focus on providers of financial capital as the primary audience should be articulated more clearly in the various sections, if this remains the IIRC's focus. Considering this, GRI recommends:
    a. In combination with the focus on providers of financial capital as the primary audience, the consultation draft also includes references in

prominent places to wider sets of stakeholders (i.e., paragraphs 1.7, 3.13-3.21). As a result it remains unclear how the focus on providers of financial capital as primary audience and the interests of wider sets of stakeholders are intended to be combined when preparing the different parts of <IR>. A narrative on whether and how the interests of a wider set of stakeholders relate to the interests of the primary audience – the providers of financial capital – is missing.

b. Furthermore, the description of the 'Materiality and conciseness' Principle (3D) does not mention the focus on financial capital providers when assessing materiality. This is a critical matter to be clarified for those using the IRF: if the proposed main audience is financial capital providers and the materiality analysis should be focused on their interests. In this context, the application of the 'Stakeholder responsiveness' Principle (3.13 -3.21), as proposed in conjunction with the 'Materiality and conciseness' Principle, also warrants further explanation.

c. The IIRC might reconsider whether this focus is advisable and tenable in the long term. GRI would propose the following questions to assess this:

    i. Will companies opt to have a report specifically for providers of capital, or would companies see more purpose in integrating their reporting for a wider audience?

    ii. If integrated thinking is the goal for the company, why would integration not account for the providers of human, social and natural capital, whose interests would be integral to a well-functioning, sustainable market economy?

6. Value: The concept of 'value' remains unclear in the consultation draft, but is proposed as a fundamental concept that must be used. This leaves the interpretation of the concept of 'value' in the IRF draft to the reader. Considering this, GRI recommends:

    a. Given the many established theories and interpretations around the concept of 'value', mainly in the context of economics, philosophy, psychology and sociology, the IRF should specify on which theory or theories, if any, it bases its concept of value creation, and provide references to external sources to help users of the IRF better understand the concept of value and the related concepts of value creation and capitals.

    b. GRI recommends that a chosen definition for this term is offered as part of the IRF. E.g., in various paragraphs it is currently possible to apply a number of definitions of 'value': exchange value, user value, financial value. Depending on the concept choice the resulting reports would be quite different.

c. The difference between the terms 'value', 'value creation' and 'capital' should also be further clarified. These terms are not distinguished sufficiently in the consultation draft.

7. Future of reporting: There is an expectation that the IIRC and IRF contribute to building a vision for the future of corporate reporting, particularly considering the coalition of players around these developments.

Related to many of GRI's general comments on the consultation draft, a number of questions are still unclear: What is the IIRC's vision of the future – One Report or standalone Integrated Reporting? What is the envisaged relationship with other standards?

How does this relate to the stated IIRC objective to reduce the reporting burden? GRI recommends that statements on how the corporate reporting field is expected to evolve in the coming years, and whether reporters should choose one type of reporting over the other, are added to the section on 'Interaction with other reports and communications' (paragraphs 1.18 – 1.20).

Chapter 1: Overview

Principles-Based Requirements

To be in accordance with the Framework, an integrated report should comply with the principles-based requirements identified throughout the Framework in bold italic type (paragraphs 1.11-1.12).

1. *Should any additional principles-based requirements be added or should any be eliminated or changed? If so, please explain why.*

The most critical missing elements and proposals for change are explained in the text with GRI's general comments ('Key Points') on the IRF consultation draft. Please consult that text for detailed comments.

The text covers the following topics:

- IIRC framework-based reports as a 'summary'
- Relation between the IRF, other frameworks, and other reporting requirements

- Relation between <IR> and Sustainability Reporting
- On the link between 'materiality' and the <IR> content elements
- Audience for <IR>
- Value
- Future of reporting

Interaction With Other Reports and Communications

The <IR> process is intended to be applied continuously to all relevant reports and communications, in addition to the preparation of an integrated report. The integrated report may include links to other reports and communications, e.g., financial statements and sustainability reports. The IIRC aims to complement material developed by established reporting standard setters and others, and does not intend to develop duplicate content (paragraphs 1.18-1.20).

2. *Do you agree with how paragraphs 1.18-1.20 characterize the interaction with other reports and communications?*

GRI proposes that this section be extended, as detailed in the general comments text.

The main recommendations to these paragraphs are also listed below.

"The consultation draft states that a report prepared based on the <IR> framework (IRF) is a 'stand-alone' report, with details or indicators to be found in other reports such as financial statements and sustainability reports (paragraphs 1.18, 1.19, 1.20 in the consultation draft).

Considering this, GRI recommends:

- The text positions an <IR> report as an extra report, potentially as a strategic summary. As such its value, scope and remit has to be discussed and precisely defined by reporters and the main report audience (providers of financial capital, as mentioned in 1.7). Otherwise, the preparation of an IRF-based <IR> report will represent an unjustified extra burden for reporters, and might be difficult to combine with the current reporting needs and with new regulations on reporting in several countries around the world.
- In this respect, it is particularly important to describe what a 'concise communication' is (as mentioned, e.g., on page 6 – Content Elements)
- Some explanation should also be offered on how this <IR> concept aligns with, or relates to, the 'one report' concept: For instance, if

considering its future evolution an IRF-based report is intended to become a comprehensive corporate report (One Report) that integrates all material information and will replace – perhaps over time – other types of reports and disclosure frameworks. On this point GRI has noticed that even reporting entities that are familiar with the IRF consultation draft are not entirely clear on this question.

- The IRF includes a section containing explanations of how it relates to the concept of sustainability and sustainability reporting/sustainability disclosure standards.
- The IRF makes explicit the necessity of having sustainability reporting processes in place to develop an IRF-based report.
- The IRF provides a narrative on the relation of <IR> and sustainability reporting processes, including related synergies and benefits, as part of paragraphs 1.18-1.20.
- The IRF clarifies the relationship – now and in the future – of the IRF with financial and sustainability reporting."

In summary, GRI believes it is of critical importance that established reporting standard setters are referenced to give the user of the IRF sufficient orientation on how <IR> relates to other connected reporting efforts.

The IRF should make explicit the necessity of having sustainability reporting processes in place to develop an <IR> report.

The IRF should provide a narrative on the relation of <IR> and sustainability reporting processes, including related synergies and benefits, as part of the paragraphs 1.18-1.20.

3. *If the IIRC were to create an online database of authoritative sources of indicators or measurement methods developed by established reporting standard setters and others, which references should be included?*

The Standard Disclosures included in the GRI G4 Sustainability Reporting Guidelines and GRI Sector Disclosures, and other globally-accepted topic-specific standards or references mentioned in the G4 Guidelines.

Other

4. *Please provide any other comments you have about Chapter 1.*

GRI strongly recommends further development of paragraphs 1.6, 1.7 and 1.8, as mentioned in its general comments document.

GRI also strongly recommends further development of paragraphs 1.18, 1.19 and 1.20, as mentioned in its general comments document.

Chapter 2: Fundamental Concepts

The Capitals (Section 2B)

The Framework describes six categories of capital (paragraph 2.17). An organization is to use these categories as a benchmark when preparing an integrated report (paragraphs 2.19-2.21), and should disclose the reason if it considers any of the capitals as not material (paragraph 4.5).

5. *Do you agree with this approach to the capitals? Why/why not?*

GRI agrees with the approach to the capitals, but considers as insufficient the guidance offered on how to link this approach to the 'value creation' concept, which is also not well defined. See details in GRI's general comments document. Particularly, the difference between the terms 'value', 'value creation' and 'capital' should also be further clarified. These terms are not distinguished sufficiently in the consultation draft.

6. *Please provide any other comments you have about Section 2B?*

None.

Business Model (Section 2C)

A business model is defined as an organization's chosen system of inputs, business activities, outputs and outcomes that aims to create value over the short, medium and long term (paragraph 2.26).

7. *Do you agree with this definition? Why/why not?*

GRI agrees with 2.26.

Outcomes are defined as the internal and external consequences (positive and negative) for the capitals as a result of an organization's business activities and outputs (paragraphs 2.35-2.36).

8. *Do you agree with this definition? Why/why not?*

GRI accepts the description in 2.35 and 2.36.

9. *Please provide any other comments you have about Section 2C or the disclosure requirements and related guidance regarding business models contained in the Content Elements Chapter of the Framework (see Section 4E)?*

GRI has comments and recommendation on the content elements in chapter 4E of the IRF consultation draft, but they are not related to the business model concept. See GRI general comments.

Other

10. *Please provide any other comments you have about Chapter 2 that are not already addressed by your responses above.*

GRI has made recommendations for further development of section 2D 'Value Creation' in its general comments document.

Mainly:

- Given the many established theories and interpretations around the concept of 'value', mainly in the context of economics, philosophy, psychology and sociology, the IRF should specify on which theory or theories, if any, it bases its concept of value creation, and provide references to external sources to help users of the IRF better understand the concept of value and the related concepts of value creation and capitals.
- GRI recommends that a chosen definition for this term is offered as part of the IRF. E.g., in various paragraphs it is currently possible to apply a number of definitions of 'value': exchange value, user value, financial value. Depending on the concept choice the resulting report would be quite different.
- The difference between the terms 'value', 'value creation' and 'capital' should also be further clarified. These terms are not distinguished sufficiently in the consultation draft.

Chapter 3: Guiding Principles

Materiality and Conciseness (Section 3D)

Materiality is determined by reference to assessments made by the primary intended report users (paragraphs 3.23-3.24). The primary intended report users are providers of financial capital (paragraphs 1.6-1.8).

11. *Do you agree with this approach to materiality? If not, how would you change it?*

GRI recommends that the sentence above is included in 3.23: "The primary intended report users are providers of financial capital" (from paragraphs 1.6-1.8). The description of the 'Materiality and conciseness' Principle (3D) does not mention the focus on financial capital providers when assessing materiality. This is a critical matter to be clarified for those using the IRF: if the proposed main audience is financial capital providers and the materiality analysis should be focused on their interests. In this context, the application of the 'Stakeholder responsiveness' Principle (3.13 -3.21), as proposed in conjunction with the 'Materiality and conciseness' Principle, also warrants further explanation.

Explanatory materials should be developed that focus on the commonalities and differences of the materiality definitions in <IR>, financial, and sustainability reporting, to aid practitioners in using the principles.

Explanatory narrative should be developed as part of the IRF, on the linkages between this Principle and materiality principle from other established frameworks, to avoid duplication and lack of conceptual harmonization.

The application of the 'Materiality and conciseness' Principle (3D) is not clearly linked to the report elements in 2.2 and Section 4 (Report Elements). More explanation is needed on how the proposed 'materiality' analysis is expected to be used when defining specific parts of the content for the report elements 4A ('Organizational overview and external environment'), 4B ('Governance'), 4C ('Opportunities and risks'), 4D ('Strategy and resource allocation'), 4E ('Business model'), 4F ('Performance') and 4G ('Future outlook').

12. *Please provide any other comments you have about Section 3D or the Materiality determination process (Section 5B).*

GRI recommends that the sentence above is included in 3.23: "The primary intended report users are providers of financial capital" (from paragraphs 1.6-1.8). The description of the 'Materiality and conciseness' Principle (3D) does not mention the focus on financial capital providers when assessing materiality. This is a critical matter to be clarified for those using the IRF: if the proposed main audience is financial capital providers and the materiality analysis should be focused on their interests. In this context, the application of the 'Stakeholder responsiveness' Principle (3.13 -3.21), as proposed in conjunction with the 'Materiality and conciseness' Principle, also warrants further explanation.

Explanatory materials should be developed that focus on the commonalities and differences of the materiality definitions in <IR>, financial, and sustainability reporting, to aid practitioners in using the principles.

Explanatory narrative should be developed as part of the IRF, on the linkages between this Principle and materiality principle from other established frameworks, to avoid duplication and lack of conceptual harmonization.

The application of the 'Materiality and conciseness' Principle (3D) is not clearly linked to the report elements in 2.2 and Section 4 (Report Elements). More explanation is needed on how the proposed 'materiality' analysis is expected to be used when defining specific parts of the content for the report elements 4A ('Organizational overview and external environment'), 4B ('Governance'), 4C ('Opportunities and risks'), 4D ('Strategy and resource allocation'), 4E ('Business model'), 4F ('Performance') and 4G ('Future outlook').

Reliability and Completeness (Section 3E)

Reliability is enhanced by mechanisms such as robust internal reporting systems, appropriate stakeholder engagement, and independent, external assurance (paragraph 3.31).

13. *How should the reliability of an integrated report be demonstrated?*
14. *Please provide any other comments you have about Section 3E.*

For Section 3 (The Guiding Principles) 3C, 3D, 3E and 3F, related to existing and in-use reporting principles ('Stakeholder responsiveness', 'Materiality and conciseness',

'Reliability and completeness', 'Consistency and comparability'), GRI recommends to develop explanatory narrative as part of the IRF, on the linkages between these Principles and those from other established frameworks, to avoid duplication and lack of conceptual harmonization.

Other

15. *Please provide any other comments you have about Chapter 3 that are not already addressed by your responses above.*

GRI has no comments related to the content of 3D, 3E and 3F. GRI remarks that the principles mentioned in the IRF consultation draft and are existing ones; the fact that this content already exists should be explicitly mentioned, and the relationships between the new IRF principles and existing principles used in other reports should be clearly explained.

As the IRF-based report will rely on details from other reports (paragraphs 1.18), this is a critical point from the reporter's perspective.

Chapter 4: Content Elements

16. *Please provide any comments you have about Chapter 4 that are not already addressed by your responses above (please include comments on the Content Element Business Model [Section 4E] in your answer to questions 7-9 above rather than here).*

In its general comments document, GRI gives recommendations for improvements related to Section 4. They are mainly:

Many of the Content Elements in the IRF consultation draft ('Strategy and resource allocation', 'Opportunities and risks', 'Organization overview and external environment', 'Governance', 'Performance') are already covered by other types of reports and disclosure frameworks (i.e., financial and sustainability), and regional legislation.

It is recommended to develop explanatory narrative as part of the IRF on the linkages between these content elements and the disclosures from other established frameworks, to avoid duplication and lack of conceptual harmonization. Furthermore, GRI recommends that the link between the materiality analysis and the report elements is clarified, and that the concept of 'value' is clarified – including clarification on its link to the concept of 'capitals'.

Chapter 5: Preparation and Presentation

Involvement of Those Charged With Governance (Section 5D)

Section 5D discusses the involvement of those charged with governance, and paragraph 4.5 requires organizations to disclose the governance body with oversight responsibility for <IR>.

17. *Should there be a requirement for those charged with governance to include a statement acknowledging their responsibility for the integrated report? Why/why not?*
18. *Please provide any other comments you have about Involvement of those charge with governance (Section 5D).*

Credibility (Section 5E)

The Framework provides reporting criteria against which organizations and assurance providers assess a report's adherence (paragraph 5.21).

19. *If assurance is to be obtained, should it cover the integrated report as a whole, or specific aspects of the report? Why?*

GRI's experience shows that reporters are not always ready to expose all elements of non-financial reports to external assurance. From GRI's perspective, in order to promote external verification it is recommended that the IRF accepts both types.

20. *Please provide any other comments you have about Credibility (Section 5E). Assurance providers are particularly asked to comment on whether they consider the Framework provides suitable criteria for an assurance engagement.*

Other

21. *Please provide any other comments you have about Chapter 5 that are not already addressed by your responses above (please include comments on the materiality determination process [Section 5B] in your answer to question 11 above rather than here).*

GRI recommends that the IRF explains how the information presented in other reports/documents (which will provide detail on the IRF-based report), which might have been prepared considering other 'boundaries', should be presented as part of <IR>.

Overall View

22. *Recognizing that <IR> will evolve over time, please explain the extent to which you believe the content of the Framework overall is appropriate for use by organizations in preparing an integrated report and for providing report users with information about an organization's ability to create value in the short, medium and long term?*

GRI observes that many companies and other players, to promote integrated thinking and also to reduce the reporting burden, are inclined to believe that the most adequate report format for future reporting is a 'one report' approach which would capture - in an integrated manner - the value creation and destruction of an organization.

Integrated thinking and reporting should then address the full spectrum of value (created or destroyed). Much of companies' value is nowadays made up of intangibles.

Intangibles relate to trust, which is related closely to stakeholder confidence and the license to operate. These in turn affect the cost of capital and brand value.

Environmental and social issues are increasingly factors that affect stakeholders' trust.

Sustainability is therefore a key component. A company's assessment of trust should therefore take account of stakeholders' views and their effect on trust, the license to operate, cost of capital and brand value and through this be aware of the extent to which sustainability issues are a factor to be considered.

In this context the definitions of 'value' and 'value creation' have to be accepted by the organization's stakeholders. The IRF should offer a clear perspective on value creation taking the importance of stakeholder views into account, and within this the reality that performance and impacts can lead to different value assessments by stakeholders (i.e. is their value perspective based on exchange value or user value?).

Development of <IR>

23. *If the IIRC were to develop explanatory material on <IR> in addition to the Framework, which three topics would you recommend be given priority? Why?*

 a. Clear definition of value creation taking the importance of stakeholder views into account.
  i. Because of the reasons described above (question 22).
 b. Technical guidance on how IRF relates to other reporting standards, particularly to sustainability reporting.
  i. Because IRF describes <IR> as a concise report supported by other reports (financial and sustainability) without explaining how this relation would be - Because IRF refers to existing concepts from other reporting standards
  ii. Because in order to implemented an 'integrated reporting' process – even to result in a report that focus on financial capital providers- financial and sustainability reporting processes have to be considered and this is not mentioned in the IRF
  iii. Because thousands of organizations are currently preparing financial and sustainability reports and will have to understand how these processes are related to IRF reporting process

Other

24. *Please provide any other comments not already addressed by your responses to Questions 1-23.*

Consultation questions

The IIRC welcomes comments on all aspects of the Draft International <IR> Framework (Draft Framework) from all stakeholders, whether to express agreement or to recommend changes.

The following questions are focused on areas where there has been significant discussion during the development process. Comments on any other aspect of the Draft Framework are also encouraged through the questions.

Please provide all comments in English.

All comments received will be considered a matter of public record and will be posted on the IIRC's website (www.theiirc.org).

Comments should be submitted by Monday 15th, July 2013.

Name: Laura Buijs
Email: laura.buijs@fee.be
Stakeholder group: Other
If replying on behalf of an Organization please complete the following:
Organization name: Federation of European Accountants
Industry sector: Not applicable
Geographical region: Western Europe

Key Points

If you wish to briefly express any key points, or to emphasize particular aspects of your submission, or add comments in the nature of a cover letter, then the following space can be used for this purpose. Please do not repeat large amounts of material appearing elsewhere in your comments.

FEE is pleased to provide you with its comments on the IIRC Consultation Draft of the Draft International <IR> Framework (the Draft Framework). This response should be seen in light of FEE's continued support for <IR> and its appreciation for the gradual transition towards <IR>. This letter first highlights our key points, followed by the answers to the consultation questions in the appendix.

Strong and continued support for the work of the IIRC and for developing <IR>

- FEE commends the IIRC for the significant achievement of issuing the Draft Framework and recognises that redesigning the direction and focus of corporate reporting is a journey. Making the step towards integrated thinking and integrated reporting takes time; the Draft Framework is an important and laudable milestone in this process.
- The IIRC is strongly encouraged in advancing the Draft Framework and in engaging all stakeholders, including policymakers, regulators, and private sector entities, in creating a shared vision on <IR>.
- FEE supports the IIRC's objective of gaining as much practical experience with the Draft Framework as possible, such as provided by the Pilot Programme and Emerging Integrated Reporting Database. The lessons learnt from the Pilot Programme will be instrumental in

further developing the Draft Framework. When the final Framework is instated, it is expected this will need to be reviewed and updated periodically, depending on the practical experiences with <IR>.

- FEE fully endorses the way in which <IR> is currently being developed, by largely drawing on stakeholders' involvement and gaining practical experience. FEE is convinced that, at least for the time being, <IR> should continue to be market driven instead of being mandated by public authorities. Legislation on this matter could in fact hinder such promising evolution and stifle innovation. However, it is necessary to involve public authorities as stakeholders in developing <IR> as regulators can be influential in promoting the widespread acceptance and use of <IR> or in removing obstacles to the application or adoption of <IR>. The focus on a principal audience for <IR> is very useful
- In our view, it is very useful that the IIRC has chosen to focus <IR> in the first instance on the information needs of providers of financial capital. This pragmatic approach aids in making the Draft Framework operational. FEE fully agrees with the Draft Framework's recognition (Paragraph 1.7) that <IR> benefits all stakeholders who are interested in an organisation's ability to create value over time. The IIRC is encouraged to investigate further how information needs of other stakeholders align with, or differ from, those of providers of financial capital.
- FEE also finds the principles of <IR> useful for reports prepared by not-for-profit organisations and the public sector, as well as reports prepared for specific stakeholder groups. In such reports, different materiality considerations may apply.
- The desirability and practicability of applying the Framework's principles to small and medium-sized enterprises (SMEs) merits consideration, in particular to explore ho w<IR> can play a role in improving access to capital for SMEs. However, FEE also acknowledges that there is a balance to be struck between the potential benefits of <IR> for SMEs, market pressure that imposes <IR> participation on SMEs (for example as part of the supply chain of a listed food manufacturer) and the risk of adding unnecessary administrative burdens for SMEs. Whilst the initial focus of <IR> has primarily been on reporting by larger companies, it is recommended that the IIRC keeps including some larger SMEs in the Pilot Programme. The transition towards <IR> is a gradual one.

- The interaction between <IR> and other reports and communications largely depends on how the transition towards <IR> is being made. FEE expects that the shift towards <IR> will have a significant impact on the current corporate reporting cycle. The Draft Framework anticipates that <IR> will lead to an additional stand-alone report, in addition to other reports and communications. FEE would like the IIRC to address the concern that it might be difficult to convince stakeholders of the benefits of <IR>, when this leads to an additional report and a perceived need for extra resources. In our view, it is important that <IR> contributes to reducing the overall reporting burden for organisations.
- To ease the shift to <IR>, a transition process for the organisation and preparation of corporate reports is needed. This could include practical guidance on changing the current reporting towards <IR> and making recommendations for (temporary) solutions, such as incorporating the Draft Framework principles in the management commentary.

FEE advocates the Draft Framework's principles-based approach 10) FEE welcomes the principles-based approach of the requirements in the Draft Framework, as opposed to setting detailed rules. Based on the Draft Framework, companies will be able to tell their value creation story by focusing on the relevant principles. However, consideration should be given to the need for suitable and clear criteria to guide preparers in applying the Draft Framework, see also paragraph 17) below. FEE believes suitable criteria will be needed for an organisation to substantiate its decision for including or excluding particular information within its integrated report.

However, the specific matters to be included in an integrated report should be dictated by the circumstances of the individual organisation.

- The Draft Framework sets minimum requirements that integrated reports need to comply with in order for them to be in accordance with the Draft Framework. FEE supports this approach and encourages the IIRC to continue identifying these minimum requirements.
- If the Framework is applied effectively, FEE believes that <IR> could contribute three essential features to the quality of understanding that users can derive from business reporting:
    - A better explanation of the key resources ('capitals') on which the business depends
    - A more comprehensive view of operating performance

- ◦ A better basis for understanding the future outlook of the business.

More connectivity within the text of the Draft Framework would make it more user-friendly

- FEE supports connectivity of information as one of the Draft Framework's Guiding Principles, meaning that <IR> should show the combination, inter-relatedness and dependencies between the components that are material to the organisation's ability to create value over time.
- The text of the Draft Framework also features connectivity by linking the different principles, concepts and elements related to value creation. Making this linkage even more apparent would make the Draft Framework more user-friendly. FEE expects that there will be a demand for external assurance on <IR>
- FEE considers external independent assurance essential in making the information in the integrated report more reliable and credible. External assurance can increase the confidence of investors and other users of <IR> as they rely more and more on the information provided in an integrated report. Therefore, FEE assumes that in the process of further developing <IR> a market demand for external assurance will arise, which calls for all relevant stakeholders to adopt a proactive approach in this regard. The accountancy profession is willing and able to innovate in order to develop assurance techniques that can provide a suitable level of assurance on <IR>.
- Specific standards are needed for providing external assurance on <IR, for which the International Auditing and Assurance Standards Board (IAASB), as standard setter for assurance, would be the designated authority. FEE would be happy to contribute to any work undertaken by the IAASB to adapt its current standards to respond to needs for new or adapted forms of assurance that may emerge as a result of the gradual transition to <IR>.
- The level of assurance that can be provided depends on the type of information underpinning the report; this is not self-evident for <IR> which combines past, present and forward looking, financial and non-financial information. In developing external assurance on <IR>, it will be necessary to distinguish between the different types of information to be presented in the integrated report whereby different

levels of assurance might need to be provided on different elements of the integrated report.

- In further developing the Draft Framework, as pointed out in paragraph 10) above, suitable criteria will need to be established that preparers can use to prepare the information in their integrated report. Those criteria would provide the benchmark against which assurance can be provided on the integrated report.

FEE is highly committed to supporting the IIRC in its next steps in advancing <IR>. It is particularly looking forward to the initial version of the Framework to be issued in December 2013.

Please do not hesitate to contact us if you wish to further discuss any of the points raised in our response, or if we can contribute to the IIRC achieving its objectives in developing the International <IR> Framework.

For further information on this letter, please contact Laura Buijs, Project Manager, at the FEE Secretariat on +32 2 285 40 71 or via e-mail at laura.buijs@fee.be.

Chapter 1: Overview

Principles-Based Requirements

To be in accordance with the Framework, an integrated report should comply with the principles-based requirements identified throughout the Framework in bold italic type (paragraphs 1.11-1.12).

1. *Should any additional principles-based requirements be added or should any be eliminated or changed? If so, please explain why.*

FEE agrees with the current principles-based requirements. The specific matters to be included in an individual organisation's integrated report will be governed by the circumstances of the individual organisation. Thus, while detailed reporting rules might be counterproductive FEE believes suitable criteria will be needed for an organisation to substantiate its decision for including or excluding particular information within its integrated report.

Interaction With Other Reports and Communications

The <IR> process is intended to be applied continuously to all relevant reports and communications, in addition to the preparation of an integrated report. The integrated report may include links to other reports and communications, e.g., financial statements and sustainability reports. The IIRC aims to complement material developed by established reporting standard setters and others, and does not intend to develop duplicate content (paragraphs 1.18-1.20).

2. *Do you agree with how paragraphs 1.18-1.20 characterize the interaction with other reports and communications?*

FEE suggests the IIRC clarify Paragraph 1.18 in Chapter 1: Overview, which states that a stand-alone integrated report will be prepared annually in line with the statutory financial reporting cycle in addition to all other relevant reports and communications.

More specifically, FEE believes there is a need for further clarification on how in practice this stand-alone integrated report

- Relates to the relevant existing reports on financial and non-financial information?
- Replaces all, or some, of the current reports, or serves solely as an addition?

FEE commends the IIRC for deepening its cooperation with the International Accounting Standards Board (IASB) and the Global Reporting Initiative (GRI) by signing a Memorandum of Understanding with each organisation. Coordination with the IASB and GRI reporting frameworks will be essential in further developing the Draft Framework.

3. *If the IIRC were to create an online database of authoritative sources of indicators or measurement methods developed by established reporting standard setters and others, which references should be included?*

FEE suggests that the Sustainability Reporting Guidelines, set by the GRI, and the Sustainability Accounting Standards, set by the Sustainability Accounting Standards Board, be considered for inclusion in the proposed database.

Other

4. *Please provide any other comments you have about Chapter 1.*

Audience (Paragraphs 1.6 and 1.8)

As mentioned in the cover letter, FEE believes it is very useful that the IIRC has chosen to focus <IR> in the first instance on the information needs of providers of financial capital. This pragmatic approach aids in making the Draft Framework operational. The IIRC is recommended to investigate further how information needs of other stakeholders align with, or differ from, those of providers of financial capital.

Disclosure of Competition-Sensitive Information (Paragraphs 1.11 and 1.12)

FEE commends the IIRC for addressing the confidentiality issues which arise from the disclosure of relevant information (Paragraphs 1.11 and 1.12). The addition of competitive harm to the two other reasons for allowing non-disclosure of material information (unavailability of reliable data and specific legal prohibitions) has resolved this issue.

FEE suggests altering the wording in Paragraphs 1.11 and 1.12 from competitive harm to significant competitive harm. This would indicate that only serious harm would be a reason for non-disclosure. This proposed change aligns more closely with Paragraph 3.42 which refers to (…) information … that would significantly harm its competitive advantage.

Chapter 2: Fundamental Concepts

The Capitals (Section 2B)

The Framework describes six categories of capital (paragraph 2.17). An organization is to use these categories as a benchmark when preparing an integrated report (paragraphs 2.19-2.21), and should disclose the reason if it considers any of the capitals as not material (paragraph 4.5).

5. *Do you agree with this approach to the capitals? Why/why not?*

FEE agrees with this approach to capitals. Capitals are essential to an organisation's existence, its operation and its ability to create value. Therefore, it is very important for an organisation to report on various capitals that it uses or affects.

Paragraph 2.24 of the Draft Framework on quantitative and qualitative information, states that when quantitative indicators do not suffice, qualitative indicators (or narrative reporting) should explain the organisation's use of and effects on capitals. According to Paragraph 3.38 narrative reporting should provide information on capitals that is consistent over time and in a way that enables comparison with other organizations to the extent it is material to the organization's own value creation story. Further guidance should be developed on how to use narrative reporting in practice in order to achieve this comparability and consistency.

As stated in Paragraph 2.23, an organisation does not control all capitals that it uses or affects. Some (non-financial) capitals are held by other parties who also have a stake in maintaining or increasing their value. It would be helpful if the IIRC would provide more guidance on how an organisation should report on capitals outside its span of control. For example, how far down the value chain organisations should go to report on these capitals? This item is not resolved in the section relating to the reporting boundaries of the integrated report in Section 5G of the Draft Framework.

6. *Please provide any other comments you have about Section 2B?*

N/A

Business Model (Section 2C)

A business model is defined as an organization's chosen system of inputs, business activities, outputs and outcomes that aims to create value over the short, medium and long term (paragraph 2.26).

7. *Do you agree with this definition? Why/why not?*

FEE agrees in principle with this definition of an organization's business model, but would like to ask the IIRC to further clarify this. The current use of the word chosen implies the organisation's responsibility and accountability for its business model and the resulting outcomes (both positive and negative) this choice entails. It would be helpful for this definition to reflect that organisations cannot fully choose the outcomes of their business model as these are also influenced by many external factors.

Outcomes are defined as the internal and external consequences (positive and negative) for the capitals as a result of an organization's business activities and outputs (paragraphs 2.35-2.36).

8. *Do you agree with this definition? Why/why not?*

FEE agrees with this definition.

9. *Please provide any other comments you have about Section 2C or the disclosure requirements and related guidance regarding business models contained in the Content Elements Chapter of the Framework (see Section 4E)?*

N/A

Other

10. *Please provide any other comments you have about Chapter 2 that are not already addressed by your responses above.*

The concept of value creation (Section 2D) is paramount to the Draft Framework. FEE would consider it useful for the IIRC to further develop this concept. In addition, the resources allocation and the monetization of intangibles and externalities are the subject of extensive research. However, there does not yet seem to be an applicable methodological framework or much relevant practical experience. Any future work of the IIRC in this regard should consider the demands of providers of financial capital.

Regarding an organisation's value drivers as referred to in Paragraph 2.45 of the Draft Framework; FEE considers a company's strategy as one of the main drivers for its success. Strategy namely forms the linking pin between capitals and value creation. FEE therefore supports the IIRC's emphasis on the importance of strategy in the Draft Framework by identifying strategic focus and future orientation as a Guiding Principle (Section 3A) and strategy and resource allocation as a Content Element (Section 4D) of the integrated report.

Chapter 3: Guiding Principles

Materiality and Conciseness (Section 3D)

Materiality is determined by reference to assessments made by the primary intended report users (paragraphs 3.23-3.24). The primary intended report users are providers of financial capital (paragraphs 1.6-1.8).

11. *Do you agree with this approach to materiality? If not, how would you change it?*

a) FEE agrees in principle with the Draft Framework's approach to materiality.

12. *Please provide any other comments you have about Section 3D or the Materiality determination process (Section 5B).*

Materiality and Conciseness (Section 3D)

FEE applauds the inclusion of conciseness as (part of) this Guiding Principle in the Draft Framework. This will prevent <IR> from leading to very sizeable reports which would lack accessibility and user-friendliness. In order to achieve a concise integrated report, FEE support the alternatives of linking it to additional detailed information as suggested in the Draft Framework (Paragraph 3.29) or compiling a multi-tier report, consisting of varying levels of detail.

Materiality Determination Process

The Draft Framework states that a matter is only material if the primary intended report users (the providers of financial capital) could be substantively influenced by it. As mentioned in our cover letter, FEE finds it is very useful that the IIRC has chosen to focus <IR> in the first instance on the information needs of providers of financial capital, as a pragmatic approach. Without this focus, materiality would be hard to determine. FEE believes that the principles of <IR> are also useful for reports to specific stakeholder groups. In such reports, different materiality considerations may apply.

Whereas Paragraph 2.24 of the Draft Framework distinguishes between quantitative and qualitative information, the difference between quantitative and qualitative materiality does not yet become clear in the Draft Framework. Financial impacts can differ greatly from non-financial impacts, such as reputation damage. FEE would find it useful for this distinction to be reflected in the materiality determination process as set out in the Draft Framework.

Reliability and Completeness (Section 3E)

Reliability is enhanced by mechanisms such as robust internal reporting systems, appropriate stakeholder engagement, and independent, external assurance (paragraph 3.31).

13. *How should the reliability of an integrated report be demonstrated?*

FEE welcomes the Draft Framework's acknowledgement of external assurance as a mechanism to enhance the reliability (Paragraph 3.31) and credibility of information (Paragraph 5.20). External assurance is essential in making the information in the integrated report more reliable and credible and thereby increasing the confidence of users. FEE expects that in the process of further developing <IR> a need for external assurance will arise.

Specific standards are needed for providing external assurance on specific subject matters. FEE would be more than willing to contribute actively to considerations as to how global assurance standards may have to be adapted for <IR>. The IAASB, as standard setter for assurance, would be the designated authority to lead this work. In our view, it is in the public interest for these standards to tie into a robust system of quality control for those organisations or individuals providing these assurance services. For example, International Standard on Quality Control (ISQC) 1 currently applies to firms that provide services covered by the IAASB's international standards.

The level of assurance that can be provided depends on the type of information on which the report is based; this is not self-evident for <IR> which combines past, present and forward looking, financial and non-financial information. FEE finds it crucial that the information underpinning the integrated report is assumable in accordance with generally accepted global standards. This means that it is supported by sufficient evidence and is prepared according to specific criteria so that it can be checked against these criteria. This insurability is not necessarily obvious for future-oriented and non-financial information (as referred to in Paragraph 3.46 and 3.47 of the Draft Framework).

Therefore, in developing external assurance on <IR>, it may be necessary to distinguish between the different types of information to be presented in the integrated report so that challenges that could be associated with providing assurance on these different types of information can be considered. Different levels of assurance might need to be provided on different elements of the integrated report.

There is also a need to develop clear criteria which preparers can use to prepare the information in their integrated report which would also be the criteria or benchmark against which assurance can be provided on the integrated report.

FEE expects that there will be market demand for assurance over an integrated report, because assurance enhances the credibility of information, which is of value to investors and other users of <IR> as they increasingly come to rely on the information provided in an integrated report.

Regarding the provision of assurance by the auditor, the following should at least be considered: competences, experience and skill sets required, and the need to use independent experts.

14. *Please provide any other comments you have about Section 3E.*

The accountancy profession is willing and able to innovate in order to develop assurance techniques that can provide a suitable level of assurance on <IR>. It is recommended the IIRC work with the IAASB in this area, as they are the responsible global standards setter for assurance. FEE is more than happy to contribute to any work undertaken by the IAASB to adapt its current standards to respond to needs for new or adapted forms of assurance that may emerge as a result of the gradual transition to <IR>.

FEE suggests altering the wording in Paragraph 3.30 from material error to material error or bias, to align with Paragraph 3.33.

Other

15. *Please provide any other comments you have about Chapter 3 that are not already addressed by your responses above.*

Connectivity within the text of the Framework

FEE is very supportive of stating connectivity of information as one of the Draft Framework's Guiding Principles in Section 3B. This means that <IR> should show the combination, inter-relatedness and dependencies between the components that are material to the organisation's ability to create value over time.

FEE recognizes that the text of the Draft Framework also features connectivity by linking the different principles, concepts, and elements related to value creation. FEE finds that making this linkage even more apparent would make the Draft Framework more user-friendly. This could be accomplished by explicitly and consistently cross referencing within the Draft Framework, such as by inserting hyperlinks.

Examples of where the interconnection between concepts stated in the Draft Framework could be improved include:

Capitals and Stakeholders

FEE fully supports the IIRC in focusing the Draft Framework on a principal audience being the information needs of providers of financial capital while the IIRC is also encouraged to consider how the information needs of other stakeholders align of those of providers of financial capital, see paragraph 5) above Within this context, FEE would like to point out that paragraph 3.24 of the Draft Framework points to capitals in determining whether a matter is material, but does not explicitly link the capitals, which the organisation uses or affects, to the stakeholders of the organisation.

The Materiality Background Paper for <IR> makes the connection between stakeholders and the concept of capitals more explicit. For example, in identifying relevant matters for <IR> purposes, this background paper (page 3, Paragraph 16, bullet 2) makes a direct link between stakeholders and the organisation's effects on capitals. FEE suggests that this critical interconnection should become apparent in the Draft Framework as well and not be left to indirect or implicit references.

Strategy, Materiality, and Capitals

The interconnection between strategy and the concept of materiality is not adequately reflected in the Draft Framework. An organisation's strategy has a material effect on its value creation ability (see section 2.4 above), but other than in Paragraph 1.17, this connection is not specifically made in the Draft Framework. The Draft Framework does not make an explicit link between strategy and capital. Namely, the preparer of an integrated report should provide insight into how an organisation's strategy relates to capitals it depends on for its value creation.

Chapter 4: Content Elements

16. *Please provide any comments you have about Chapter 4 that are not already addressed by your responses above (please include comments on the Content Element Business Model [Section 4E] in your answer to questions 7-9 above rather than here).*

FEE recommends keeping the <IR> Framework principles-based, including Chapter 4.

Chapter 5: Preparation and Presentation

Involvement of Those Charged With Governance (Section 5D)

Section 5D discusses the involvement of those charged with governance, and paragraph 4.5 requires organizations to disclose the governance body with oversight responsibility for <IR>.

17. *Should there be a requirement for those charged with governance to include a statement acknowledging their responsibility for the integrated report? Why/why not?*

Requiring such a statement by those charged with governance could add value to the report, in light of their oversight responsibilities for <IR>.

18. *Please provide any other comments you have about Involvement of those charged with governance (Section 5D).*

N/A

Credibility (Section 5E)

The Framework provides reporting criteria against which organizations and assurance providers assess a report's adherence (paragraph 5.21).

19. *If assurance is to be obtained, should it cover the integrated report as a whole, or specific aspects of the report? Why?*

The demand for assurance with respect to <IR> may equally develop gradually over time, similar to the fact that the development of <IR> in practice is expected to be a gradual process. FEE could envisage that assurance on different elements of the report would be useful in an initial stage. However, over time, we expect that assurance on the integrated report as a whole would be considered most useful by investors, and which in our view can be provided if and when suitable criteria have been further developed, including through significant practical experience.

20. *Please provide any other comments you have about Credibility (Section 5E). Assurance providers are particularly asked to comment on whether they consider the Framework provides suitable criteria for an assurance engagement.*

The current format of the Draft Framework seems less practical and more conceptual and high level, which would make it difficult to provide assurance on <IR>. The Draft Framework thus does not contain suitable criteria for an assurance engagement, nor for preparers, at this point. As previously stated, FEE is well aware of the emerging nature of <IR>, especially with regard to external assurance. Therefore, FEE encourages the IIRC to consider the need for criteria to determine the content of an integrated report.

The Draft Framework would need to be further developed to guide preparers and to enable a suitable assurance framework to be developed.

Other

21. *Please provide any other comments you have about Chapter 5 that are not already addressed by your responses above (please include comments on the materiality determination process [Section 5B] in your answer to question 11 above rather than here).*

Aggregation and Disaggregation (Section 5H, Paragraph 5.33)

The Draft Framework (in Paragraph 5.33) makes an important link between the way the organisation (dis)aggregates information and how the organisation is managed. FEE notes that this connection may reveal issues that may be material to the organisation'sability to create value, such as a concern regarding human rights.

Aggregation and disaggregation of information have both a financial and a nonfinancial dimension. The financial one presents financial information based on the business or geographical segments that are commonly used for financial reporting purposes (Paragraph 5.33). The non-financial dimension shows how other capitals (such as natural or social capital) are taken into account. FEE agrees with this approach, but also seeks to identify if information which is based on the business or geographical segments, primarily aimed at financial reporting, would also address material nonfinancial disclosure.

FEE encourages the IIRC to further explore the non-financial dimension of (dis) aggregation of information. In particular, the IIRC should assess whether (dis)aggregating information for non-financial reporting is manageable for companies and whether this information can be compared between and within different business and geographical segments.

XBRL (Section 5I, Paragraph 5.40-41)

FEE welcomes the IIRC's suggestion of using XBRL as a standardized technology platform for <IR>. When <IR> is in a later stage of development, it would be helpful to have more guidance on how an integrated report can be best captured in XBRL.

Overall View

22. *Recognizing that <IR> will evolve over time, please explain the extent to which you believe the content of the Framework overall is appropriate for use by organizations in preparing an integrated report and for providing report users with information about an organization's ability to create value in the short, medium and long term?*

As previously stated, FEE thinks that the Draft Framework taken as a whole is appropriate for preparing an integrated report. The Draft Framework is still in its initial and conceptual stages. More practical experience is needed to enable large scale implementation of the Draft Framework to be a smooth development.

Development of <IR>

23. *If the IIRC were to develop explanatory material on <IR> in addition to the Framework, which three topics would you recommend be given priority? Why?*

FEE actually does not consider it to be the role of the IIRC to develop extensive guidance on <IR>. The IIRC can give priority to keep providing examples and best practices of implementing <IR> and structuring the integrated report, as is being done via the Emerging Integrated Reporting Database.

Other

24. *Please provide any other comments not already addressed by your responses to Questions 1-23.*

N/A

Avenue d'Auderghem 22-28 • B-1040 Brussels • Tel: +32 (0)2 285 40 85 • Fax: +32 (0)2 231 11 12 • secretariat@fee.be • www.fee.be

Association Internationale reconnue par Arrêté Royal en date du 30 décembre 1986

Professor Mervyn E. King
Chairman
International Integrated Reporting Council
(IIRC)
Submitted through:
http://www.theiirc.org/consultationdraft2
013/feedback/
16 July 2013
Ref.: CRPG/AKI/LBU/IDS

Dear Professor King,
Re: FEE Comments on the IIRC Consultation Draft of the Draft International

Integrated Reporting <IR> Framework

FEE is pleased to provide you with its comments on the IIRC Consultation Draft of the Draft International <IR> Framework (the Draft Framework).

This response should be seen in light of FEE's continued support for <IR> and its appreciation for the gradual transition towards <IR>. This letter first highlights our key points, followed by the answers to the consultation questions in the appendix.

Strong and Continued Support for the Work of the IIRC and for Developing <IR>

- FEE commends[1] the IIRC for the significant achievement of issuing the Draft Framework and recognizes that redesigning the direction and focus of corporate reporting is a journey. Making the step towards integrated thinking and integrated reporting takes time; the Draft Framework is an important and laudable milestone in this process.
- The IIRC is strongly encouraged in advancing the Draft Framework and in engaging all stakeholders, including policymakers, regulators, and private sector entities, in creating a shared vision on <IR>.
- FEE supports the IIRC's objective of gaining as much practical experience with the Draft Framework as possible, such as provided by the Pilot Programme and Emerging Integrated Reporting Database. The lessons learnt from the Pilot Programme will be instrumental in further developing the Draft Framework. When the final Framework is instated, it is expected this will need to be reviewed and updated periodically, depending on the practical experiences with <IR>.

[1] See the press release of 16 April 2013 in which FEE has welcomed the issuance of the Draft Framework. Hereby FEE summed up its view as follows: *<IR> is the most promising development to improve the quality of businesses' and investors' decision-making and help make our economy more sustainable and stable.*

Page 2 of 13

Avenue d'Auderghem 22-28 • B-1040 Brussels • Tel: +32 (0)2 285 40 85 • Fax: +32 (0)2 231 11 12 • secretariat@fee.be • www.fee.be

Association Internationale reconnue par Arrêté Royal en date du 30 décembre 1986

- FEE fully endorses the way in which <IR> is currently being developed, by largely drawing on stakeholders' involvement and gaining practical experience. FEE is convinced that, at least for the time being, <IR>

should continue to be market driven instead of being mandated by public authorities. Legislation on this matter could in fact hinder such promising evolution and stifle innovation. However, it is necessary to involve public authorities as stakeholders in developing <IR> as regulators can be influential in promoting the widespread acceptance and use of <IR> or in removing obstacles to the application or adoption of <IR>.

The Focus on a Principal Audience for <IR> Is Very Useful

- In our view, it is very useful that the IIRC has chosen to focus <IR> in the first instance on the information needs of providers of financial capital. This pragmatic approach aids in making the Draft Framework operational. FEE fully agrees with the Draft Framework's recognition (Paragraph 1.7) that <IR> benefits all stakeholders who are interested in an organisation's ability to create value over time. The IIRC is encouraged to investigate further how information needs of other stakeholders align with, or differ from, those of providers of financial capital.
- FEE also finds the principles of <IR> useful for reports prepared by not-for-profit organisations and the public sector, as well as reports prepared for specific stakeholder groups. In such reports, different materiality considerations may apply.
- The desirability and practicability of applying the Framework's principles to small and medium-sized enterprises (SMEs) merits consideration, in particular to explore how <IR> can play a role in improving access to capital for SMEs. However, FEE also acknowledges that there is a balance to be struck between the potential benefits of <IR> for SMEs, market pressure that imposes <IR> participation on SMEs (for example as part of the supply chain of a listed food manufacturer) and the risk of adding unnecessary administrative burdens for SMEs. Whilst the initial focus of <IR> has primarily been on reporting by larger companies, it is recommended that the IIRC keeps including some larger SMEs in the Pilot Programme.

The Transition Towards <IR> Is a Gradual One

- The interaction between <IR> and other reports and communications largely depends on how the transition towards <IR> is being made. FEE expects that the shift towards <IR> will have a significant impact on the current corporate reporting cycle. The Draft Framework anticipates that <IR> will lead to an additional standalone report, in addition to other reports and communications. FEE would like the IIRC to address the concern that it might be difficult to convince stakeholders of the benefits of <IR>, when this leads to an additional report and a perceived need for extra resources. In our view, it is important that <IR> contributes to reducing the overall reporting burden for organisations.
- To ease the shift to <IR>, a transition process for the organisation and preparation of corporate reports is needed. This could include practical guidance on changing the current reporting towards <IR> and making recommendations for (temporary) solutions, such as incorporating the Draft Framework principles in the management commentary.

2 See Paragraphs 1.6 - 1.8 of the Draft Framework and the answer to Consultation Question 4.

3 See Paragraph 1.18 of the Draft Framework and the answer to Consultation Question 2.

Page 3 of 13

Avenue d'Auderghem 22-28 • B-1040 Brussels • Tel: +32 (0)2 285 40 85 • Fax: +32 (0)2 231 11 12 • secretariat@fee.be • www.fee.be

Association Internationale reconnue par Arrêté Royal en date du 30 décembre 1986

FEE Advocates the Draft Framework's Principles-Based Approach

- FEE welcomes the principles-based approach of the requirements in the Draft Framework, as opposed to setting detailed rules. Based on the Draft Framework, companies will be able to tell their value creation story by focussing on the relevant principles. However, consideration should be given to the need for suitable and clear criteria to guide preparers in applying the Draft Framework, see also paragraph 17) below. FEE believes suitable criteria will be needed for an organisation to substantiate its decision for including or excluding particular information within its integrated report. However, the specific matters to be included in an integrated report should be dictated by the circumstances of the individual organisation.

- The Draft Framework sets minimum requirements that integrated reports need to comply with in order for them to be in accordance with the Draft Framework. FEE supports this approach and encourages the IIRC to continue identifying these minimum requirements.
- If the Framework is applied effectively, FEE believes that <IR> could contribute three essential features to the quality of understanding that users can derive from business reporting:
    - A better explanation of the key resources ('capitals') on which the business depends
    - A more comprehensive view of operating performance
    - A better basis for understanding the future outlook of the business.

More Connectivity Within the Text of the Draft Framework Would Make It More User-Friendly

- FEE supports *connectivity of information* as one of the Draft Framework's Guiding Principles, meaning that <IR> should show the combination, inter-relatedness and dependencies between the components that are material to the organisation's ability to create value over time.
- The text of the Draft Framework also features connectivity by linking the different principles, concepts and elements related to value creation. Making this linkage even more apparent would make the Draft Framework more user-friendly.

FEE Expects That There Will Be a Demand for External Assurance on <IR>

- FEE considers external independent assurance essential in making the information in the integrated report more reliable and credible. External assurance can increase the confidence of investors and other users of <IR> as they rely more and more on the information provided in an integrated report. Therefore, FEE assumes that in the process of further developing <IR> a market demand for external assurance will arise, which calls for all relevant stakeholders to adopt a proactive approach in this regard. The accountancy profession is willing and able to innovate in order to develop assurance techniques that can provide a suitable level of assurance on <IR>.

See Paragraphs 1.13 and 1.14 of the Draft Framework.

See Section 3B of the Draft Framework and the answer to Consultation Question 15.

See Paragraphs 3.31 and 5.20-21 of the Draft Framework and the answer to Consultation Question 13.

Avenue d'Auderghem 22-28 • B-1040 Brussels • Tel: +32 (0)2 285 40 85 • Fax: +32 (0)2 231 11 12 • secretariat@fee.be • www.fee.be

Association Internationale reconnue par Arrêté Royal en date du 30 décembre 1986

- Specific standards are needed for providing external assurance on <IR, for which the International Auditing and Assurance Standards Board (IAASB), as standard setter for assurance, would be the designated authority. FEE would be happy to contribute to any work undertaken by the IAASB to adapt its current standards to respond to needs for new or adapted forms of assurance that may emerge as a result of the gradual transition to <IR>.
- The level of assurance that can be provided depends on the type of information underpinning the report; this is not self-evident for <IR> which combines past, present and forward looking, financial and non-financial information. In developing external assurance on <IR>, it will be necessary to distinguish between the different types of information to be presented in the integrated report whereby different levels of assurance might need to be provided on different elements of the integrated report. 18) In further developing the Draft Framework, as pointed out in paragraph 10) above, suitable criteria will need to be established that preparers can use to prepare the information in their integrated report. Those criteria would provide the benchmark against which assurance can be provided on the integrated report. FEE is highly committed to supporting the IIRC in its next steps in advancing <IR>. It is particularly looking forward to the initial version of the Framework to be issued in December 2013.

Please do not hesitate to contact us if you wish to further discuss any of the points raised in our response, or if we can contribute to the IIRC achieving its objectives in developing the International <IR> Framework.

For further information on this letter, please contact Laura Buijs, Project Manager, at the FEE Secretariat on +32 2 285 40 71 or via e-mail at laura.buijs@fee.be.

Yours sincerely,

André Kilesse Olivier Boutellis-Taft
President Chief Executive
Page 5 of 13

Avenue d'Auderghem 22-28 • B-1040 Brussels • Tel: +32 (0)2 285 40 85 • Fax: +32 (0)2 231 11 12 • secretariat@fee.be • www.fee.be

Association Internationale reconnue par Arrêté Royal en date du 30 décembre 1986

ANSWERS TO THE CONSULTATION QUESTIONS

Chapter 1: Overview

Principles-Based Requirements

To be in accordance with the Framework, an integrated report should comply with the principles-based requirements identified throughout the Framework in bold italic type (Paragraphs 1.11-1.12).

1. *Should any additional principles-based requirements be added or should any be eliminated or changed? If so, please explain why.*

FEE agrees with the current *principles-based requirements.* The specific matters to be included in an individual organisation's integrated report will be governed by the circumstances of the individual organisation. Thus, while detailed reporting rules might be counterproductive FEE believes suitable criteria will be needed for an organisation to substantiate its decision for including or excluding particular information within its integrated report.

Interaction With Other Reports and Communications

The <IR> process is intended to be applied continuously to all relevant reports and communications, in addition to the preparation of an integrated report. The integrated report may include links to other reports and communications, e.g., financial statements and sustainability reports. The IIRC aims to complement material developed by established reporting standard setters and others, and does not intend to develop duplicate content (Paragraphs 1.18-1.20).

2. *Do you agree with how Paragraphs 1.18-1.20 characterize the interaction with other reports and communications?*

FEE suggests the IIRC clarify Paragraph 1.18 in Chapter 1: Overview, which states that a stand-alone integrated report will be prepared annually in line with the statutory financial reporting cycle in addition to all other relevant reports and communications.

More specifically, FEE believes there is a need for further clarification on how in practice this *stand-alone integrated report*

- Relates to the relevant existing reports on financial and non-financial information?
- Replaces all, or some, of the current reports, or serves solely as an addition?

FEE commends the IIRC for deepening its cooperation with the International Accounting Standards Board (IASB) and the Global Reporting Initiative (GRI) by signing a Memorandum of Understanding with each organisation. Coordination with the IASB and GRI reporting frameworks will be essential in further developing the Draft Framework.

Page 6 of 13

Avenue d'Auderghem 22-28 • B-1040 Brussels • Tel: +32 (0)2 285 40 85 • Fax: +32 (0)2 231 11 12 • secretariat@fee.be • www.fee.be

Association Internationale reconnue par Arrêté Royal en date du 30 décembre 1986

3. *If the IIRC were to create an online database of authoritative sources of indicators or measurement methods developed by established reporting standard setters and others, which references should be included?*

FEE suggests that the Sustainability Reporting Guidelines, set by the GRI, and the Sustainability Accounting Standards, set by the Sustainability Accounting Standards Board, be considered for inclusion in the proposed database.

4. *Please provide any other comments you have about Chapter 1.*

Audience (Paragraphs 1.6 and 1.8)

As mentioned in the cover letter, FEE believes it is very useful that the IIRC has chosen to focus <IR> in the first instance on the information needs of providers of financial capital. This pragmatic approach aids in making the Draft Framework operational. The IIRC is recommended to investigate further how information needs of other stakeholders align with, or differ from, those of providers of financial capital.

Disclosure of Competition-Sensitive Information (Paragraphs 1.11 and 1.12)

FEE commends the IIRC for addressing the confidentiality issues which arise from the disclosure of relevant information (Paragraphs 1.11 and 1.12). The addition of *competitive harm* to the two other reasons for allowing non-disclosure of material information (unavailability of reliable data and specific legal prohibitions) has resolved this issue.

FEE suggests altering the wording in Paragraphs 1.11 and 1.12 from *competitive harm* to *significant competitive harm*. This would indicate that only serious harm would be a reason for non-disclosure. This proposed change aligns more closely with Paragraph 3.42 which refers to (…) *information … that would significantly harm its competitive advantage.*

Chapter 2: Fundamental Concepts

The Capitals (Section 2B)

The Framework describes six categories of capital (Paragraph 2.17). An organization is to use these categories as a benchmark when preparing an integrated report (Paragraphs 2.19-2.21), and should disclose the reason if it considers any of the capitals as not material (Paragraph 4.5).

5. *Do you agree with this approach to the capitals? Why/why not?*

FEE agrees with this approach to capitals. Capitals are essential to an organisation's existence, its operation and its ability to create value. Therefore, it is very important for an organisation to report on various capitals that it uses or affects.

Paragraph 2.24 of the Draft Framework on quantitative and qualitative information, states that when quantitative indicators do not suffice, qualitative indicators (or narrative reporting) should explain the organisation's use of and effects on capitals. According to Paragraph 3.38 narrative reporting should provide information on capitals that is *consistent over time and in a way that enables comparison with*

Avenue d'Auderghem 22-28 • B-1040 Brussels • Tel: +32 (0)2 285 40 85 • Fax: +32 (0)2 231 11 12 • secretariat@fee.be • www.fee.be

Association Internationale reconnue par Arrêté Royal en date du 30 décembre 1986 *other organizations to the extent it is material to the organization's own value creation story*. Further guidance should be developed on how to use narrative reporting in practice in order to achieve this comparability and consistency.

As stated in Paragraph 2.23, an organisation does not control all capitals that it uses or affects. Some (non-financial) capitals are held by other parties who also have a stake in maintaining or increasing their value. It would be helpful if the IIRC would provide more guidance on how an organisation should report on capitals outside its span of control. For example, how far down the value chain organisations should go to report on these capitals? This item is not resolved in the section relating to the reporting boundaries of the integrated report in Section 5G of the Draft Framework.

6. *Please provide any other comments you have about Section 2B?*

N/A

Business Model (Section 2C)

A business model is defined as an organization's chosen system of inputs, business activities, outputs and outcomes that aims to create value over the short, medium and long term (Paragraph 2.26).

7. *Do you agree with this definition? Why/why not?*

FEE agrees in principle with this definition of an organization's business model, but would like to ask the IIRC to further clarify this. The current use of the word *chosen* implies the organisation's responsibility and accountability for its business model and the resulting outcomes (both positive and negative) this choice entails. It would be helpful for this definition to reflect that organisations cannot fully choose the outcomes of their business model as these are also influenced by many external factors.

Business Model (Section 2C) Continued

Outcomes are defined as the internal and external consequences (positive and negative) for the capitals as a result of an organization's business activities and outputs (Paragraphs 2.35-2.36).

8. *Do you agree with this definition? Why/why not?*

FEE agrees with this definition.

9. *Please provide any other comments you have about Section 2C or the disclosure requirements and related guidance regarding business models contained in the Content Elements Chapter of the Framework (see Section 4E)?*

N/A

Page 8 of 13

Avenue d'Auderghem 22-28 • B-1040 Brussels • Tel: +32 (0)2 285 40 85 • Fax: +32 (0)2 231 11 12 • secretariat@fee.be • www.fee.be

Association Internationale reconnue par Arrêté Royal en date du 30 décembre 1986

10. *Please provide any other comments you have about Chapter 2 that are not already addressed by your responses above.*

The concept of value creation (Section 2D) is paramount to the Draft Framework. FEE would consider it useful for the IIRC to further develop this concept. In addition, the resources allocation and the monetisation of intangibles and externalities are the subject of extensive research. However, there does not yet seem to be an applicable methodological framework or much relevant practical experience. Any future work of the IIRC in this regard should consider the demands of providers of financial capital.

Regarding an organisation's value drivers as referred to in Paragraph 2.45 of the Draft Framework; FEE considers a company's strategy as one of the main drivers for its success. Strategy namely forms the linking pin between capitals and value creation. FEE therefore supports the IIRC's emphasis on the importance of strategy in the Draft Framework by identifying *strategic focus and future orientation* as a Guiding Principle (Section 3A) and *strategy and resource allocation* as a Content Element (Section 4D) of the integrated report.

Chapter 3: Guiding Principles

Materiality and Conciseness (Section 3D)

Materiality is determined by reference to assessments made by the primary intended report users (Paragraphs 3.23-3.24). The primary intended report users are providers of financial capital (Paragraphs 1.6-1.8).

11. *Do you agree with this approach to materiality? If not, how would you change it?*

FEE agrees in principle with the Draft Framework's approach to materiality.

12. *Please provide any other comments you have about Section 3D or the Materiality determination process (Section 5B).*

Materiality and Conciseness (Section 3D)

FEE applauds the inclusion of *conciseness* as (part of) this Guiding Principle in the Draft Framework. This will prevent <IR> from leading to very sizeable reports which would lack accessibility and user-friendliness. In order to achieve a concise integrated report, FEE support the alternatives of linking it to additional detailed information as suggested in the Draft Framework (Paragraph 3.29) or compiling a multi-tier report, consisting of varying levels of detail.

Materiality Determination Process

The Draft Framework states that a matter is only material if the primary intended report users (the providers of financial capital) could be substantively influenced by it. As mentioned in our cover letter, FEE finds it is very useful that the IIRC has chosen to focus <IR> in the first instance on the information needs of providers of financial capital, as a pragmatic approach. Without this focus, materiality would be hard to determine. FEE believes that the principles of <IR> are also useful for reports to specific stakeholder groups. In such reports, different materiality considerations may apply.

Page 9 of 13 d'Auderghem 22-28 • B-1040 Brussels • Tel: +32 (0)2 285 40 85 • Fax: +32 (0)2 231 11 12 • secretariat@fee.be • www.fee.be

Association Internationale reconnue par Arrêté Royal en date du 30 décembre 1986

Whereas Paragraph 2.24 of the Draft Framework distinguishes between quantitative and qualitative information, the difference between quantitative and qualitative materiality does not yet become clear in the Draft Framework. Financial impacts can differ greatly from non-financial impacts, such as reputation damage.

FEE would find it useful for this distinction to be reflected in the materiality determination process as set out in the Draft Framework.

Reliability and Completeness (Section 3E)

Reliability is enhanced by mechanisms such as robust internal reporting systems, appropriate stakeholder engagement, and independent, external assurance (Paragraph 3.31).

13. *How should the reliability of an integrated report be demonstrated?*

FEE welcomes the Draft Framework's acknowledgement of external assurance as a mechanism to enhance the reliability (Paragraph 3.31) and credibility of information (Paragraph 5.20). External assurance is essential in making the information in the integrated report more reliable and credible and thereby increasing the confidence of users. FEE expects that in the process of further developing <IR> a need for external assurance will arise.

Specific standards are needed for providing external assurance on specific subject matters. FEE would be more than willing to contribute actively to considerations as to how global assurance standards may have to be adapted for <IR>. The IAASB, as standard setter for assurance, would be the designated authority to lead this work. In our view, it is in the public interest for these standards to tie into a robust system of quality control for those organisations or individuals providing these assurance services. For example, International Standard on Quality Control (ISQC) 1 currently applies to firms that provide services covered by the IAASB's international standards.

The level of assurance that can be provided depends on the type of information on which the report is based; this is not self-evident for <IR> which combines past, present and forward looking, financial and non-financial information. FEE finds it crucial that the information underpinning the integrated report is *assurable* in accordance with generally accepted global standards. This means that it is supported by sufficient evidence and is prepared according to specific criteria so that it can be checked against these criteria. This *assurability* is not necessarily obvious for future-oriented and non-financial information (as referred to in Paragraph 3.46 and 3.47 of the Draft Framework). Therefore, in developing external assurance on <IR>, it may be necessary to distinguish between the different types of information to be presented in the integrated report so that challenges that could be associated with providing assurance on these different types of information can be considered. Different levels of assurance might need to be provided on different elements of the integrated report.

There is also a need to develop clear criteria which preparers can use to prepare the information in their integrated report which would also be the criteria or benchmark against which assurance can be provided on the integrated report.

FEE expects that there will be market demand for assurance over an integrated report, because assurance enhances the credibility of information, which is of value to investors and other users of <IR> as they increasingly come to rely on the information provided in an integrated report.

Avenue d'Auderghem 22-28 • B-1040 Brussels • Tel: +32 (0)2 285 40 85 • Fax: +32 (0)2 231 11 12 • secretariat@fee.be • www.fee.be

Association Internationale reconnue par Arrêté Royal en date du 30 décembre 1986

Regarding the provision of assurance by the auditor, the following should at least be considered: competences, experience and skill sets required, and the need to use independent experts.

14. *Please provide any other comments you have about Section 3E.*

The accountancy profession is willing and able to innovate in order to develop assurance techniques that can provide a suitable level of assurance on <IR>. It is recommended the IIRC work with the IAASB in this area, as they are the responsible global standards setter for assurance. FEE is more than happy to contribute to any work undertaken by the IAASB to adapt its current standards to respond to needs for new or adapted forms of assurance that may emerge as a result of the gradual transition to <IR>.

FEE suggests altering the wording in Paragraph 3.30 from *material error* to *material error or bias*, to align with Paragraph 3.33.

15. *Please provide any other comments you have about Chapter 3 that are not already addressed by your responses above.*

Connectivity Within the Text of the Framework

FEE is very supportive of stating *connectivity of information* as one of the Draft Framework's Guiding Principles in Section 3B. This means that <IR> should show the combination, inter-relatedness and dependencies between the components that are material to the organisation's ability to create value over time.

FEE recognises that the text of the Draft Framework also features connectivity by linking the different principles, concepts, and elements related to value creation. FEE finds that making this linkage even more apparent would make the Draft Framework more user-friendly. This could be accomplished by explicitly and consistently cross referencing within the Draft Framework, such as by inserting hyperlinks.

Examples of where the interconnection between concepts stated in the Draft Framework could be improved include:

Capitals and Stakeholders

FEE fully supports the IIRC in focusing the Draft Framework on a principal audience being the information needs of providers of financial capital while the IIRC is also encouraged to consider how the information needs of other stakeholders align of those of providers of financial capital, see paragraph 5) above Within this context, FEE would like to point out that paragraph 3.24 of the Draft Framework points to *capitals* in determining whether a matter is material, but does not explicitly link the capitals, which the organisation uses or affects, to the *stakeholders* of the organisation.

The Materiality Background Paper for <IR> makes the connection between *stakeholders* and the concept of *capitals* more explicit. For example, in identifying relevant matters for <IR> purposes, this background paper (page 3, Paragraph 16, bullet 2) makes a direct link between stakeholders and the organisation's effects on capitals. FEE suggests that this critical interconnection should become apparent in the Draft Framework as well and not be left to indirect or implicit references.

Page 11 of 13

Avenue d'Auderghem 22-28 • B-1040 Brussels • Tel: +32 (0)2 285 40 85 • Fax: +32 (0)2 231 11 12 • secretariat@fee.be • www.fee.be

Association Internationale reconnue par Arrêté Royal en date du 30 décembre 1986

Strategy, Materiality, and Capitals

The interconnection between *strategy* and the concept of *materiality* is not adequately reflected in the Draft Framework. An organisation's strategy has a material effect on its value creation ability (see section 2.4 above), but other than in Paragraph 1.17, this connection is not specifically made in the Draft Framework.

The Draft Framework does not make an explicit link between *strategy* and *capital.*

Namely, the preparer of an integrated report should provide insight into how an organisation's strategy relates to capitals it depends on for its value creation.

Chapter 4: Content Elements

16. *Please provide any comments you have about Chapter 4 that are not already addressed by your responses above (please include comments on the Content Element Business Model [Section 4E] in your answer to questions 7- 9 above rather than here).*

FEE recommends keeping the <IR> Framework principles-based, including Chapter 4.

Chapter 5: Preparation and Presentation

Involvement of Those Charged With Governance (Section 5D)

Section 5D discusses the involvement of those charged with governance, and Paragraph 4.5 requires organizations to disclose the governance body with oversight responsibility for <IR>.

17. *Should there be a requirement for those charged with governance to include a statement acknowledging their responsibility for the integrated report? Why/why not?*

Requiring such a statement by those charged with governance could add value to the report, in light of their oversight responsibilities for <IR>.

18. *Please provide any other comments you have about involvement of those charged with governance (Section 5D).*

N/A

Credibility (Section 5E)

The Framework provides reporting criteria against which organizations and assurance providers assess a report's adherence (Paragraph 5.21).

19. *If assurance is to be obtained, should it cover the integrated report as a whole, or specific aspects of the report? Why?*

The demand for assurance with respect to <IR> may equally develop gradually over time, similar to the fact that the development of <IR> in practice is expected to be a gradual process. FEE could envisage that assurance on different elements of the report would be useful in an initial stage. However, over time, we expect that assurance on the integrated report as a whole would be considered most useful by.

Avenue d'Auderghem 22-28 • B-1040 Brussels • Tel: +32 (0)2 285 40 85 • Fax: +32 (0)2 231 11 12 • secretariat@fee.be • www.fee.be

Association Internationale reconnue par Arrêté Royal en date du 30 décembre 1986 investors, and which in our view can be provided if and when suitable criteria have been further developed, including through significant practical experience.

20. *Please provide any other comments you have about Credibility (Section 5E). Assurance providers are particularly asked to comment on whether they consider the Framework provides suitable criteria for an assurance engagement.*

The current format of the Draft Framework seems less practical and more conceptual and high level, which would make it difficult to provide assurance on <IR>. The Draft Framework thus does not contain suitable criteria for an assurance engagement, nor for preparers, at this point. As previously stated, FEE is well aware of the emerging nature of <IR>, especially with regard to external assurance.

Therefore, FEE encourages the IIRC to consider the need for criteria to determine the content of an integrated report. The Draft Framework would need to be further developed to guide preparers and to enable a suitable assurance framework to be developed.

21. *Please provide any other comments you have about Chapter 5 that are not already addressed by your responses above (please include comments on the materiality determination process [Section 5B] in your answer to question 11 above rather than here).*

Aggregation and Disaggregation (Section 5H, Paragraph 5.33)

The Draft Framework (in Paragraph 5.33) makes an important link between the way the organisation (dis)aggregates information and how the organisation is managed. FEE notes that this connection may reveal issues that may be material to the organisation's ability to create value, such as a concern regarding human rights.

Aggregation and disaggregation of information have both a financial and a nonfinancial dimension. The financial one presents financial information based on the business or geographical segments that are commonly used for financial reporting purposes (Paragraph 5.33). The non-financial dimension shows how other capitals (such as natural or social capital) are taken into account. FEE agrees with this approach, but also seeks to identify if information which is based on the business or geographical segments, primarily aimed at financial reporting, would also address material non-financial disclosure.

c) FEE encourages the IIRC to further explore the non-financial dimension of (dis) aggregation of information. In particular, the IIRC should assess whether (dis)aggregating information for non-financial reporting is manageable for companies and whether this information can be compared between and within different business and geographical segments.

XBRL (Section 5I, Paragraph 5.40-41)

FEE welcomes the IIRC's suggestion of using XBRL as a standardized technology platform for <IR>. When <IR> is in a later stage of development, it would be helpful to have more guidance on how an integrated report can be best captured in XBRL.

Avenue d'Auderghem 22-28 • B-1040 Brussels • Tel: +32 (0)2 285 40 85 • Fax: +32 (0)2 231 11 12 • secretariat@fee.be • www.fee.be

Association Internationale reconnue par Arrêté Royal en date du 30 décembre 1986

22. *Recognizing that <IR> will evolve over time, please explain the extent to which you believe the content of the Framework overall is appropriate for use by organizations in preparing an integrated report and for providing report users with information about an organization's ability to create value in the short, medium and long term?*

As previously stated, FEE thinks that the Draft Framework taken as a whole is appropriate for preparing an integrated report. The Draft Framework is still in its initial and conceptual stages. More practical experience is needed to enable large scale implementation of the Draft Framework to be a smooth development.

23. *If the IIRC were to develop explanatory material on <IR> in addition to the Framework, which three topics would you recommend be given priority? Why?*

FEE actually does not consider it to be the role of the IIRC to develop extensive guidance on <IR>. The IIRC can give priority to keep providing examples and best practices of implementing <IR> and structuring the integrated report, as is being done via the Emerging Integrated Reporting Database.

24. *Please provide any other comments not already addressed by your responses to Questions 1-23.*

N/A

Reporting against performance outcomes was the least well done, inputs were satisfactory and to a more limited extent outputs too.

Consultation Questions

The IIRC welcomes comments on all aspects of the Draft International <IR> Framework (Draft Framework) from all stakeholders, whether to express agreement or to recommend changes.

The following questions are focused on areas where there has been significant discussion during the development process. Comments on any other aspect of the Draft Framework are also encouraged through the questions.

Please provide all comments in English.

All comments received will be considered a matter of public record and will be posted on the IIRC's website (www.theiirc.org).

Comments should be submitted by Monday 15th, July 2013.

Name: Brian Singleton-Green
Email: brian.singleton-green@icaew.com
Stakeholder group: Professional bodies – Accounting
If replying on behalf of an Organization please complete the following:
Organization name: ICAEW
Industry sector: Not applicable
Geographical region: Global

Key Points

If you wish to briefly express any key points, or to emphasize particular aspects of your submission, or add comments in the nature of a cover letter, then the following space can be used for this purpose. Please do not repeat large amounts of material appearing elsewhere in your comments.

INTRODUCTION

ICAEW welcomes the opportunity to comment on the Consultation Draft of the International <IR> Framework published by the International Integrated Reporting Council (IIRC) in April 2013.

WHO WE ARE

ICAEW is a world-leading professional accountancy body. We operate under a Royal Charter, working in the public interest. ICAEW's regulation of its members, in particular its responsibilities in respect of auditors, is overseen by the UK Financial Reporting Council (FRC). We provide leadership and practical support to over 140,000 member chartered accountants in more than 160 countries, working with governments, regulators and industry in order to ensure that the highest standards are maintained.

ICAEW members operate across a wide range of areas in business, practice and the public sector. They provide financial expertise and guidance based on the highest professional, technical and ethical standards. They are trained to provide clarity and apply rigor, and so help create long-term sustainable economic value.

Integrated reporting is a subject that crosses traditional boundaries of expertise, raising issues of financial and broader corporate reporting, assurance, corporate governance and sustainability. Through the work of its Financial Reporting Faculty, Audit and Assurance Faculty and Corporate Governance and Sustainability teams, ICAEW is recognised as a leading authority in all of these areas. Our thought leadership work is at the forefront of global debates on the future evolution of corporate reporting, assurance, corporate governance, and sustainable business practices. ICAEW's own Annual Review continues to move towards an integrated reporting model.

MAJOR POINTS

Support for the Work of the IIRC

ICAEW supports the vision of the IIRC, and believes that the <IR> initiative has the potential to act as a catalyst for major improvements in business reporting and the adoption of sustainable business practices. Our comments and recommendations below should be read in this context.

We welcome publication of the consultation draft (CD), and believe, notwithstanding our reservations on a number of important issues, that it marks a significant step towards the realization of integrated reporting. Clearly, a great deal of work has been done since publication of the 2011 discussion paper on integrated reporting in a relatively short space of time, and many of the questions that we and other commentators raised on the earlier document have now been addressed. This is a considerable achievement. In our view, though, a number of difficulties still need to be dealt with before the case for <IR> is sufficiently compelling to ensure that is taken up voluntarily by more than a minority of companies and is regarded by mainstream investors as essential information. We explain these points in our responses to the various questions posed in the CD and highlight the more important points in the paragraphs immediately below.

<IR> and Other Business Reporting

An <IR> report is intended to be a standalone document (CD 5.2) that would be additional to companies' existing reports, but would be linked or referenced to them. It may or may not form part of the annual report; this would be for each company to decide. We think that leaving this matter for companies to decide for themselves is the right approach. This is partly because existing reports are usually produced in accordance with requirements that vary from jurisdiction to jurisdiction and are not about to disappear. But it is also because, while <IR> is still in the experimental phase, it would be premature to replace any of the established components of corporate reporting. Unfortunately, this means that <IR> seems likely to impose additional costs and disclosure requirements on companies at a time when there is already a strong drive to streamline the disclosure regime.

How far <IR> will provide additional information to that currently reported is something that will vary from jurisdiction to jurisdiction, depending on companies' existing reporting practices. For some companies in certain jurisdictions – in the UK, for example – the inclusion of the type (though not necessarily the range) of disclosures suggested by the draft framework may not be a radical departure from existing practice.

For such companies, it may be most sensible to integrate with their existing disclosures any additional points arising from the issues raised by the framework, rather than to take the approach of preparing a separate report. Indeed, as business reporting evolves, and the principles set out in the framework are increasingly accepted over time, we would expect to see increasing integration of integrated reporting with existing reports, so that standalone <IR> reports may become less common.

Timing and Due Process

We note the IIRC's firm plans to publish the final framework in December 2013. This is an ambitious timetable. It may be achievable, but this will depend critically on the nature of the comments received by the IIRC from respondents during the formal consultation process and how much further work they give rise to. Given the large number of responses that we understand the IIRC has already received, the timetable seems to be especially ambitious. The IIRC should moreover continue to be receptive to stakeholder comment following the end of the formal consultation period; indeed, it should welcome further comments and plan to meet with stakeholders to discuss their key concerns and to validate any major changes proposed to the current draft. A less ambitious timetable would allow more time for this and allow the IIRC to take into account the results of the Pilot Programme (see below). The publication of a widely supported and high quality document is far more important than meeting self-imposed deadlines for publication. If, as we suggest, publication of the final framework is deferred, it would be advisable to take this decision and announce it sooner rather than later.

We would also point out that, at least from a US and European perspective, December is not the best time of year to publish new reporting proposals that it is hoped will be adopted as soon as possible, as it will be too late for those many companies and other organisations with December financial reporting dates to reflect them in their 2013 reports. From this point of view, publication in March or April 2014 would be better as it would allow adequate time for boards to start thinking about how to incorporate the proposals in their 2014 reports. No doubt in choosing the publication date for the final framework, the IIRC will take into account when companies in different parts of the world might be most receptive to new ideas for the annual reporting cycle.

Results of the Pilot Programme

There is a real prospect that improvements in communication might flow from the proposals in the draft framework, and we are keen to see these improvements realised. But this will often require organisations to disclose much more than they do now, particularly non-financial information, which may put them at a disadvantage against competitors. For this reason, many organisations are likely to find the proposals challenging when they try to apply them in practice. The experience of companies engaged in the Pilot Programme would be of great interest in this respect, and it would have been helpful if the draft framework could have included a clear analysis of experiences to date. We understand that a number of major companies will be experimenting with integrated reporting in 2013, and it would also be useful to be able to learn from their experiences before finally issuing the framework. All this adds to our concerns about the timetable for publication of the framework.

Focus

We support the draft framework's stated position that integrated reports 'should be prepared primarily for providers of financial capital' (CD 1.6). However, the CD's wording sometimes suggests an uncertain focus. We believe that the framework's focus needs to be more clearly on the providers of financial capital for for-profit companies. We recognize that such a focus may be unwelcome to some of those who have supported the idea of integrated reporting, but we believe that it is essential if it is to be accepted voluntarily by more than a minority of businesses and their investors. We would not, of course, want this focus to dilute or undermine the potential of the <IR> initiative to catalyze more sustainable business practices. In particular, integrated reporting should seek to demonstrate to businesses and their investors that sustainable business practices are consistent with their long-term interests.

The concept of the six capitals is very important and has the potential to improve business practices, as well as reporting. It may be helpful in this context to distinguish more clearly between the capitals as objectives in their own right and as tools to help thinking about what drives value creation in a business. At the moment, the draft framework gives equal weight to each of the six capitals, which may be helpful as a means for telling the business's story. However, the implication of the investor focus of integrated reporting is that references to the various capitals should be made for the specific purpose of explaining how shareholder value has been created for the providers of financial capital – ie, how the earnings or future earnings prospects of the business have been enhanced. This in turn suggests that priority should be given throughout the framework to a focus on thinking about the effects of the other five capitals on financial capital.

At CD 2.17, 'financial capital' is defined to include grants. Some think grant providers should not be regarded as providers of financial capital (though they would be more relevant perhaps for non-commercial organisations). This highlights, in our view, an ambiguity that currently exists in the concept of capital.

Investor Engagement

Although <IR> is primarily aimed at the providers of financial capital (investors), it is still not clear that it will give mainstream investors and the investment analysts who serve them the information that they want. Investors and investment analysts are not a homogeneous group, and there are important differences in their information needs. To achieve widespread recognition, <IR> will need to provide useful information to mainstream investors, not just to those with an explicit focus on socially responsible investment (SRI). There are important aspects of <IR> that should appeal to mainstream investors and investment analysts, but we do not believe that this is as widely recognised as it should be. We are concerned that illustrations and language in the draft framework may reinforce the view that <IR> is purely or mainly for SRI investors, and we would encourage the IIRC to emphasise how information provided in accordance with the framework should support fundamentals-based assessments of shareholder value.

For these reasons, we believe that it is very important that the IIRC should maintain its efforts to engage with mainstream investors and analysts, in order to ensure that <IR> gains their active support. This may well mean that <IR> is in significant respects experimental for some time to come; not only because preparers will at first be unfamiliar with it, but because it will not be immediately clear how it can best be adapted to meet those users' needs.

It will also be important for individual companies to engage with investors so as to understand their particular information needs.

Structure and Scope of the Document

The draft framework is a rather difficult document to read, and it will be important in the final version to provide an accessible overview at the beginning. It is also difficult to see many small and medium-sized organisations being willing to make the investment of time and effort that the document requires, and if it is intended that they should adopt its principles, a simplified version would be essential.

Assurance

While the most effective way of demonstrating reliability is external assurance, at this experimental stage in the development of integrated reporting, we think it is too early to establish principles on how much of it should be assured or exactly what form of assurance should be provided. We believe that these matters should be left to businesses to decide for themselves, in consultation with their investors.

Looking Ahead

There remains important work for the IIRC to undertake. However, at some point reasonably soon after the framework and any associated guidance has been issued the IIRC might wish to consider initiating a debate with and between its stakeholders about the future role of the IIRC, and indeed about whether or not in the long run integrated reporting will need a standing body to keep the framework updated and to encourage and monitor its application. We understand that the IIRC intends to issue next year a consultation document on its future governance structure, and this may provide an opportunity for stakeholders to comment on what the organisation's future should be.

Chapter 1: Overview

Principles-Based Requirements

To be in accordance with the Framework, an integrated report should comply with the principles-based requirements identified throughout the Framework in bold italic type (paragraphs 1.11-1.12).

1. *Should any additional principles-based requirements be added or should any be eliminated or changed? If so, please explain why.*

On the guiding principles (Chapter 3), as we explain below (paragraph 53), we believe that the stakeholder responsiveness principle needs to be significantly revised; stakeholder responsiveness should not be an objective in its own right. We believe that the reliability and completeness principle needs to be moved towards a requirement that <IR> should be fair, balanced and understandable (paragraphs 44-45 below). We also suggest a rewording of the consistency and comparability principle (paragraph 54 below) and a re-ordering of the content elements in order to emphasize the connectivity between the different elements in an integrated report (paragraph 57).

On the content elements (Chapter 4), we think that – contrary to the principle expressed at CD 4.4 – standalone <IR> reports should not be the only way of doing integrated reporting. As explained above (paragraphs 7-8), in the short term a requirement to prepare an additional report may well be a deterrent to adopting <IR>, and in the longer term we expect that integrated reporting will be increasingly integrated with other reports. We have doubts about some of the disclosures required in the principle at CD 4.5 (see paragraph 59 below). The principle that an integrated report should answer the question 'To what extent is the organisation's business model resilient?' (CD 4.21) is open to objection, and we suggest below (paragraph 36) that it should be changed to deal instead with allowing users to make their own judgements on a company's resilience. We question (paragraph 64 below) whether reporting effects on all the capitals should be a principle in its own right (CD 4.27).

Interaction With Other Reports and Communications

The <IR> process is intended to be applied continuously to all relevant reports and communications, in addition to the preparation of an integrated report. The integrated report may include links to other reports and communications, e.g., financial statements and sustainability reports. The IIRC aims to complement material developed by established reporting standard setters and others, and does not intend to develop duplicate content (paragraphs 1.18-1.20).

2. *Do you agree with how paragraphs 1.18-1.20 characterize the interaction with other reports and communications?*

As already explained, we think that integrated reports will increasingly either overlap with firms' other reports or – and this might be the more sensible solution – be integrated with them, so that standalone integrated reports would gradually disappear or become less common.

3. *If the IIRC were to create an online database of authoritative sources of indicators or measurement methods developed by established reporting standard setters and others, which references should be included?*

We do not think that an online database of authoritative sources would be a good idea. If they are deemed to be authoritative, this implies that people should comply with them, which would put the IIRC into the inappropriate position of a sort of accreditation body for other bodies.

Other

4. *Please provide any other comments you have about Chapter 1.*

We have no other comments on Chapter 1.

Chapter 2: Fundamental Concepts

The Capitals (Section 2B)

The Framework describes six categories of capital (paragraph 2.17). An organization is to use these categories as a benchmark when preparing an integrated report (paragraphs 2.19-2.21), and should disclose the reason if it considers any of the capitals as not material (paragraph 4.5).

5. *Do you agree with this approach to the capitals? Why/why not?*

We agree with the approach of using the six capitals as benchmarks in preparing an integrated report, subject to the point we made earlier (in paragraph 13) about giving priority to thinking about the effects on financial capital of the other five capitals. We are not sure, though, that useful disclosures would result from any requirement to disclose why something is not material. Something either is or is not material, and there may be nothing that can usefully be said to elaborate the point. The assumption that all six capitals will usually be material for all organisations also seems to be inconsistent with the approach taken at CD 2.19-2.21. We are also concerned that the description of social and relationship capital is too narrow. We have suggested (paragraph 28) a wider definition that places greater emphasis on relationships, which we think will usually be of most interest in practice to investors.

6. *Please provide any other comments you have about Section 2B?*

It would be helpful to explain why it is right to include 'shared norms, and common values and behaviours' as social and relationship capital. Elsewhere, the draft framework stresses the value of diversity, which presumably includes diversity of norms, values and behaviours. Norms operate at different levels, so that is possible for diversity of norms at one level to co-exist with a shared, higher level norm of respect for such diversity. If the current wording is to be retained, it needs to be explained why, in some instances, uniformity rather than diversity of norms is desirable.

We recognise that 'social capital' is a commonly used term in the social sciences, where it refers to trust as well as relationships. Trust is of course helpful for business, even – or perhaps especially – in communities where there are diverse norms, values and behaviours. But except where there is a question about an entity's licence to operate, relationship capital is typically of more immediate relevance to a business than other aspects of social capital, and we suggest 'relationship and social capital' would be a more appropriate term than 'social and relationship capital'. In our view, the importance of relationships does not come across clearly from the description of this capital as currently drafted.

The term 'reporting boundary' appears at paragraph CD 2.25, although it is not explained until Section 5G. This term will be unfamiliar to readers, and it may be useful to explain it at this point in the framework. Alternatively, perhaps the glossary should appear at the front of the framework rather than at the back.

Business Model (Section 2C)

A business model is defined as an organization's chosen system of inputs, business activities, outputs and outcomes that aims to create value over the short, medium and long term (paragraph 2.26).

7. *Do you agree with this definition? Why/why not?*

We agree with this definition, although the inclusion of outcomes goes beyond what is conventionally regarded as belonging to a firm's business model. We would not expect business model disclosures in accordance with The UK Corporate Governance Code, for example, to include outcomes unless the disclosures were deliberately extended for the purposes of integrated reporting.

Outcomes are defined as the internal and external consequences (positive and negative) for the capitals as a result of an organization's business activities and outputs (paragraphs 2.35-2.36).

8. *Do you agree with this definition? Why/why not?*

We agree with the definition, but it needs to be recognised that it will be difficult to get people to report on the negatives as fully as on the positives; greater emphasis on the connectivity between different content elements may help in this respect. The examples of relevant outcomes at CD 2.35 are perhaps not the most persuasive that could be found. Staff morale, for example, is a difficult matter to report on objectively or for an organisation as a whole, and it is also difficult to know what the results of staff surveys (for instance) imply for future success. Perhaps turnover of critical personnel would be a better illustration.

9. *Please provide any other comments you have about Section 2C or the disclosure requirements and related guidance regarding business models contained in the Content Elements Chapter of the Framework (see Section 4E)?*

CD 2.40 notes that 'Business strategies that are overly focused on optimizing short term financial performance can impede the ability to create long term value.' This is of course true, but it is equally true that business strategies that are overly focused on the creation of long-term value can impede the ability to survive in the short term. We doubt whether advice of this sort adds anything useful to the framework.

The second sentence of CD 2.43 also dispenses unnecessary advice, but is arguably self-contradictory as well as it appears to say that the maximisation of financial capital does not necessarily maximise financial capital. Perhaps in this section generally ('The meaning of value' – CD 2.41-2.44) it would be better to focus on explaining the meaning of shareholder value. This should be done by reference to the future earnings capability of the business and by explaining how an integrated report provides information on value created in all relevant capitals in order to support better investor assessments of this capability.

CD 4.21 would require organisations not only to describe their business model, but also to say how resilient it is. We think that it will be very difficult for organisations to provide a useful answer on resilience, and so the temptation will be for them to give bland assurances that they are indeed resilient. Perhaps more fundamentally, it is the business's resilience that is important rather than that of its business model. Business models are constantly changing in response to changing circumstances and opportunities; this is an important part of how a business stays resilient.

The question of resilience overlaps with the financial reporting and auditing question of going concern. This is currently under consideration in the UK, largely as a result of the financial crisis. The 2012 report of the Sharman Inquiry, Going Concern and Liquidity Risks: Lessons for Companies and Auditors, provides a good review of the issues, and it may be worthwhile for the IIRC to consider it in deciding what can usefully be said about resilience. The UK debate on this subject continues as the Financial Reporting Council's January 2013 proposals on implementation of the Sharman Inquiry's recommendations – recommendations that we support – were, in our view, in need of improvement (see ICAEW Rep 65/13). As we pointed out in our response to the FRC: 'Directors are able to take a clear view on their company's short term liquidity and solvency but the future is inherently uncertain. The longer the assessment period, the less confident directors can be.' Any reporting on resilience would face similar limitations.

We suggest that rather than reporting on resilience directly, the emphasis should be on providing investors with sufficient information to form their own judgements on resilience. It would also be helpful for the framework to define 'resilience' clearly in the Glossary, and for the term to be explained when it appears at CD 4.21.

Other

10. *Please provide any other comments you have about Chapter 2 that are not already addressed by your responses above.*

We have no further comments on Chapter 2.

Chapter 3: Guiding Principles

Materiality and Conciseness (Section 3D)

Materiality is determined by reference to assessments made by the primary intended report users (paragraphs 3.23-3.24). The primary intended report users are providers of financial capital (paragraphs 1.6-1.8).

11. *Do you agree with this approach to materiality? If not, how would you change it?*

While the draft framework's definition of materiality is a reasonable one, we are concerned that there should not be a multiplicity of authoritative statements on what constitutes materiality in corporate reporting. The definition of materiality used by the International Accounting Standards Board (IASB) is: 'Information is material if omitting it or misstating it could influence decisions that users make on the basis of financial information about a specific reporting entity' (2010 Conceptual Framework, QC11). The reference to 'financial information' is too restrictive for <IR>, but we suggest that, apart from a necessary modification on this point, the framework should adopt the IASB's definition. Engagement with investors should help to determine what is material to them.

The description of the materiality determination process is also reasonable, but we are not sure that it adds much to the framework, and we wonder whether it could be dispensed with. The draft framework proposes (CD 3.28) that the materiality determination process should be disclosed, but we doubt whether, as far as most organisations are concerned, such disclosures would provide more than boilerplate.

CD 3.29 says that there should be a balance between conciseness and completeness. In our view, the need to disclose all material information should not be constrained by a desire for conciseness, desirable though this is. The requirement should be to disclose all material information (completeness), but to do so as concisely as possible.

12. *Please provide any other comments you have about Section 3D or the Materiality determination process (Section 5B).*

Notwithstanding the comments above, we support the materiality and conciseness principle. If standalone reports described as integrated reports are too long – and we understand that experience in South Africa highlights the risk of this outcome – some of the value of <IR> will be lost.

Reliability and Completeness (Section 3E)

Reliability is enhanced by mechanisms such as robust internal reporting systems, appropriate stakeholder engagement, and independent, external assurance (paragraph 3.31).

13. *How should the reliability of an integrated report be demonstrated?*

We assume that external stakeholders would not have access to an organisation's internal records, so we do not see how engagement with them would either enhance or demonstrate the reliability of an integrated report. And while it is true that robust internal reporting systems enhance reliability, users of an integrated report will not be in a position to judge how far this is the case in relation to the report. As noted earlier, the most effective way of demonstrating reliability, in our view, is external assurance.

We do not think, though, that the question of external assurance needs to be settled at this stage. External assurance imposes additional costs and, if the assurance is to be useful, may impose constraints on what can usefully be disclosed; both points may diminish <IR>'s attractiveness to potential adopters. While integrated reporting is still at an early stage of development, there would be advantages in allowing organisations to decide for themselves, in consultation with investors, how far they want reported information to be externally assured. They may decide that some parts of an integrated report should be subject to assurance and some not. To avoid confusing readers, the assured parts might be printed on different colour paper or visually distinguished in some other way – and there are of course other ways of explaining what is assured and what is not. But the IIRC is right to flag the question of how reliability can be demonstrated, which will be important for the long-term success of <IR>.

14. *Please provide any other comments you have about Section 3E.*

Subject to the comments below, we support the reliability and completeness principle, though it would be more accurate to call it the 'reliability, completeness and balance' principle.

We are doubtful how far the guidance set out at CD 3.33 is practical. At the moment, it reads like a counsel of perfection. The 2012 revision of The UK Corporate Governance Code includes a requirement (C.1) that 'The board should present a fair, balanced and understandable assessment of the company's position and prospects', which seems to us to be a sensible approach. Perhaps it would be sufficient to say that <IR> should be 'fair, balanced and understandable'.

While no one would suggest that <IR> should contain errors, we wonder whether 'freedom from error' is the right concept for what is essentially a forward-looking report. It seems more appropriate for something backward-looking and factual.

While there will always be some managements that rely on poor information and inadequate systems, CD 3.41 rather carries the flavor that the authors of the framework know better than the people who run businesses how the latter ought to do their jobs – which will not help sell <IR> to them. It may therefore be worth considering whether this paragraph needs to be retained.

We support the proposal (CD 3.42) that organizations should not have to disclose information for <IR> that would damage their interests. But the draft framework's caution that this exemption should not be used inappropriately is pertinent, and obviously there is a risk that it will be used as an excuse for all sorts of non-disclosures. This is a point on which some examples of when the exemption might or might not be used in practice would be helpful.

Other

15. *Please provide any other comments you have about Chapter 3 that are not already addressed by your responses above.*

We support the strategic focus and future orientation principle (CD 3.2).

The connectivity principle (CD 3.7) is also a good one, but it will be difficult in practice to comply with it well. This is a question for which examples of good practice would be very helpful to preparers.

On a point of detail, it is debatable whether every organization has a 'unique value creation story'. While in a sense every organization is indeed unique, it is also true that organizations in the same line of business are often pretty well identical in important respects. Perhaps 'particular' would be better than 'unique'.

We suggest that CD 3.9 should be deleted. It gives the impression that those issuing the framework know better than the people currently running organizations how they ought to think. This is likely to put people off.

In our view, the stakeholder responsiveness principle (CD 3.13) needs to be significantly revised. The avowed primary focus of <IR> is reporting to capital providers, but this paragraph gives the opposite impression, apparently putting all 'key' stakeholders on an equal footing. It also raises questions about what stakeholders' legitimate needs are. And while it is true that 'value is … created through relationships with others' (CD 3.14), these relationships may be purely commercial, in which case there may not be much to be said about them. We suggest a redraft of the principle along the following lines: 'An integrated report should provide insight into the organization's relationships with key stakeholders so far as these are relevant to the providers of financial capital'. Understanding of the capitals on which a firm depends may also be enhanced by engagement with stakeholders, but this does not require responsiveness to stakeholders as an objective in its own right.

We support the consistency and comparability principle (CD 3.48), subject to some rewording, as follows:

- Consistency over time: Changes in the way in which information is prepared or presented should not be made arbitrarily, but corporate reporting improves progressively over time, and we would not want it to be tied to old practices just for the sake of consistency.
- Comparability with other organizations: This is desirable, but especially for nonfinancial information, can lead to an inappropriate one-size-fits-all approach.

Organizations will no doubt be under pressure from users to disclose the information that their competitors in the same sector disclose, but different disclosures will be right for different sectors.

We suggest accordingly that the principle should be redrafted as follows:

'To the extent that this is useful to the providers of financial capital, the information in an integrated report should be presented on a basis that is consistent over time and in a way that enables comparison with other organizations'.

Chapter 4: Content Elements

16. *Please provide any comments you have about Chapter 4 that are not already addressed by your responses above (please include comments on the Content Element Business Model [Section 4E] in your answer to questions 7-9 above rather than here).*

As explained at paragraphs 7-8 and 22 above, we do not think that it should be a principle that an integrated report has to be a standalone document (CD 4.4).

We like the question-based approach to describing the various content elements. This should encourage organizations to think more about what they should disclose and should therefore help secure more helpful and relevant disclosures than would a detailed list of required contents.

We suggest that a more logical ordering for the content elements, which would 'organizational overview'); strategy; business model; performance; governance; future outlook and risks.

We believe that the reference to stakeholders at CD 4.4 should be restricted to the providers of financial capital, rather than to stakeholders generally. Organizations may of course wish to communicate with other stakeholders, but bringing them within the scope of integrated reporting is likely to lead to a loss of focus.

We have various concerns about CD 4.5, as follows:

- We have already commented (paragraph 39) that most organizations' disclosures on their materiality determination process are unlikely to be useful.
- On the question of the governance body with oversight responsibilities for <IR>, it seems inevitable, in the case of companies, that it will be the board, which cannot escape responsibility for the company's external reporting.
- On the question of the reporting boundary, we doubt whether this is a key issue for <IR>; materiality, rather than boundaries, should determine what is reported.
- The proposed requirement to disclose 'the nature and magnitude of material trade-offs' is a very difficult one. Every decision an organization makes is a trade-off, but we doubt whether the framework really means that <IR> should report on all important decisions, and it is difficult to envisage what sort of useful disclosures organizations would be likely in practice to make about them. Perhaps a requirement

to discuss any material depletion of a particular capital would be more to the point, if this is what this particular proposal is getting at.

- Finally, we would expect that the requirement to explain why a capital is immaterial to an organization will often generate bland and unhelpful disclosures (see paragraph 26 above).

CD 4.6 as currently drafted overlaps with the business model question at CD 4.21. We suggest that it is redrafted to focus on the external environment and business context.

The reference to diversity in the first bullet at CD 4.11 could be understood as referring to matters such as gender, race or age. In our view, the important diversity for a board will usually be to have a range of different backgrounds and skills.

Also at CD 4.11, we doubt whether the fourth and sixth bullets – 'governance practices that go beyond legal requirements' and 'responsibility ... for promoting and enabling innovation' – will produce useful disclosures.

We agree that it is desirable that organizations should avoid boilerplate in their reporting, but suggest that exhortations to avoid boilerplate (as in CD 4.17) should be left out of the framework as they can give it a slightly hectoring tone. 64. We believe that most providers of financial capital will be interested primarily in financial capital, and we therefore suggest that the focus of Section 4F should be on this form of capital and how changes to other capitals affect it. In particular, the principle that an organization should report on outcomes in terms of effects on the capitals (CD 4.27) does not focus on what is of interest to the company's financial capital providers. In most cases, we would expect effects on other capitals to be of interest only to the extent that they ultimately impact on financial capital. However, financial capital providers' interests may differ from business to business.

Chapter 5: Preparation and Presentation

Involvement of Those Charged With Governance (Section 5D)

Section 5D discusses the involvement of those charged with governance, and paragraph 4.5 requires organizations to disclose the governance body with oversight responsibility for <IR>.

17. *Should there be a requirement for those charged with governance to include a statement acknowledging their responsibility for the integrated report? Why/why not?*

This proposal seems to us to be reasonable provided such an acknowledgement does not create new legal responsibilities for those concerned, which would be a deterrent to adopting ‹IR›.

18. *Please provide any other comments you have about Involvement of those charged with governance (Section 5D).*

The phrase 'collective mind' at CD 5.18 (second bullet) sounds odd to us, but the IIRC may perhaps be aware of a jurisdiction where it would be appropriate.

We are not confident that the framework has yet reached the point where it will be possible for the governance body to assert that any report is in accordance with it. This is not a criticism of the draft; integrated reporting is still in an early experimental phase.

Credibility (Section 5E)

The Framework provides reporting criteria against which organizations and assurance providers assess a report's adherence (paragraph 5.21).

19. *If assurance is to be obtained, should it cover the integrated report as a whole, or specific aspects of the report? Why?*

As stated above (paragraph 43), we believe that it would be appropriate to have a period of experimentation with assurance on integrated reports. This might well include some assurance reports that cover a complete integrated report and others that cover only parts of it.

20. *Please provide any other comments you have about Credibility (Section 5E). Assurance providers are particularly asked to comment on whether they consider the Framework provides suitable criteria for an assurance engagement.*

While we believe that, subject to a satisfactory conclusion on the question of resilience, it would certainly be possible to provide assurance on an integrated report, this does not mean that it is possible to develop universally applicable criteria specifically for such engagements. This process will be easier after the period of experimentation that we have suggested, but even then it may be appropriate to tailor assurance engagements for different sizes of enterprise and for different types of integrated report that may emerge in different jurisdictions. More generally, we would expect criteria for such engagements to be developed in accordance with the framework provided by ISAE 3000, Assurance Engagements other than Audits or Reviews of Historical Financial Information (which is currently being revised). Firms providing assurance on sustainability reporting already do so in accordance with this standard's requirements. We expect useful criteria to emerge from the period of experimentation, and we consider it probable that a single assurance opinion could be offered over <IR> reports once this has occurred.

Other

21. *Please provide any other comments you have about Chapter 5 that are not already addressed by your responses above (please include comments on the materiality determination process [Section 5B] in your answer to question 11 above rather than here).*

For the reasons indicated at paragraphs 7-8 above, we do not believe that an integrated report should invariably be a separate report additional to the rest of a company's reports. In some jurisdictions it may be better to integrate integrated reporting with existing reports.

It will be helpful for preparers to have some examples of how to do integrated reporting. This should be done in a way that does not become a template that would be adopted by businesses regardless of how appropriate it is to their particular circumstances. Each company will have to make its own decisions on what needs to be reported and how best to report it, but at the moment it will be difficult for them to work out exactly what they should be doing.

Investors do not seem to have a place in the list of stakeholders in the diagram at Figure 7. Perhaps they come under the heading 'Others', in which case they do not have the central position that we would expect given the stated focus of integrated reporting.

Overall View

22. *Recognizing that <IR> will evolve over time, please explain the extent to which you believe the content of the Framework overall is appropriate for use by organizations in preparing an integrated report and for providing report users with information about an organization's ability to create value in the short, medium and long term?*

We agree that <IR> will evolve over time, and as its principles become accepted it is likely that it will be integrated with other reporting rather than remain a standalone report. As we indicated earlier (paragraphs 15-16), we believe that more work needs to be done to talk with mainstream investors and analysts about their information needs. Until these consultations have made further progress and there is more experience of <IR> in practice, it will not be clear how much useful new information it is able to deliver for users. However, it is a journey that should be well worth undertaking.

Development of <IR>

23. *If the IIRC were to develop explanatory material on <IR> in addition to the Framework, which three topics would you recommend be given priority? Why?*

While practical examples of <IR> would be useful for preparers, we think that it is too early to identify specific topics where explanatory material is needed. We are also concerned that guidance could lead down the road to ever-greater detail. We believe that it is important to keep an approach based on principles rather than detailed requirements.

Other

24. *Please provide any other comments not already addressed by your responses to Questions 1-23.*

It would be helpful to define 'value' in the Glossary.

REFERENCES

Bansal, P., & Clelland, I. (2004). Talking Trash: Legitimacy, impression management, and unsystematic risk in the context of the natural environment. *Academy of Management Journal*, *47*(1), 93–103.

Brown, N., & Deegan, C. (1998). The public disclosure of environmental performance information – a dual test of media agenda setting theory and legitimacy theory. *Accounting and Business Research*, *29*(1), 21–42.

Cho, C. H., & Patten, D. M. (2007). The role of environmental disclosures as a tool of legitimacy: A research note. *Accounting, Organizations and Society*, *32*, 639–647.

Deegan, C., & Gordon, B. (1996). A study of environmental disclosure practices of Australian corporations. *Accounting and Business Research*, *26*(3), 187–199.

Deegan, C., & Rankin, M. (1996). Do Australian companies report environmental news objectively? An analysis of environmental disclosures by firms prosecuted successfully by the Environmental Protection Authority. *Accounting, Auditing & Accountability Journal*, *2*, 50–67.

Deegan, C., Rankin, M., & Tobin, J. (2002). An examination of the corporate social and environmental disclosures of GHP from 1983-1997: A test of legitimacy theory. *Accounting, Auditing & Accountability Journal*, *15*(3), 312–343.

Deloitte. (2012). *Integrated reporting: Navigating your way to a truly integrated report.* Deliotte.

Farrell, A., Kadous, K., & Towry, K. (2008). Contracting on contemporaneous versus forward-looking measures: An experimental investigation. *Contemporary Accounting Research*, *25*(3), 773–802.

Festinger, L. (1957). *A Theory of Cognitive Dissonance*. Palo Alto, CA: Stanford University Press.

Guthrie, J., & Parker, L. (1989). Corporate social reporting: A rebuttal of legitimacy theory. *Accounting and Business Research*, *9*(76), 343–352.

Kaplan, R. S., & Norton, D. P. (1996). *The Balanced Scorecard: Translating Strategy into Action*. Boston, MA: Harvard Business School Press.

Luft, J., & Shields, M. (2009). Psychology models of management accounting. *Foundations and Trends in Accounting*, *4*(3/4), 199–345.

Milne, M. J., & Patten, D. M. (2002). Securing organizational legitimacy: An experimental decision case examining the impact of environmental disclosures. *Accounting, Auditing & Accountability Journal*, *15*(3), 372–405.

Moore, D. A., Tanlu, L., & Bazerman, M. (2010). Conflict of interest and the intrusion of bias. *Judgment and Decision Making*, *5*(1), 37–53.

O'Donovan, G. (2002). Environmental disclosures in the annual report: Extending the applicability and predictive power of legitimacy theory. *Accounting, Auditing & Accountability Journal*, *15*(3), 344–371.

Paharia, N., Kassam, K. S., Greene, J. D., & Bazerman, M. H. (2009). Dirty work, clean hands: The moral psychology of indirect agency. *Organizational Behavior and Human Decision Processes*, *109*, 134–141.

Patten, D. M. (1991). Exposure, legitimacy, and social disclosure. *Journal of Accounting and Public Policy*, *10*, 297–308.

Patten, D. M. (1992). Intra-industry environmental disclosures in response to the Alaskan Oil Spill: A note on legitimacy theory. *Accounting, Organizations and Society*, *17*(5), 471–475.

Patten, D. M. (1995). Variability in social disclosure: A legitimacy-based analysis. *Advances in Public Interest Accounting*, *6*, 273–285.

Patten, D. M. (2005). The accuracy of financial report projections of future environmental capital expenditures: A research note. *Accounting, Organizations and Society*, *30*, 457–468.

Peters, G. F., & Romi, A. M. (2013a). Discretionary compliance with mandatory environmental disclosures: Evidence from SEC filings. *Journal of Accounting and Public Policy*, *32*, 213–236.

Peters, G. F., & Romi, A. M. (2013b). *Does the voluntary adoption of corporate governance mechanisms improve environmental risk disclosures? Evidence from greenhouse gas emission accounting* (Working Paper). Texas Tech University.

Sveiby, K. E. (1997). *The new organizational wealth.* Berett-Koehler Publishers, Inc.

Walden, W. D., & Schwartz, B. N. (1997). Environmental disclosures and public policy pressure. *Journal of Accounting and Public Policy*, *16*, 125–154.

About the Author

Ioana-Maria Dragu obtained her Doctoral diploma in Accounting and Audit in July 2015, after four years of research on integrated reporting – the topic of her book. She has published many papers, studies and book chapters in the field of corporate social responsibility, sustainability, and integrated reporting. Currently, she continues her research in the sphere of integrated reports, as a Research Assistant of the Accounting and Audit Department, within the Faculty of Economics and Business Administration, Babes-Bolyai University, Cluj-Napoca, Romania.

Index

N

P

R

S

T

www.ingramcontent.com/pod-product-compliance
Lightning Source LLC
LaVergne TN
LVHW081331300926
849161LV00008B/1940